Review and Remediation Skill Book

Bronze Level

Prentice Hall
LITERATURE
Timeless Voices, Timeless Themes

Prentice
Hall

Upper Saddle River, New Jersey
Glenview, Illinois
Needham, Massachusetts

ISBN 0-13-063329-1

1 2 3 4 5 6 7 8 9 10   05 04 03 02 01

Contents

Acknowledgments

VOCABULARY

Adapted from "Two Faces of Alaska's Youth" from *American Youth* Magazine (July/August 1968), published for General Motors Corporation. Reprinted by permission of Ceco Publishing Company.

READING

"I Have No Fears . . ." by Joy Silverstein from *I Heard a Scream in the Street: Poems by Young People in the City*, collected by Nancy Larrick. Originally appeared in "What Is a City? Young People Reply." Reprinted by permission of the Trustees of the Public Library of the City of Boston, Massachusetts.

From "The Mystery of Rommel's Missing Treasure" by Ken Krippene from *The Saturday Evening Post* January/February 1980. Copyright © 1980 by The Saturday Evening Post Company. Reprinted by permission of the Saturday Evening Post.

Adapted by permission of Alfred A. Knopf, Inc., and James Seligmann Agency from *Free Woman: The Life and Times of Victoria Woodhull* by Marion Meade. Copyright © 1976 by Marion Meade.

Adapted from "I Leave You Love: Mary McLeod Bethune" from *Contributions of Women: Education* by Mary W. Burgess. Copyright © 1975 by Dillon Press, an imprint of Silver Burdett Press, Simon & Schuster Elementary. Used by permission.

Selection 3 from "Woodworking Is My Hobby" by Glenn Wagner from *Boys' Life* (March 1968). Published by The Boy Scouts of America.

From *The Land of the Pharaohs*. Copyright © 1992 by Childrens' Press, Chicago.

From "Ghost of the Wild" in National Geographic *World*, July 1992.

From *American Indian Women* by Marion E. Gridley. Copyright © 1974 by Marion E. Gridley. Reprinted by permission of the publisher, E. P. Dutton, Inc.

From "The Crystal Skull" from *Strange Mysteries from Around the World* by Seymour Simon. Copyright © 1980 by Seymour Simon. By permission of Morrow Junior Books, a division of William Morrow & Co., Inc.

Adapted from "Pounding Hooves and Helicopter Wings," *American West*, January/February 1981. Reprinted by permission.

From *Woodswoman* by Anne La Bastille. Copyright © 1976 by Anne La Bastille. Reprinted by permission of the publisher, E.P. Dutton, Inc., and the author.

Adapted from "Fast . . . Faster . . . Fastest!" by Marcia Muller. Reprinted by permission from *American Girl*, March 1970, © Girl Scouts of the U.S.A.

Paul Annixter, *Swiftwater*. New York: Hill and Wang, Inc., 1950, pp. 48-49.

"The Toaster" from *Laughing Time: Collected Nonsense* by William Jay Smith. Copyright © 1990 by William Jay Smith. Reprinted by permission of Farrar, Straus and Giroux, Inc.

"The Death of a Cat" from *The Collected Poems of Louis MacNeice*, edited by E.R. Dodds, copyright © 1966. The Estate of Louis MacNeice. Reprinted by permission of David Higham Associates.

"A Cat" by John Gittings from *Miracles: Poems by children of the English-Speaking World*, edited by Richard Lewis. Copyright © 1966 by Richard Lewis. Reprinted by permission of Richard Lewis and The Touchstone Center, New York, 1996.

Adapted from *A Dream of Ghosts* by Frank Bonham. Copyright © 1973 by Frank Bonham. Reprinted by permission of the publisher, E.P. Dutton, Inc., and Harold Matson Company, Inc.

"A Fabulous Creature" adapted and reprinted with the permission of Atheneum Books for Young Readers, an imprint of Simon & Schuster Children's Publishing Division from *A Fabulous Creature* by Zilpha Keatley Snyder. Copyright © 1981 Zilpha Keatley Snyder.

From "The Case of the Coin Collector" from *Two-Minute Mysteries* by Donald J. Sobol. Copyright © 1967 by Donald J. Sobol. Reprinted by permission of the author and McIntosh and Otis, Inc.

From *Stranger on the Road* by Caroline Crane. Copyright © 1971 by Caroline Crane Kiyabu. Reprinted by permission of Random House, Inc.

From "Mascots" by Stanley Schmidt from *The Magazine of Fantasy and Science Fiction*, February 1982. Copyright © 1981 by Mercury Press, Inc. Reprinted by permission of the author and the author's agents, Scott Meredith Literary Agency, Inc., 845 Third Avenue, New York, New York 10022.

Walter Oleksy, *Quacky and the Crazy Curve Ball*, New York: McGraw-Hill Publishing Company, 1981, pp. 7-8.

From *Streets of Gold* by Karen Branson, copyright © 1981 by Karen Branson Wardlaw. Reprinted by permission of The Putnam and Grosset Group.

Zane Spencer and Jay Leech, *Branded Runaway*. Philadelphia: The Westminster Press, 1980, pp. 68-69.

"Snake Dance" by Corey Ford. Copyright 1934 Liberty Publishing Corp. Reprinted by permission of Liberty Library Corporation.

Robert Silverberg, *Before the Sphinx: Early Egypt*. New York: Thomas Nelson, Inc., 1971, p. 159.

Richard L. Knudson, *Classic Sports Cars*. Minneapolis: Lerner Publications Company, 1979, p. 14.

Reprinted by permission of Dodd, Mead & Company, Inc. from *Nature Invented It First* by Ross E. Hutchins. Copyright © 1980 by Ross E. Hutchins.

From *Hocus Focus: The World's Weirdest Cameras* by Carl Glassman. Copyright © 1976 by Carl Glassman. Adapted by permission of Franklin Watts, Inc.

Example paragraph and exercise items based on information in "The Mouse That Soared: Animators Recall Great Days at Disney," by Knights News Service, in The Baltimore *Sun*, December 2, 1981.

Pages 1–6 "Secrets of a Tropical Rain Forest" reprinted with the permission of Atheneum Books for Young Readers, an imprint of Simon & Schuster from *Earth's Vanishing Forests* by Roy A. Gallant. Copyright © 1992 by Roy A. Gallant.

WRITING

Marjorie Kinnan Rawlings, *The Yearling*. New York: Charles Scribner's Sons, 1938.

N. Scott Momaday, *The Names*. New York: Harper & Row, Publishers, Inc., 1976, pp. 5-6.

Rosa Guy, *Paris, Pee Wee, and Big Dog*. New York: Delacorte Press, 1984, p. 84.

From "The Circuit" by Francisco Jiménez. Reprinted by permission of the author.

From "Lucas and Jake" from *I Thought You Were a Unicorn and Other Stories* by Paul Darcy Boles. Copyright © 1963 by Paul Darcy Boles. First appeared in *Seventeen* Magazine. Reprinted by permission of Little, Brown and Company and Russell & Volkening, Inc. as agents for the author.

Winifred Madison, *Maria Luisa*. New York: J. B. Lippincott Company, 1971, p. 41.

Nicholasa Mohr, *El Bronx Remembered*. New York: Harper & Row, Publishers, Inc., 1975, pp. 48-49.

From "One Smart Bird" by Katherine Hauth. Appeared in *Cricket*, November 1983. Reprinted by permission of the author.

From *All About Horses* by Marguerite Henry. Copyright © 1962 by Marguerite Henry. Reprinted by permission of Random House, Inc.

From *Readers' Guide to Periodical Literature*. Copyright © 1986, 1987 by The H.W. Wilson Company. Material reproduced by permission of the publisher.

From "guide dog" in *Encyclopaedia Britannica*, 15th edition (1982), IV: 784-785. Copyright © 1982 by Encyclopaedia Britannica, Inc. Reprinted by permission.

Carl Burger, *All About Dogs*. New York: Random House, Inc., 1972, pp. 42-43.

Lesson 1
The Value of Context

Exercise A

In the paragraph below, some words have been left out. First, read the entire paragraph. This will give you a general idea of what it is about. Then go back and write on each blank a word that makes sense to you.

With only about 39,000 men and women, the United States Coast Guard is 1. _____ than any of the other Armed Forces. However, this little group is very important to the nation. Every year they save many 2. _____ and millions of 3. _____ worth of goods and ships. They also rescue people during hurricanes, floods, and other 4. _____. The Coast Guard is a sea going police force that can arrest anyone who breaks the 5. _____. They watch for oil 6. _____ and make safety rules. They protect fish and other sea 7. _____. Coast Guard icebreakers help ships that become trapped in frozen lakes and rivers during the 8. _____. The Coast Guard uses radio, lighthouses, and markers to help captains 9. _____ their ships. They also broadcast weather information to warn ships about dangerous 10. _____.

How do you know that *smaller* is the word that belongs on the first blank? You know because the rest of the sentence contains information that provides clues.

First, it is clear that the Coast Guard is being compared with the other Armed Forces—the Army, the Navy, and so on.

Second, since the number of Coast Guard personnel is given, the comparison probably deals with the number of people in the different services.

Third, since the word *only* is used about the number Coast Guard personnel, it is probably *smaller* than other Armed Forces.

You can often figure out the meaning of an unfamiliar word by using the other information in the sentence in which it appears. This information is called the **context** of the word.

Exercise B

Read each sentence below and try to figure out the meaning of the italicized word. Then choose a word or phrase from the list that follows that means about the same as the italicized word. Write the letter of your choice on the line in front of the sentence.

_____ 1. The *modicum* of food on my plate hardly began to fill me up.

_____ 2. She was in too much of a hurry to get the children home to allow any more *procrastination*.

_____ 3. The little girl was standing in the middle of a *gaggle* of geese.

_____ **4.** The telephone call brought good *tidings*.

_____ **5.** After the touchdown there was a great *clamor* from the crowd.

_____ **6.** They held a *caucus* to decide how they would vote.

_____ **7.** We went out in the boat and caught a dozen *shad*.

_____ **8.** I spread a crisp *rusk* with some jam.

_____ **9.** The coach had a whistle attached to the *lanyard* around his neck.

_____ **10.** Before the movie began, we bought some candy in the *foyer*.

_____ **11.** Satellites looking for storms *survey* tropical oceans.

_____ **12.** We refused to give into *despondency* and remained hopeful about solving the problem.

_____ **13.** Bob spent the afternoon looking through old pictures, *reminiscing* about his boyhood.

_____ **14.** During a hurricane, winds swirl and blow at a tremendous *velocity*.

_____ **15.** The fire in the downtown warehouse was quite a *calamity*.

a. hopelessness
b. lettuce
c. examine
d. lobby
e. cord
f. flock
g. horns
h. disaster
i. remembering
j. meeting
k. small amount
l. shouting
m. fish
n. news
o. speed
p. delay
q. toast

Lesson 2
Context and Multiple Meanings

Some words have only one meaning, but others can mean many different things. The meaning in each case depends on the *context*.

For example, the students who take part in a play are the *cast*, meaning "a group of actors." But *cast* can also mean "a plaster support for a broken bone" or "to throw a fishing line" or "to give a vote in an election," as well as a number of other things.

Exercise A

Each sentence below has a different meaning for the word *cast*. Find the meaning in the list below that fits each sentence and write its letter on the line in front of the sentence.

_____ 1. The sky had a pink *cast* during last night's sunset.

_____ 2. They will *cast* the metal after it has melted.

_____ 3. Did he *cast* the stone that broke the window?

_____ 4. The director will *cast* Maria as the leading character.

_____ 5. The man had a *cast* in his left eye.

     a. pour into a mold   **d.** small amount of color
     b. throw   **e.** a slight squint
     c. an insect's skin   **f.** choose for a part

Exercise B

Each sentence below has a different meaning for the word *spring, plot, crop* or *round*. Find the meaning in the list on the next page that fits each sentence. Then write the letter of that meaning on the line in front of the sentence.

_____ 1. *Spring* came early this year with its rains and its flowers.

_____ 2. The detective discovered a *plot* to steal the crown jewels.

_____ 3. There was a good wheat *crop* last year in the Midwest.

_____ 4. To end the program, the children sang a *round*.

_____ 5. We got some water from a nearby *spring* to wash the dishes.

_____ 6. The *plot* of the movie was silly, to say the least.

_____ 7. The angry rider lashed her horse with the small *crop* she carried.

_____ 8. He asked the butcher for a *round* of beef.

_____ 9. The dog made a *spring* at the low branch where the cat crouched and hissed.

_____ 10. There was a small *plot* behind the house where they grew a few vegetables.

_____ **11.** He wore a hat to hide his too-short *crop*.

_____ **12.** There is only a single *round* left in the gun.

_____ **13.** The *spring* in the child's jack-in-the-box had come loose.

_____ **14.** The builder unrolled a *plot* of the housing development.

_____ **15.** In the afternoon they played a *round* of golf.

a. stream	**f.** map	**k.** whip
b. story	**g.** harvest	**l.** season
c. cut	**h.** scheme	**m.** game
d. leap	**i.** song	**n.** piece of ground
e. coil	**j.** shot	**o.** haircut

Exercise C

Each of the italicized words below has more than one meaning. Use context clues to determine how the word is being used. Circle the definition in parentheses that gives the correct meaning of the word.

1. That *shade* of blue will be perfect for the new cafeteria. (hue, tint; curtain)

2. The storm tore roofs off houses across town; it was a scene of *utter* destruction. (speak; total)

3. After the earthquake, the old building's walls were not *stable*. (where horses are kept; solid, sturdy)

4. Dr. Medrano's *patient* called this morning to cancel her appointment. (client; untiring)

5. Be sure to stir the paint carefully so you get a *uniform* color—we don't want some parts to be lighter. (consistent; outfit)

Lesson 3
Context and Unfamiliar Words

Context clues can also help you figure out the meaning of unfamiliar words. Sometimes the clue will be a word or words that mean about the *same* as the unfamiliar word:

> The eagle flew *aloft*; his strong wings took him high into the sky.

The phrase "high into the sky" means about the same thing as *aloft*.

Sometimes the clue is a word or words that mean the *opposite* of the unfamiliar word:

> Bill's biggest problem as a swimmer is laziness; greater *exertion* could have won him the prize.

Here "laziness" means roughly the opposite of *exertion*. Therefore, *exertion* must mean something like "effort."

In other sentences you may get a clue when you find that one thing *caused* another:

> An untended campfire caused a *conflagration* in the woods after a rainless September had left them very dry.

Here, we know that the *conflagration* was caused by an untended campfire. What could an untended campfire cause? A forest fire. Therefore, a *conflagration* must be a large, destructive fire, like a forest fire.

Exercise A
Read the paragraph below. Notice how the italicized words are used in the sentences. Then answer the questions that follow.

> As the oceanliner was sinking, five people scrambled overboard to get into the *dinghy*. Although the small boat was designed for four, everyone managed to *nestle* themselves in. They huddled together to keep warm. Everyone wondered how they would get out of this *dilemma* until they heard the blast of the Coast Guard's horn.

1. What words in the passage mean roughly the same as *dinghy*?

   _____

2. What words in the passage mean roughly the same as *nestle*?

   _____

3. What *dilemma* did the people in the dinghy have?

   _____

Exercise B

Choose the best meaning for each of the italicized words and write its letter on the line in front of the sentence.

_____ 1. The captain of the ship had *sacrificed* himself to save his passengers and crew.
    a. given up
    b. quit
    c. cried
    d. saved

_____ 2. The *valiant* efforts of the brave crew saved the lives of many of the passengers.
    a. brave
    b. silly
    c. unnecessary
    d. wasted

_____ 3. When all of the passengers were safe in the hospital, they were given fluids because they were so *dehydrated*.
    a. angry
    b. tired
    c. dry
    d. hungry

_____ 4. The oceanliner had been set on fire by an *anonymous* person. No one would ever know who did the horrible deed.
    a. friendly
    b. nameless
    c. familiar
    d. annoyed

_____ 5. One of the *affluent* owners of the ship even offered a $500,000 reward for any information about the fire.
    a. older
    b. wealthy
    c. unhappy
    d. artistic

Lesson 4
Direct and Indirect Context Clues

A. The *coelacanth* (sē/ lə kanth) is a kind of primitive fish with heavy, leg-like fins.

Sometimes context clues are *direct*; that is, the unfamiliar word is followed immediately by a word or words that explain it. In sentence A, for example, the word *coelacanth* is explained as "a kind of primitive fish with heavy, leg-like fins."

Explanations of this kind are called **direct context clues**. Such clues often immediately follow the words they explain, and may be set off with punctuation such as parentheses, dashes, or commas, as in sentence B:

B. A large amount of *adipose* (fatty) tissue found in these fish suggests that they once had lungs as well as gills.

Often, however, there are no direct clues to the meaning of an unfamiliar word. Then you must look for **indirect context clues** in the information contained in the rest of the sentence.

C. The coelacanth was supposed to have become *extinct* around sixty million years ago, until a living one was netted in the Indian Ocean off the southeast coast of Africa in 1938.

The clues to the meaning of *extinct* are contained in the general information given in the sentence. The fish was thought to be *extinct* until it was discovered "living" in the Indian Ocean. Therefore, *extinct* must mean something like "dead" or "vanished."

Exercise

Read each of the following sentences and decide if the clues to the meaning of the italicized word are direct or indirect. Place a check on the correct line. Then write a meaning for the word on the line below.

1. Coelacanths are closely related to the ancestors of the land *vertebrates*—animals with backbones.

   direct _____   indirect _____

   _____

2. These ancestors were the first *amphibians*, creatures living both in water and on land.

   direct _____   indirect _____

   _____

3. Coelacanths first appeared about 350,000,000 years ago and quickly became *abundant*, thriving in many parts of the world.

    direct _____   indirect _____

    _____

4. Although they were thought to be extinct, coelacanths were rediscovered in 1938 when some fishermen netted one in a *trawl* at a depth of about 250 feet.

    direct _____   indirect _____

    _____

5. Coelacanths are *denizens* of deep water, living in depths near the Comoro Islands in the Indian Ocean.

    direct _____   indirect _____

    _____

6. The natives of the Comoro Islands consider coelacanths to be *edible* when they are dried and salted.

    direct _____   indirect _____

    _____

7. The coelacanths are powerful *predators*, one being found with the remains of a fish of at least fifteen pounds in its stomach.

    direct _____   indirect _____

    _____

Lesson 5
More Indirect Context Clues

As we have seen, writers sometimes tell you exactly what they mean by the words they use:

Some scientists think that the dinosaurs disappeared as a result of a collision between the Earth and an *asteroid*, one of the many minor planets that revolve around the sun between the orbits of Mars and Jupiter.

However, the clues to unfamiliar words are not always so easy to find. A writer may give only general clues to the meaning of a word:

In the *tumulus*, buried along with the body of the warrior to whom they belonged, were weapons, armor, and a set of chessmen carved of walrus ivory.

The word *tumulus* is not defined, but there are several indirect clues to its meaning. Things from a bygone age—"weapons," "armor," "chessmen carved of walrus ivory"—are "buried" in the *tumulus*, and they are buried along with the body of a "warrior." Therefore, a *tumulus* is probably an ancient grave.

Sometimes the indirect clues lead up to an unfamiliar word, so that it appears to summarize them:

The yearbook photographer took a number of shots of each cheerleader doing a different cheer or stunt and then put them together in one large photo *montage* to introduce the sports section.

Montage summarizes three clues: (1) a photographer takes a number of shots; (2) the subjects are different; (3) the shots are put together in one large picture. Therefore, a *montage* must be "a combination of several separate pictures to make one picture."

Exercise
Each following sentence contains indirect context clues to the meaning of the unfamiliar word. Read each sentence carefully and then use those clues to help figure out the meaning of the unfamiliar word. Write the letter of the best meaning for the word on the line in front of the sentence.

_____ 1. The *itinerant* salesman told me that in his work he went from town to town and state to state, sometimes more than a thousand miles a month.
   a. important
   b. angry
   c. traveling
   d. wealthy

_____ 2. With all the candidates for office shouting at each other, and their supporters cheering, booing, and throwing things, the student council debate was turning into a *fray*.
   a. chat
   b. quarrel
   c. lecture
   d. meeting

_____ 3. Allen never gives in even when he knows that he's wrong—a really *obstinate* person.
   a. friendly
   b. truthful
   c. stubborn
   d. lazy

_____ 4. The woman's *haggard* face was thin, pale, and lined, with dark circles beneath her eyes.
   a. cheerful
   b. careworn
   c. silly
   d. angry

_____ 5. He always carried the rabbit's foot as a *talisman* to bring him luck in a race.
   a. charm
   b. friend
   c. sign
   d. prayer

_____ 6. Jason seems to *thrive* on challenge; he's only happy when he has a difficult project to complete.
   a. struggle
   b. weaken
   c. do well
   d. fall apart

_____ 7. She claims to have made a *momentous* discovery, but some scientists think her work is unimportant.
   a. quick
   b. important
   c. small
   d. unhappy

Lesson 6
Common Sense and Context

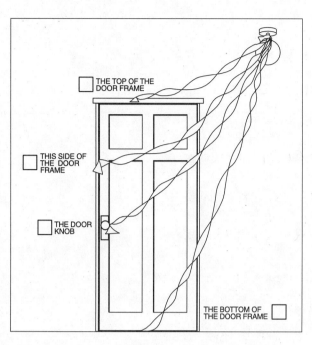

To decorate for Marilee's surprise party, we hung crepe paper streamers from the ceiling light to the curtain rods, the door *lintel*, and the tops of the taller pieces of furniture.

Does *lintel* mean the doorknob, the top of the door frame, the bottom or the side of the door frame? Try to visualize the situation. Study these possibilities; then check the box where the streamers are the most likely to be attached.

You were using your common sense if you decided that the top of the door frame was the only good place to fasten the streamers. If they were attached to any other of the other three places they would be in the way of anyone entering the room. A person entering the room could not open the door without breaking them.

You need to use your common sense every time you look for context clues to help you with the meaning of an unfamiliar word. Sometimes it is easy. Sometimes it is difficult. And sometimes context clues don't help you at all. When that happens, you may need to use the dictionary. Practice and your common sense will tell you when the context of an unfamiliar word is helpful and when it isn't.

Exercise

Read the following paragraph.

We left the sickroom and went down the hall, but the odor followed us. The smell was not only of sickness and medicine, but also of stale air and yesterday's cooking and last week's garbage. I looked at the cracked and peeling walls. There were large damp patches on the ceiling where the roof had leaked. A single dim light bulb dangled from a frayed cord. I thought, "It's bad enough to be as sick as Mrs. Harrison is. But it must be ten times worse to be ill in such a *squalid* place."

Each of the following statements is a student's attempt to use context to figure out the meaning of the word *squalid*. Read the statements carefully. Write the letter of the one that answers each of the questions below on the line in front of the question.

A. I think I've heard that word before. Doesn't it mean "stormy," or "rain-soaked," or something like that?

B. Somebody is very sick. Maybe she's in pain and crying out. *Squalid* could mean something like "unpleasantly noisy."

C. But it's the place that's *squalid*. It smells bad. It needs painting. It's damp. It's dark. *Squalid* must mean "shabby" or "miserable."

D. The writer mentions that the place is lit by a single dim light bulb. Maybe *squalid* means "poorly lit."

_____ **1.** Which person notices what *squalid* describes, but finds a clue that has to do with only one detail?

_____ **2.** Which person seems to be mistaking *squalid* for an entirely different word?

_____ **3.** Which person notices what *squalid* describes, and looks for clues in the whole paragraph?

_____ **4.** Which person does not notice what *squalid* describes, and uses a clue that refers to something else?

_____ **5.** Which person is making the best use of common sense?

Lesson 7
Recognizing Word Structure

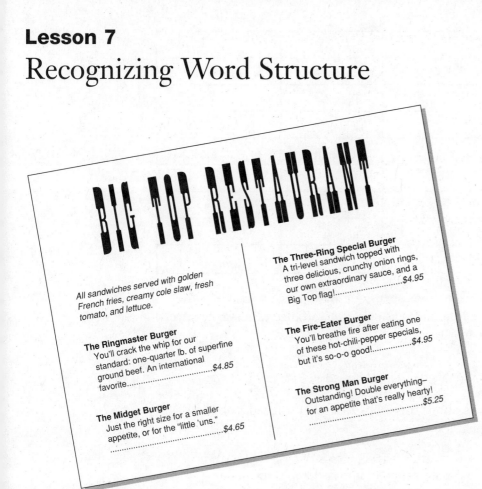

Look at the restaurant menu above. Simple food has been given fancy names. All the food on this menu, however, is one basic kind, but with a lot of "trimmings" added. What is the one basic food item mentioned? Write it below.

The answer you wrote is the basic food in the menu. Its name is part of each choice, whether described as "Midget Burger," "Ringmaster Burger," or some other burger.

Examine some of the words in the menu. "Ringmaster" is really two words put together: *ring* and *master*. "Three-ring" is two words, *three* and *ring*, joined by a hyphen. "Golden" from "golden French fries" is *gold* and *-en* added.

Exercise
The chart on the next page shows how other words in the menu can be broken down into parts. In the blank boxes write the part or parts of each word that are missing.

1. creamy	cream	
2. smaller	small	
3. favorite	favor	
4. tri-level	level	
5. extraordinary	ordinary	
6. everything	thing	
7. international	nation	
8. fire-eater	eat	
9. outstanding	stand	

As you can see, each word above consists of one basic word part with other parts added. Words that are long, like *international*, are not necessarily harder to understand than shorter words.

Look at the next word:

superpowerful

You probably know more about this word than you think. Look at its different parts: super power ful.

Read it in an example sentence.

The United States has been called a *superpowerful* nation.

By putting the word parts *super* + *power* + *ful* together, you can figure out the meaning of the word *superpowerful*. This is called using structure to understand an unfamiliar word. Write your own definition of *superpowerful* below.

10. _____

You will come across many unfamiliar words in your reading. These words will contain familiar word parts. When you try to understand the meanings of such words by using their different parts, you are using **structure**.

Lesson 8
Compound Words

Exercise A

Show time in the *Big Top*! The *ringmaster* announces by *loudspeaker*: "Ladies and *Gentlemen*. . ." The *bandleader*, looking like a *brigadier general* with all his braid, signals his band to play for the Grand Entry. The ringmaster blows his whistle, and the parade, a *time-honored* custom, begins. *Bright-eyed* performers march around the tent. Then the acts begin under the *spotlights*.

1. Two italicized words are formed by joining two words with a hyphen (-). Write them here.

   _____

2. Other italicized words are made of two complete words written together as one. Write two of them here.

   _____

3. Some italicized words are usually thought of as one word but are written as two separate words. Write them here.

   _____

    The six words you have written are all compound words. A **compound word** is made from two or more words joined to form a new word. Compounds may be written as one word (*shortcut*), as two or more words (*short story*), or as a hyphenated word (*short-range*). All are treated as one word, no matter how they are joined. To find their meanings, combine the meanings of the two or more words

Exercise B

Read the paragraphs below. Underline the compound words. Then write their meanings on the blanks. There are eight compounds in all.

    As the sunlight streams through the tent door, the show begins. Bareback riders come galloping out at breakneck speed. They do handstands and tricks while riding at full gallop. The music changes, and the horses do a high-stepping dance. Overhead, trapeze artists wearing earrings do flips timed to the split second.
    It's time for the human cannonball. The cannon is rolled out, there is a boom, a puff of smoke, and a man soars into the net. With that dramatic event the show is ended.

1. _____

2. _____

3. _____

4. _____

5. _____

6. _____

7. _____

8. _____

Although compounds can be written three different ways, they are always thought of as one word in meaning.

Exercise C

Now think of ten more compound words that you have heard. List them on the lines below. You can use a dictionary if you get stuck.

1. _____

2. _____

3. _____

4. _____

5. _____

6. _____

7. _____

8. _____

9. _____

10. _____

Lesson 9
Recognizing Root Words

FRIENDLY
BEFRIEND
FRIENDSHIP
UNFRIENDLY
FRIENDLESS

Look at the words above. They have one thing in common: the same root word, friend. A **root word** is the basic part from which other words can be made. When a root is combined with other word parts, it forms a **derivative**, like *friendless*.

Exercise A
Use the derivatives in the list above to complete the next sentences. Be sure the words make sense in the context of the sentences.

1. Ben's harsh greeting was very _____.

2. Laura tried to _____ the new student.

3. The immigrant arrived _____ in the strange city.

4. Their _____ lasted over fifteen years.

5. Everyone in the club was very _____ to the visitor.

To find root words, remove all the parts that have been added. When you can't take away any more letters or parts, and the remainder is a whole word, you probably have found the root.

Exercise B
In the list below look for roots that have no parts added to them. Underline the words. Example: <u>tear</u>.

cream	faultless	dislike	recoverable
painful	pride	lemonade	muscle
unknown	stately	age	turn

Exercise C

Study the derivatives below. Identify the root in each derivative and underline it.

1. prewash
2. statement
3. darkness
4. greatly
5. tasteful

6. sheepish
7. airless
8. deface
9. nonsense
10. reread

11. singable
12. semicircle
13. subway
14. management
15. basically

Exercise D

Read the derivative at the head of each column of blanks. Circle the root. Then fill in the blanks with derivatives from the list below based on the same root.

1. development

_____

_____

_____

_____

_____

3. actor

_____

_____

_____

_____

_____

2. discolor

_____

_____

_____

_____

4. payable

_____

_____

_____

_____

redevelop
colorless
overdevelop
reaction
payment

bicolor
interact
prepay
developmental
nonpayment

activist
colorfully
underdevelop
payless
discoloration

repay
transaction
inactive
colorful
developable

Lesson 10
Root Words with Spelling Changes

Dear Denise,

Everyone has happy *memories* of summer camp, or so I'm always told! Well, I'll be *happiest* when camp is only a memory. Each morning we get up at 6 A.M., eat, have housekeeping *activities*, then are *hurried* off to our classes.

Cheryl, my cabinmate, is *busily* cleaning up now and *whistling* off-key. I'm *waiting* for the bell to ring for *diving* lessons. But we may not go *swimming* at all. It's so *foggy* out, you can't see the *leaves* on the trees.

Yesterday I was *paddling* around the dock when something *grabbed* my leg. I let out a *piercing* screech and started *scrambling* for shore. Then I saw Cheryl's *grinning* face. I was *furious!* But she thought it was *funny.*

Outside Cheryl's *craziness*, not much is going on.

Your friend,
Vickie

Each italicized word in the letter is formed from a root word with a word part added at the end. The spelling of the root word was changed, however, when the ending was added.

There are four common spelling changes:

1. final *e* dropped . . . . ice + y = icy
2. *y* changed to *i* . . . . dry + ed = dried
3. *f* changed to *v* . . . . life + s = lives
4. final consonant doubled . . . . . sit + ing = sitting

Although other kinds of spelling changes are sometimes made, the four above are the most common. If you remember them, you can spot the root more easily in an unfamiliar word.

Exercise A

On the blanks below write the root word of each italicized word in the story.
Three have been done for you.

1. memory
2. happy
3. activity
4. _____
5. _____
6. _____

7. _____
8. _____
9. _____
10. _____
11. _____
12. _____

13. _____
14. _____
15. _____
16. _____
17. _____
18. _____

Exercise B

Below is a list of words in which spelling changes have taken place in the roots.
After each word write the spelling change that has taken place. The first is
done for you.

halves _____ f changed to v _____

1. baggy _____
2. merriest _____
3. worrier _____
4. calves _____
5. having _____

6. leaving _____
7. funniest _____
8. imaginable _____
9. shelves _____
10. leggy _____

Lesson 11
Using Prefixes

John Faulkner

Imagine that you are in a race. Which would you rather ride: a *unicycle*, a *bicycle*, or a *tricycle*? Why?

_____

You know that the root word of the three words above is *cycle*. Each root is preceded by a word part. All word parts added to roots are called **affixes**. A word part that comes before the root is called a **prefix**. Prefixes can change or add to the meaning of the root word. Also, when a prefix is added to a root, the new word is a derivative.

Now look again at the words *unicycle*, *bicycle*, and *tricycle*. What do you think the prefixes mean?

uni- _____   bi- _____   tri- _____

Exercise A
Study the derivatives in the list below. Each has a prefix that has been added to the root. Circle the prefixes.

recover	misbehave	adverb
subsoil	supermarket	antifreeze
unhappy	incorrect	preheat
abnormal	intercity	postwar
debug	underground	remake

Exercise B

Read the questions and write your answers on the blanks.

1. If you were on a picnic, would you be happier to see the sun *disappear* or *reappear*?

   _____

2. Which is held before a football game, a *postgame* or *pregame* session?

   _____

3. Would you rather be *overpaid* or *underpaid* for doing a chore at a neighbor's house?

   _____

4. Does a basketball bounce better when it is *deflated* or when it is *inflated*?

   _____

5. Would the *vice-president* or the *ex-president* be more likely to address Congress?

   _____

Exercise C

Each sentence has one derivative. Underline the derivative, then write the prefix in the blank. The first is done for you.

fore-   What I need is someone to <u>foretell</u> my errors before I make them!

_____ 1. The United States is often described as a superpower in the press.

_____ 2. If Perry grows any more, he'll outgrow his new suit before he's really used it.

_____ 3. Why not redecorate the room in blue for the anniversary party?

_____ 4. The key was copied by making an imprint of the key on clay and taking the clay to a locksmith.

_____ 5. Our old car will misfire if it is driven below twenty-five miles an hour.

Lesson 12
Negative Prefixes

Suppose you were having your arm examined by a doctor. Which statement would you rather hear?

> "Just as I thought—it's broken."
> "Just as I thought—it's unbroken."

One statement contains a word with a prefix. Write the word below.

_____

Because the prefix means "not," it is called a **negative prefix**. Such prefixes change the meaning of the root. *Broken* in the first statement is changed to *unbroken* in the second, completely changing the doctor's statement.

Exercise A

Look at the italicized words in the paragraph below. They have negative prefixes.

What began as a friendly neighborhood game of touch football turned into an *unpleasant* experience for Charles. The two teams were *mismatched*, though the players didn't care as long as the game was fun. They played *nonstop* until noon, when Charles broke his arm.

1. List the three prefixes from the italicized words:

_____

The three prefixes you listed all have similar meanings. They mean *not*. All negative prefixes mean *not*, but depending upon their use in a sentence, they can be understood as *wrong, bad, without, lack of, the opposite of*, etc.

2. Write each italicized word from the example paragraph (*unpleasant, mismatched, nonstop*) beside the meaning of its prefix.

not _____

without _____

badly _____

Exercise B

On the next page are words with negative prefixes. Look at them, then write the prefix and its meaning in the blanks. The first is done for you.

WORD LIST	NEGATIVE PREFIX	MEANING PREFIX
unbroken	un- _____	not _____
1. irresponsible	_____	_____
2. nonfiction	_____	_____
3. illogical	_____	_____
4. imperfect	_____	_____
5. disregard	_____	_____

Exercise C

Below is a list of derivatives with negative prefixes. Complete the sentences by using the proper words from the list.

misspell	unbuckle	incorrect
impossible	illegal	nonstop
dislike	irregular	unaware

1. The cliff was difficult, but not _____ to climb.

2. Janice had only two _____ answers on her test.

3. The policeman told Tony that it was _____ to make a left turn at this intersection.

4. Maine's _____ coast has many sheltered harbors.

5. Most teachers _____ handwriting that is not easy to read.

Lesson 13
Prefixes with Several Meanings

The prefix *in-* can have several meanings.

> "The crude passageways **inside** the old fortress looked **incomplete**."

Exercise A

In the word *incomplete*, *in-* is used as a negative prefix. But in a word like *inside*, it means "within." Read the sentences that follow. Pay attention to the prefixes of the italicized words.

    A. Because of the detour, my father had to take an *indirect* route to the campground.

    B. It's Tomas's job to handle the *incoming* company mail and deliver it to the proper persons.

    C. Many northern animals are *inactive* during the cold winter months.

    D. We sailed *inland* in order to find a protected place and escape the threatening storm.

1. Which sentences use *in-* as a negative prefix?

_____

2. Which sentences use *in-* to mean "in," "into," or "within"?

_____

    Another prefix, *un-*, also has several meanings. It can be used as a negative prefix or used to mean the opposite of something.

    E. At midnight everyone must *unmask* so we can find out who each person is.

    F. If the radio you bought is *unsatisfactory*, why don't you just take it back to the store?

    G. Harriet wanted to *untie* her dog so it could run around freely.

3. Which sentence uses *un-* as a negative prefix?

_____

4. Which sentences use *un-* to mean "do the opposite of" or "do something that will reverse what has been done"?

_____

    Like *in-* and *un-*, many prefixes have different meanings, depending on the root words and on the context in which they are used.

    The prefix *im-* (another way to spell *in-*) can mean "not," "upon," or "in."

Exercise B

In the blanks write the meaning of *in-*, *un-*, or *im-* that applies in each sentence.

in-   not; within; into
un-   not; opposite of; reverse
im-   not; upon; in

_____ 1. We left the *imprints* of our hands on the wet cement.

_____ 2. Claire left the room with an *unhappy* expression on her face.

_____ 3. Roger's shorts were *inappropriate* for the fancy dress party.

_____ 4. The water was *impure*, and we were told not to drink any of it.

_____ 5. Mr. Watson's hands shook as he *unfolded* the old letter.

_____ 6. Bill felt it was *improper* for his brother to borrow his bicycle without asking him.

_____ 7. Flight 308 is *inbound* from Chicago and should arrive at 4:15.

_____ 8. Jill felt *imprisoned* in the classroom when she had to stay after school.

_____ 9. Don't be so *impatient*; the bus is on its way.

_____ 10. The fierce winds *uncovered* a passageway into the tomb.

Lesson 14
Using Suffixes

Exercise A

As he set his fish equip down on the wood pier, Harry John note how differ the bright of the water was from yesterday and felt thank that a sun day was clear predict.

If the paragraph above doesn't look right to you, it's because many words in it have something missing. Here is the same paragraph with the words corrected:

As he set his fishing equipment down on the wooden pier, Harry John noted how different the brightness of the water was from yesterday and felt thankful that a sunny day was clearly predictable.

1. Circle the word parts that have been added in this second paragraph.

2. Are these word parts added to the beginning, middle, or the end of the root words?

A prefix is a word part, or affix, that is added to the beginning of a root word. An affix that is added to the *end* of a root word is called a **suffix**.

Suffixes can change or add to the meaning of the root word. A suffix also can change the way a word is used in a sentence.

Just as a derivative can contain more than one prefix, so can it also have more than one suffix. Example: pain-ful-ly.

Exercise B

Read the paragraph below. Study the italicized words; then separate each root and suffix in the chart. The first one is done for you.

"The salmon are running!" Each June this cry brings the entire John family to the flooded banks of the Copper River for two *eventful* months of *excitement* and hard work. Harry and his father have *previously* completed *construction* of their fish wheel. The wheel turns *rapidly* in the energetic current and scoops up the *pinkish* salmon. If they are *lucky*, the John family will catch three thousand salmon.

WORD	ROOT	SUFFIX
eventful	event	-ful
1. excitement		
2. previously		
3. construction		
4. pinkish		
5. lucky		

Exercise C

Read the sentences below and underline the words that contain a suffix. Write each suffix on the line below the sentence. The first one has been done for you.

1. The man was <u>barely</u> <u>breathing</u> when they <u>pulled</u> him ashore.

   -ly, -ing, -ed

2. Some people can be quite unfriendly when they are tired.

   _____

3. Our math teacher was a diver on her college swim team.

   _____

4. Today we are going to go hiking in the canyon.

   _____

5. I was so proud to be a finalist in the talent performances.

   _____

6. Hal's history assignment is finally complete.

   _____

7. Going to the store last night, we passed several crews working on the roads.

   _____

8. It was a joyful day of celebration and fun.

   _____

9. Sylvia's father is approaching retirement.

   _____

10. Our bus driver has been working for the school district for many years.

    _____

Lesson 1
Reading for Different Purposes

For Tuesday
1. Social Studies - find a newspaper
article that tells what the new
import tax is and how it will affect
the average citizen.

2. Science - read pages 151-156 on cells.
What are five parts of a cell? How are
cells and tissues related?

3. English - read page 36 in I Heard
a Scream in the Street. Consider how
this particular young person feels about
the city. Look for the reasons she
gives for not being afraid in the city.

Exercise A

Suppose a page in your notebook has assignments like the three shown above.

1. In order to do the social studies assignment, will you need to read all the articles in a newspaper? Will you be able to tell from headlines which articles you need to look at more closely?

_____

2. The questions in the science assignment tell you to pay special attention to two things. Circle them on the notebook page.

When you are given an assignment, listen to the directions. As you do the reading, look for the things that have been mentioned. Directions and questions set a purpose for you and should help you better understand what you read. They should also help you decide how carefully—or how quickly—to read the material assigned.

Sometimes it is necessary to read slowly and carefully in order to understand and remember detailed information. At other times you may read quickly for enjoyment or to get a general idea of what is said. And sometimes you need to look up one particular fact, and you can do this by skimming without reading all the material.

Your purpose will determine *what* you read. It will also determine your method—the *way* in which you do your reading.

Exercise B

The book referred to in the English assignment is a collection of poems written by young people. Reread the assignment carefully. Then read the poem and answer the questions.

I HAVE NO FEARS . . .
by Joy Silverstein

Everyone
seems to be saying
how lonely
the city is.
To me
it is a paradise where
one can
talk and
laugh out loud and
stare at people . . .
I have no
fears in the
city;
for I believe that
humans
are more gentle than
we think them
to be.
Outside
of all that smog
and fake confidence
lies the true city . . .
full of love
and not afraid
of being laughed at.

1. What does the speaker say others are saying about the city?

_____

2. What three activities does the speaker enjoy in the city?

_____

3. What is the speaker's attitude toward the city?

_____

4. What quality do human beings possess more of than we think?

_____

5. Did you read the poem quickly or carefully in order to do this exercise?

_____

Lesson 2

Helps for Setting Purpose

The beginning of an article is printed below. The *title*—"The Mystery of Rommel's Missing Treasure"—may arouse your curiosity. *Who is Rommel? How did he get his treasure? What happened to it?*

Stories and articles sometimes have *headnotes*. The headnote for this article, "Coins and jewels worth millions," may raise further questions. *What sort of coins? What kinds of jewels? How many millions?*

Exercise

Quickly read the first paragraph of the article. What questions does it suggest?

Coins and jewels worth millions

THE MYSTERY OF ROMMEL'S MISSING TREASURE
by Ken Krippene

Buried somewhere among the windswept sand dunes of southern Tunisia are ninety small metal trunks. They are filled to the brim with gold coins. In addition, there is one steel box about two feet in diameter in which can be found a fortune in priceless jewels. These include sparkling diamonds, blood-red rubies, flashing emeralds and star sapphires, as well as dozens of other precious stones. All together, the treasure is valued at approximately $100 million.

If you ask questions about an article *before* you read it, you will improve your reading. Purpose-setting questions—based on such features as the title, headnote, pictures, captions, and opening paragraph—serve as reading guides.

The process of looking over an article before beginning to read it is called **making a survey**. Regardless of your general purpose for reading, making a survey will help you set more definite purposes.

Articles are sometimes divided into sections that are headed by *subtitles*. For example, in the article about Rommel's missing treasure, which continues on the next page, the subtitle is "Rommel confused the enemy." The subtitles of a selection will often provide additional clues to the subject matter.

There is one more thing you can do before you read the article—read the *last* paragraph. This paragraph may summarize the points covered in the material or it may state a conclusion.

1. Write a purpose-setting question based on the subtitle "Rommel confused the enemy."

_____

2. Read the last paragraph of the article and add one more purpose-setting question.

_____

Now read the article, keeping your questions in mind.

Why should such a valuable treasure as this lie buried in the burning sands of the Sahara? For one thing, not many people know about the loot. If they do, they think it's at the bottom of the Mediterranean Sea. Others who know about it have avoided the desert and searched elsewhere.

But where did this treasure come from? To whom does it belong? Why was it buried in such a forbidding place? To find the answer it is necessary to turn back the pages of history to World War II, to March, 1943, and to Erwin Rommel, one of the ablest generals to come out of Germany.

The end had come and Rommel knew it. Recently he had fought and lost his last battle near a small desert outpost. Desperate, and with only 140 tanks remaining, he had attacked British General Montgomery's desert forces in a final effort to turn the tide of battle. But it was no use. As night approached, fifty-two of his tanks had been destroyed and his panzer (armored) units had retreated in the direction of Tunis.

In the beginning, of course, everything had gone well. German submarines based in southern Italy had carried to Tunis a fortune in gold coins for Rommel to use. He was to bribe important Arab leaders in order to win them over to the German cause. But even this proved difficult, as some of the powerful Arab rulers preferred to remain out of the action. In many instances when the Arabs refused to fight for the Germans, they were executed or imprisoned, their palaces burned and their belongings stolen. It was in this way that Rommel gathered his treasure.

He was determined not to let it fall into the hands of his enemies. Many times he had thought of shipping it by sea from Tunis to southern Italy, but this was now impossible. The British had complete control of the air and sea.

Rommel confused the enemy

In order to confuse the British, Rommel used a clever tactic: he sent a fleet of fast power boats bearing several crates of objects that his troops had stolen from museums and palaces to a secret destination on the coast of Italy. The enemy had been waiting for such a move and were ready to seize or sink these small boats once their planes had spotted them.

Rommel's tactics worked perfectly. While the British bombers and naval units were making a desperate attempt to capture the swift ships, a convoy of trucks bearing most of Rommel's treasure was speeding along dirt roads in a southwesterly direction toward Douz, a small desert outpost. From there the gold was transported by camel caravan to a safe location and buried under one of the hundreds of sand dunes.

The German soldiers succeeded in safely burying the treasure on the Sahara. However, on their return they were ambushed and died, to the last man. So no one—not even Rommel—knew where his gold and jewels had been buried.

3. How did your purpose-setting questions help you as you read?

Lesson 3
Adjusting to Structure

Exercise A

Read the two paragraphs below with the purpose of understanding the main points of each. Put a check in front of the paragraph that you read more rapidly.

(A) _____ What is the responsibility of contemporary lexicographers (dictionary makers)? The successors of Noah Webster are enmeshed in a controversy. Some would maintain that lexicographers should condemn without qualification such words as *ain't*, while others argue that a lexicographer has nothing to do with deciding which words and expressions are right and which are wrong but only with citing current usages.

(B) _____ What is the duty of today's dictionary writers? The people who have followed in the footsteps of Noah Webster are involved in a debate. Some think that dictionaries should not include such words as *ain't*. Others disagree. They think dictionary writers shouldn't decide whether words and expressions are right or wrong. They should only report the way people actually use language.

1. Which paragraph has longer, more complicated sentences?

_____

2. Which paragraph were you able to understand more easily?

_____

3. Which paragraph did you have to read more carefully?

_____

Both paragraphs say about the same thing, but you were probably able to read paragraph B more rapidly. When a selection contains sentences that are long and complicated, your method of reading must be a careful one, and your rate of reading must be slow. To be a flexible reader, you must adjust your rate (slow, normal, fast) and method (careful reading, normal reading, or skimming) to your purpose and to the difficulty of words and sentences.

Look over the two selections on the next page to get an idea of their difficulty. Then read the articles, adjusting your rate and method to the difficulty of the material. Try to understand and remember the *main* points and the *important* details.

She was the first woman to seek the American presidency.

VICTORIA WOODHULL: INDEPENDENT THINKER
by Marion Meade

Victoria Woodhull ran for president of the United States in 1872. In an age when females were thought too ignorant even to vote, the notion of a woman president had sufficient power to shock most people. It was a revolutionary idea.

Perhaps others before her had shared the dream; if so, they never dared to expose themselves to ridicule. Any kind of worldly ambition was thought to be unnatural for a woman. America had been founded as a democracy with liberty and justice for all, but the question of who shall lead and who shall follow had been determined at the outset. Indeed, it had never even been debated. Politics was deemed a suitable occupation only for men.

A woman with political ambitions kept them to herself. If she were extraordinarily lucky, she might marry a man who would someday win the highest office and then she could be the First Lady. To wish for more was madness and delusion.

No doubt Victoria Woodhull was a bit odd. She rudely violated conventional ideas of what was proper behavior for a woman. Whether as presidential nominee, radical feminist, stockbroker, newspaper editor, public speaker, or divorced woman, Victoria Woodhull gloried in her independence. When she aimed for the White House, it was not an empty gesture. She meant business.

Because she happened to be an extraordinarily beautiful woman and a compelling speaker, people were sufficiently impressed to look, listen, and read about her. Her contemporaries may not have liked her, but they couldn't ignore her.

She overcame hardships to become a leading educator.

MARY McLEOD BETHUNE: TIRELESS WORKER
by Mary W. Burgess

A loud cry came from the tiny black baby. It was July 10, 1875. "She is born free!" exclaimed Patsy McLeod.

Years later Mary Jane's mother was doing washing for a white family. One morning, Mary Jane was standing silently while her mother talked with her employer. A small white child ran up with a book in her hand, and finding her mother busy, she turned to Mary Jane.

"Read me this story, Mary Jane," the child said.

Her older sister snatched the book away. "*She* can't read!" she said scornfully.

On the way home, Mary Jane pulled at her mother's dress, saying, "I want to learn to read!"

Patsy McLeod glanced down at the eager face.

"No schools for coloreds around here," she answered. "But—the teacher and the school will come some day."

The sight of that book had made a deep impression on Mary Jane. She could not get it out of her mind. She dreamed of it as she helped her father plant cotton.

"Mary's as strong as an ox," her neighbors would say. "And smart, too."

"Mary has a risin' soul," her mother said proudly. "She will go far or break her heart."

Mary McLeod did go far. She went to school and became a teacher. After her marriage to Albertus Bethune, she started a school for black girls. It later became Bethune-Cookman College, and she was its president from 1923 to 1947. She was a special advisor to President Franklin Roosevelt and the first black woman to head a government agency. She started the National Council of Negro Women. Many national awards were given to her—tributes to a remarkable woman.

Exercise B

Without looking back at the articles, see if you can answer the following questions.

_____ 1. When was Woodhull a presidential candidate?
        a. 1775
        b. 1947
        c. 1872

_____ 2. What was the best way for a woman to have a part in politics?
        a. by marrying a successful politician
        b. by running for office herself
        c. by criticizing men in politics

_____ 3. Which of the following did Woodhull _not_ become?
        a. nominee for president
        b. wife of a state governor
        c. newspaper editor

4. Was Mary McLeod Bethune born into slavery or freedom?

_____

5. What was it that Bethune wanted to learn to do?

_____

6. Why didn't Bethune go to school as a small child?

_____

7. Name one of Bethune's accomplishments.

_____

Exercise C
Answer these questions about your rate and method of reading.

8. Look back at both articles and underline the words that were unfamiliar
   to you in each one. Then write the title of the article that had more
   unfamiliar words.

   _____

9. Which article has longer and more difficult sentences?

   _____

10. Which article required that you do a slower, more careful reading in
    order to answer the questions in Exercise B?

    _____

Lesson 4
Using Patterns to Help You Read

Time order.   Thoughts and actions are often described in time order, as the next sentences show.

(A) I picked up my camping supplies at the Last Chance Outpost. Then I drove toward the wilderness.

(B) I drove toward the wilderness. Next, I picked up my camping supplies at the Last Chance Outpost.

In which example did the speaker pick up the camping supplies first? Circle the word that gives a clue to the time order.

In A and B the events are the same. Only the order in time in which the events occurred is changed.

Time order is an easy pattern to recognize. It is often signaled by clues like dates or words such as *first, next, then, at last, three months later, finally, before*, and *after*.

Time order is just one pattern you will meet in your reading. Ideas and events can be arranged in a number of other patterns.

Listing.   Sometimes the only pattern a writer uses is a simple list. The items in the list could be in any order without changing the meaning.

The following tools might be needed to work in a yard: rake, lawn mower, hedge trimmer, spade, wheelbarrow, clippers.

Is there any reason why the list of tools couldn't be rearranged in a different order? In a case like this the order of the items does not matter.

Cause-effect.   In a cause-effect pattern, something makes something else happen: a cause brings about a result, or effect. Look at the following example.

(A) Judith got an A on the test because she studied last night.
(B) Because Jan helped her with the lesson, Judith got an A on the test.

The same clue word to the cause-effect pattern appears in both sentences. What is this word? Circle it. A cause can be written before an effect or after it. In sentence A, the cause is "she studied last night." In sentence B, the cause is "Jan helped her." It is also possible for a cause to be in one sentence and the effect in another sentence or even in another paragraph.

The cause-effect pattern can be signaled by such words and phrases as *because, since, consequently, therefore, so that, for this reason*, and *as a result*.

Comparison-contrast.   The following sentence describes how two boats are alike and how they are different.

The stubby little rowboat—square, battered, practical—bobbed up and down next to the sleek white yacht—slim, glossy, built for speed and beauty.

This sentence has a comparison-contrast pattern. It is used here to show the difference between the rowboat and the yacht.

Clue words and phrases that often signal comparison-contrast patterns include *however, on the contrary, on the one hand—on the other, but, although, yet.*

Writers use different patterns to arrange facts, ideas, and events. Your understanding of what you are reading will be better if you know the way an author has arranged the information.

Time order, listing, cause-effect, and comparison-contrast are four common patterns. Recognizing such patterns and seeing how they are used can help you remember what you have read.

Also, you can adjust your reading to suit each pattern. If you are reading a selection that uses comparison-contrast, you will be on the lookout for how things are alike or different. If the selection uses mainly a cause-effect pattern, you will pay special attention to what causes something to happen or what the results of something are. If time order is the main pattern, you will try to remember the order in which things happened. In this way, understanding patterns can affect your method of reading.

Exercise A

Decide whether the pattern in each sentence is time order, cause-effect, comparison-contrast, or listing. Then write the answer on the blank.

1. Monroe Street is a noisy neighborhood because there is a lot of traffic, and our building is behind an all-night hot-dog stand.

   Pattern: _____

2. Walk down Monroe Street to the traffic light, then turn right; after you pass the hot-dog stand, you'll come to our building.

   Pattern: _____

3. There are many different kinds of places on Monroe Street: restaurants, groceries, bakeries, and butchers, among others.

   Pattern: _____

4. Madison, a quiet street, is much less exciting than Monroe.

   Pattern: _____

5. Monroe Street is busy all the time, but it is especially lively in the evenings.

   Pattern: _____

6. People enjoy living on Monroe Street since there is so much to do there.

   Pattern: _____

7. In the morning on Monroe Street you can smell fresh bread baking at the bakery. By afternoon the aroma of the coffeehouse fills the air. When night falls the sweet scent of lilacs is carried down the street by the wind.

   Pattern: _____

Exercise B

Decide whether the main pattern in each paragraph is time order, cause-effect, comparison-contrast, or listing. Then write the answer on the blank.

1. Buzz is an outfielder, and right now he's getting in shape for this year's baseball season. His daily exercises include twenty pushups, a hundred turns of the jump rope, two miles of jogging, four miles of bicycling, and practice in batting and fielding. In addition, on weekends he swims and plays tennis.

   Main pattern: _____

2. Stalactites and stalagmites are both rock forms found in caves. Stalactites are shaped like icicles, and they hang from the roof of a cave. They are formed by dripping water containing calcium carbonate that has hardened to rock. Stalagmites are shaped like cones, and they are built up on the floor of a cave. They are formed by water dripping from stalactites.

   Main pattern: _____

3. To get started with your woodworking project, select a piece of wood that has an interesting grain pattern. Next think of something you can make from a piece that size. It is a good idea to make a cardboard pattern first and then trace it on the wood. After this, cut out the design with a coping saw, just outside the lines you traced. When you have finished sawing, remove the saw marks with a fine file, followed by sandpaper. Finally, apply a coat or two of a stain wax.

   Main pattern: _____

4. Snows, hunters, and forest fires are all very hard on migrating birds. Death on a large scale is a price birds pay for long flights. From these and other causes, many birds die every year, sometimes so many that it takes years before their numbers are restored.

   Main pattern: _____

5. Sandy got into radio as a result of a practical joke. His school had a weekly radio program. Without Sandy's knowledge, his cousin said Sandy could take over for the announcer who had quit. Because he was a huge success with the audience, he got the job.

   Main pattern: _____

6. Plateosaurus and Styracosaurus were both plant-eating dinosaurs. The Styracosaurus had a strong spiked shield to protect itself, while the Plateosaurus could watch for enemies with their big birdlike eyes.

Main pattern: _____

Lesson 5
More About Patterns

Patterns are important in long selections. As you read an article, you should adjust your reading to the different patterns you find. If you understand how a writer has arranged information in a selection, you will be better able to remember what you have read.

Exercise A

The following paragraphs discuss life in ancient Egypt. As you read look for the patterns used by the author.

(A) From Aswan in the south to the Mediterranean Sea in the north, the Nile River Valley is 560 miles (900 kilometers) long. Along its banks is a fertile strip of land 6 to 9 miles (10 to 15 kilometers) wide. Desert rises on both sides of this rich river valley. Near its mouth, the Nile splits into two main branches. The split forms a triangle-shaped area that the Greeks called the Delta, after a letter of the alphabet.

(B) Most ancient Egyptians lived in the Nile Valley. The first people to settle there arrived about 5500 B.C. Their economy was based mainly on farming. Egyptians grew grains such as barley and emmer wheat. They raised cattle, sheep, goats, and pigs. Every year, farmers looked forward to the flooding of the Nile, for this assured a rich harvest.

1. How does the author show time order in paragraph B?

_____

_____

2. What other patterns does the author use in paragraph B?

_____

_____

3. What cause and effect does the author give in paragraph B?

_____

_____

(C) In July, monsoons drenched the highlands of East Africa. The rainwater flowed northward into tributaries of the Nile, making the river overflow. As the water flooded the farmers' fields, it deposited a thin layer of rich topsoil.

(D) In November, as the water receded, men and women turned up the soil with simple, wooden plows. They planted grain by stamping it into the ground with their feet. In some areas, they piled up long mounds of earth to trap the rich floodwaters. They also dug canals to bring precious water into the desert. In the warm climate, grain ripened quickly. Most years, people could grow a second crop using irrigation.

4. What pattern does the author use in paragraphs C and D? How do you know?

_____

_____

(E) Besides grain, Egyptians grew melons, beans, lettuces, and onions. They planted date and fig trees. Vineyards in the Nile Delta produced grapes to eat and to make into wine. Egyptians also drank a nourishing, low-alcohol beer made from barley, water, and yeast. There was no sugar. Food was sweetened with honey or fruits such as dates and grapes.

(F) Flax was grown and made into linen cloth, thread, and rope. The papyrus plant, which grew in the marshes of the Delta, was made into a kind of writing paper.

(G) Compared to other ancient lands, Egypt was a rich country. Harvests were usually abundant. When neighboring countries suffered famines, Egypt sometimes sold or gave them grain.

5. What pattern is used in paragraphs E and F? Give an example.

_____

_____

6. What pattern is used in paragraph G?

_____

_____

Exercise B

The article on the next page describes the history of mountain lions in the United States and what is being done to protect them. Read the article and answer the questions about patterns.

Ghost of the Wild

(A) Feel the stare. If looks could kill, the level gaze of this mountain lion guarding captured prey could be deadly. You're not likely to see the mountain lions except in a photograph or at a zoo. In the wild they usually avoid people—and each other. These secretive cats are so seldom seen that people sometimes call them "ghosts of the wilderness."

(B) Dr. Maurice Hornocker, however, meets mountain lions all the time. He's a scientist who has been tracking and studying the cats in parts of the western United States for nearly 30 years.

(C) Mountain lions don't deserve their bad reputation he says. They won't wipe out herds of deer or elk, their main source of food. The number of lions won't grow out of control. Furthermore, Hornocker adds, they won't normally attack livestock or people.

(D) Some problem cats do attack farm animals. That's why hunters were being paid to kill mountain lions as pests, as recently as 25 years ago.

(E) Mountain lions used to roam all of North and South America. But hunters killed so many that they vanished from the eastern U.S. except for Florida. Today they're beginning to make a comeback, thanks to laws that restrict hunting. Hornocker hopes his work can make the comeback last.

(F) He and his assistants hike remote mountains and meadows in New Mexico and Idaho in search of lions. When they find the animals, they capture and tranquilize them, then fit them with radio collars. The lions are released, and the scientists follow their comings and goings by studying signals from transmitters on the collars. "Radio tracking helps us make good conservation decisions," Hornocker says. "We learn what the animals eat. When they mate, hunt, and die. When people are ready to reintroduce lions in other parts of the country, our studies will help them."

(G) Left undisturbed, mountain lions can live in almost any environment—swamp, desert, forested areas. "They've survived without much help," says Hornocker. "It's a tribute to their adaptability that they've been able to hang on."

1. What word in the first sentence of paragraph B signals a comparison-contrast pattern?

   _____

   _____

2. What pattern do you see in paragraph C?

   _____

   _____

3. The word "then" is found in the second sentence of paragraph F. What pattern does this word signal?

_____

_____

4. What pattern do you see in paragraph G?

_____

_____

5. For what reason mentioned in paragraph E did mountain lions become so scarce in the United States?

_____

_____

Lesson 6
Surveys to Guide Your Study

Exercise

Suppose that you have been asked to give a report on Native Americans. In preparing the report you have to read a number of articles and parts of books. The selection that follows is from a magazine article. Complete the following items by referring to the article.

1. What or who is the article about? Look at the title for clues.

   _____

2. Write a purpose-setting question based on the opening paragraph.

   _____

3. Based on your survey, your purpose, and the difficulty of the words and sentences, what rate of reading—slow, normal, or fast—is most suitable?

   _____

Now read the article for the purpose of understanding and remembering the main points. Be prepared to answer questions after you have finished reading.

MARIA TALLCHIEF: PRIMA BALLERINA
by Marion E. Gridley

(A) The newspapers liked to refer to her as the beautiful dancing Osage princess. Reporters begged for stories about her life on the Indian reservation in Oklahoma where she was born. She had become a celebrity, but she wanted no part of such publicity. If Maria Tallchief were to be famous, it would be for achievement in dancing, not for "being an Indian."

(B) **The beginnings**

Betty Marie Tall Chief grew up in a modern world of change and not in the traditional ways of her ancestors. She could not speak a word of Osage, for it was not used in her home. She was remote from the older people in the community who still observed Indian customs. Her pride in being an Osage came largely from her grandmother, Eliza Bigheart, who lived with Betty Marie's family and who kept alive their Indian background with stories about the old days.

(C) When she was four years old, Betty Marie began to take dancing lessons to "develop grace." Her teacher came to the house once a week and taught her to stand on her toes, to leap, and to spin about—movements that horrified a later teacher, Ernest Belcher. Belcher, who became Betty Marie's teacher after the family moved to Los Angeles when she was eight, declared it a miracle that her feet had not been damaged for life. He made her stop toe-dancing at once and "unlearn" everything she had been taught. The endless hours of practice absorbed Betty Marie. She strove for perfection, and practice, to her, was a ritual.

(D) **Training as a dancer**

Throughout her school days, as soon as she got up in the morning, Betty Marie exercised and reviewed her dancing lessons. She took music lessons during this period of her life and practiced the piano twice a day—before going to school and as soon as she returned from school. At five o'clock in the evening, she left for her ballet class, which lasted two hours. After dinner, there was school homework to do. It was a rugged schedule.

(E) The years of strict discipline were relieved by small, personal triumphs—a performance at age ten in the ballet of the Los Angeles Opera Company, a solo performance at fifteen in the Hollywood Bowl, and a Canadian tour with the Ballet Russe (rüs) after graduation from high school.

(F) **The New York years**

After the Canadian tour, Betty Marie was signed on as a regular member of the Ballet Russe in New York. The director of the company suggested that she change her name to a Russian one—most of the dancers with the Ballet Russe were Russian, and those who were not had assumed that identity. Betty Marie at first totally rejected this suggestion—she was proud of her American name. Later, however, she compromised: her first name became Maria, her last spelled as one word.

(G) Six months after her arrival in New York City, Maria Tallchief had a small part in *Rodeo*, a new ballet choreographed by Agnes de Mille. It was a tremendous success and did much to advance Maria's career. But her big break did not come until she was assigned to dance the Chopin Concerto in place of an ailing ballerina, a major soloist. Her performance was so good that she was recognized as a great dancer, one who would undoubtedly become a prima ballerina, the leading female dancer of a ballet company.

(H) From then on Maria danced the Concerto whenever it was presented. She danced the ballet's debut in New York City when she was eighteen years old to a tremendous ovation. The young girl whose only desire was to dance had become a celebrity.

4. What pattern does the author use in paragraph C? In paragraphs D and E?

_____

5. What is a prima ballerina?

_____

6. What was Tallchief's big break?

_____

If you can't answer these questions, you read the selection too quickly for your purpose and for the difficulty of the material. Go back and reread for the answers.

Lesson 7
Putting Your Reading Skills to Work

Exercise

Using all the skills you have learned in this unit, read the following article for the purpose of understanding and remembering its main points and details. Make a survey to ask purpose-setting questions. Then decide on a suitable method and rate of reading. Be prepared to answer questions on the material as you are reading.

Mysterious work of art reported to possess strange powers.

THE CRYSTAL SKULL
by Seymour Simon

In the early 1970s, the Museum of the American Indian in New York City had an unusual object on display. It was a life-size sculpture of a human skull carved from quartz. As the crystal skull turned slowly on its rotating base, it glittered and sparkled like a huge diamond.

The discovery of the skull is hidden in mystery. It is reported to have been found in 1927 in an ancient Mayan city. The Mayans were an American Indian people who lived in Central America and Mexico. The skull was discovered beneath a broken altar by Anna Mitchell-Hedges.

1. Where was the crystal skull found?

_____

2. Is the crystal skull life-size or a miniature?

_____

Description of the skull

While many carved Mayan skulls have been found, most are made from clay, wood, or bone. A few are made of crystal, but the Mitchell-Hedges skull is the only one with movable parts. Also, its workmanship is far better than that of other crystal skulls.

The skull is beautifully made from clear rock crystal. It seems to have been carved without the use of metal tools, since no scratches or tool marks have been seen under a microscope.

The lower jaw of the skull is a separate piece of quartz. The jaw fits tightly into two polished sockets and can be moved up and down so that it looks as if the mouth is opening and closing. Channels have been hollowed out in the skull, reaching from the bottom to the eye sockets. If a light is passed beneath the skull, it makes the eyes flicker in a spooky way.

The skull measures about five inches high by seven inches long and five inches wide. It weighs eleven pounds, seven ounces. If it were to be sold, it would be worth a great deal of money. But for many people it is truly priceless.

3. In the first paragraph under the subhead "Description of the skull," what is compared and contrasted?

Strange powers

Ever since the skull was found, its discoverer and other people who have examined it have claimed that is has some strange powers. Anna Mitchell-Hedges says that when she found the skull, three hundred Indians who were working nearby fell to their knees and kissed the ground.

In 1956, Frank Dorland, an art expert, started to study the skull. Some of his claims about the skull are very surprising and even frightening.

For example, Dorland claims that when he kept the skull in his house to study, weird things began to happen. When he went to sleep, he and his wife were awakened by unusual noises. They heard what sounded like a large jungle cat prowling through the house. They also heard the sounds of chimes and bells.

Dorland goes on to state that when he awoke the next morning, the rooms in his house were in a mess with things scattered all over. But the windows to the rooms had all been closed and locked.

Anna Mitchell-Hedges says that her father thought that the skull was an evil thing. He believed that the skull brought death.

Dorland and other persons who viewed the skull insist that its color changes from clear crystal to shades of green, violet, purple, red, blue, and amber. It also sometimes has a heavy odor like that of moist earth.

It is difficult to know what to make of all these claims of mysterious powers. One thing that can be said is that when the skull was displayed at the Museum of the American Indian, no special powers were noticed.

4. After the subhead "Strange powers," a listing pattern is used. What are some of the strange powers that are listed?

The mystery continues

As for the questions about who made the skull or when it was made, no proof has been found. Most observers are fairly sure that the skull is Mayan, and they believe the story of the find by the Mitchell-Hedges family.

The skull was examined in close detail by the Hewlett-Packard crystal laboratories in Santa Clara, California. Some of the laboratory people felt that the lenses and prisms in the skull show a knowledge of physics that has only recently been understood.

Perhaps in the future the crystal skull will be studied further by scientists and more will be found out. Until that time the crystal skull remains a beautiful and mysterious relic of an age long past.

5. What did the laboratory that examined the skull say about it?

Lesson 8

What Is Imagery?

Imagine that you are riding in a helicopter that is being used to corral wild horses.

1. How would the scene look from the air?

_____

2. What colors might you see?

_____

3. What sound might you hear?

_____

4. How would you feel physically as the helicopter moved?

_____

5. How would the helicopter rotor blades look?

_____

You can probably imagine the sight from the air of swiftly moving horses over the rough ground. You would probably see different shades of brown and green. You can imagine the sound of the helicopter rotor blades. You might also feel the helicopter's vibrations or a sinking feeling in your stomach as it swoops down. If you looked up, you might see the blades as a whirling blur above you. Details of smell and taste are not shown directly, but you can probably imagine the smell and taste of dust that might be blown into an open window by the revolving rotor blades and stampeding horses.

In a similar way, you can respond to the details that writers use to appeal to your senses. When writers use sensory details, they are showing with language how something looks, sounds, smells, tastes, or feels. They are creating images, or **imagery**, and they hope that their imagery helps you to create your own imagery as you read about what is being described.

Exercise

Try to imagine what happened during the attempt to corral the wild horses as it is described below. Concentrate on the images of physical sensations. Then answer the questions.

Wild horses running free have long been a part of the untamed West. Last September the Bureau of Land Management staged a helicopter roundup in a section of crowded range in western Idaho. About thirty-four horses were rounded up in one day, as the siren-equipped helicopter flew over the barren range searching for stallions traveling in bands with their mares and colts. Sleek-bodied horses stampeded through the brush with

modern ranching methods being used to capture them. A corral disguised
by sagebrush was ready to receive the stampeding horses.

1. Write an image that helps you picture how the horses looked.

   _____

2. What word does the author use to describe the West?

   _____

3. What word other than the word *running* is used to create a vivid image of
   the movement of the horses?

   _____

4. What sound was used to attract the attention of the horses?

   _____

5. What kinds of horses were the helicopters searching for?

   _____

6. How does the author let you know using helicopters is a new way of
   rounding up horses?

   _____

7. Write the words that describe the horses' final destination.

   _____

8. Write at least three words that you would use to describe the people who
   flew the helicopter and rounded up the horses.

   _____

Lesson 9
Recognizing Imagery

Exercise A

Certain words can make your senses react more strongly than others. Here are some phrases that appeal to your senses of sight, sound, smell, taste, and touch or feeling. Read each phrase and write which sense or senses it affects most.

1. tennis ball bouncing off a racket

_____

2. freshly cut pine branches

_____

3. last rays of the sun sinking over the horizon

_____

4. a mouthful of Swiss cheese and wheat crackers

_____

5. a leg cramp

_____

Exercise B

Each pair of sentences below describes the same event. Put a check in front of the one in each pair that uses more vivid imagery.

1. _____ **a.** The oil-spattered mechanic tried to calm the outraged customer who yelled about the poor service and threatened to sue the garage.

   _____ **b.** The garage mechanic talked to the upset customer who complained about the service.

2. _____ **a.** Suddenly the calf's eyes focused, its body shook, and it made a noise that could barely be heard.

   _____ **b.** The calf's eyes looked at me clearly for a moment, its body trembled in the cool spring breeze, and it bleated softly.

3. _____ **a.** After putting his suitcase on the luggage rack, Oliver sat down on the leather seat.

   _____ **b.** After tossing the battered suitcase onto the luggage rack, Oliver sank into the thickly cushioned leather seat.

4. _____ **a.** After a day of hiking everyone had hearty appetites and piled their plates high with golden-brown roasted chicken and rice.

_____ **b.** Everyone was hungry after hiking all day and had second helpings of chicken and rice.

5. _____ **a.** The room was filled with a musty, damp odor that seemed to come from the foul-smelling water that flooded the floor.

_____ **b.** There was a bad smell in the room that seemed to come from the water on the floor.

Exercise C

Read the passage that follows. Underline ten words or groups of words that create sharp, clear images.

I huddled closer to what was left of the fire and gloomily prepared myself to get through the night. In the dying light of the campfire, I opened a can of black bean soup and gulped it down in thick spoonfuls without water. Wrapped in flannel blankets and smeared with insect repellent, I tried to sleep. But without the comforting crackle of a fire, I began to hear the noises of the night. They forced their way to my attention. Some large creature was rustling through the bushes about two hundred feet away. A deer? A bear? Then a beaver slapped its tail out in the marshes. Could a canoe be coming? A Barred Owl began its screeching across the swamp. Its mate answered right above my head.

Mysterious soft murmurs, sighs, scufflings, squeaks, clawings, and scratchings filled the forest as mice, hares, owls, foxes, flying squirrels, moles, bats, and insects fled and fed upon each other in the eternal struggle for life.

Lesson 10
Responding to Imagery

Exercise A

Sara is the young daughter of a weekend racing driver. Imagine that you are with her in the scene below. Then answer the questions.

The sound of growling, throbbing engines fills the track. A slim blonde girl leans against the fence to watch the cars lining up. It's scorching hot and the air is thick with fumes. When she pushes back a strand of hair, a smear of grease runs along her forehead. She sees the starter wave his flag, his feet dangerously close to the cars. As the flag drops, the cars take off in a body.

1. What kind of sound is made by the car engines?

_____

2. What images tell how the girl looks?

_____

3. How does the air smell?

_____

4. What does the girl feel on her face?

_____

5. What image is used to indicate the start of the race?

_____

Exercise B

Read the following paragraphs and answer the questions. When questions have choices for answers, underline the correct one.

During the week, Sara spends every spare moment working with her father on his racing car. She doesn't know how much help she actually was in the beginning, though. "Dad would ask me to hand him 'that cylinder with the long handle.' Now I know it's a socket, and I can use it."

The family has to be ready by six o'clock Saturday morning when practiced ears listen intently to the roar of finely tuned engines. One faulty noise heard by Sara or another team member means stopping trouble before it starts.

On Sunday as racing time nears, yesterday's tensions double. Excitement mounts as Sara helps her father-turned-driver into his low-slung car. Now he adjusts his goggles and helmet and puts on his gloves.

Then her father joins the line of cars moving slowly toward the starting grid. To Sara it seems like forever until they get there. Then the engines blast, revving up for the start and making it even hotter in the pits. But Sara feels good—she is part of this challenging contest from the tune-up to the finish line.

1. Sara spends most of her spare time helping her father work on
   a. a new helmet design.
   b. a new engine.
   c. his racing car.

2. When checking their cars, racers rely mainly on
   a. smell.
   b. touch.
   c. hearing.
   d. sight.

3. The cars approach the starting grid
   a. in single file.
   b. bunched together.
   c. at top speed.

4. A socket wrench looks like: (Check one.)

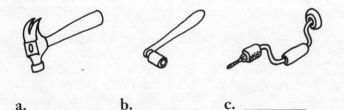

   a. _____   b. _____   c. _____

5. Sara's father's car sits
   a. high off the ground.
   b. close to the ground.

6. At the start of the race, do the engines rev quietly? How do you know?

   _____

7. How do you think Sara feels as the race starts?

   _____

8. Describe a sight, sound, smell, taste, or feeling that you might experience in the service pit as the race is starting.

   _____

   _____

Lesson 11
Visualizing What Happens

Check the sketch above that looks most like the scene described in the following paragraph.

Kate placed her bare feet down carefully on the rough planks at the shore end of the pier, enjoying the soft thudding of her feet against the wood, mingled with the soft, rhythmic slap of the water against the piles. It was hot, but the breeze blowing in from the lake felt cool and Kate enjoyed a deep breath of air.

To identify the most accurate drawing, you had to visualize—to form a mental picture of—a wooden pier sticking out from a lake shore washed by small, steadily rolling waves. If you paid close attention to the details of the paragraph, you knew that Kate was standing at the shore end of the pier. You will build up a clearer mental picture of this lakeside scene as you read more details about it.

There was no one else on the pier except Kate's six-year-old brother, Jimmy, who was dangling his legs above the water at the far end of the pier. He was lowering a tin pail on a string and hauling up water, then pouring it all over himself. Kate looked along the pebbled beach curving to her left. She saw nobody except her Uncle Frank with two other men in the distance. They seemed to be working on some fishing tackle. The men's small figures shimmered in the heat waves rippling above the beach. Kate waved, but they didn't see her.

Exercise A

Underline the correct answer to each question.

1. As you visualize the scene described in both paragraphs, the pier is probably located
   a. next to a crowded beach.
   b. near a shed where fishing nets are drying.
   c. on an almost empty stretch of shore.
   d. in front of busy shops and motels.

2. When Kate first sees Jimmy, he is
   a. running along the pier.
   b. fishing from the middle of the pier.
   c. climbing out of the water.
   d. sitting on the end of the pier.

3. Which sound could Kate probably *not* hear?
   a. a gull's cry
   b. splashing water
   c. the fishermen's voices
   d. Jimmy's laughter

4. Write the image that describes how hot the beach is as Kate looks toward her uncle and the two other men.

   _____

5. On the map below, show roughly where each of the following people is by marking **K** for Kate, **J** for Jimmy, and **F** for Uncle Frank. Then draw an arrow to show the direction of the breeze.

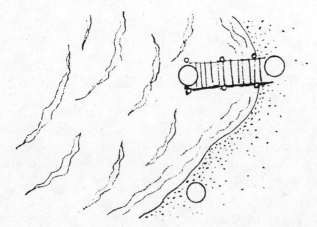

These questions and answers are the kinds of ideas you should think about whenever your read a description that does not seem clear. The answers will usually help you visualize the images and actions being described. It's also important to pay attention to the words that show the positions of people and objects in a scene. In this story, for example, you need to notice such phrases as: "the breeze blowing *in from* the lake"; "*to* her *left*"; "*in the distance*."

At first, you may want to jot down a few details like these to keep them straight. But quite soon, you'll find you can quickly ask and answer the questions in your mind. Then it will be much easier for you to follow descriptions of places and action.

Exercise B

Now that you have a clear picture in your mind of the scene around the pier, you should be able to imagine what happens next almost as if you were watching it scene by scene.

Maybe she'd go swimming, Kate thought. She looked over the side of the pier at the small, smooth, round rocks beneath the clear, shallow water. She had learned to swim right here only last year, holding onto the dock, splashing and kicking, while her uncle laughed and called encouragement from above. She remembered the one time she'd tried to swim into the deeper water at the end of the pier and the panic that had overwhelmed her because she knew she had been in over her head. She was too afraid to ever try that again. . . . Kate glanced at Jimmy, who was squealing and laughing aloud as he played. She called to him.

Jimmy looked around and then suddenly disappeared without a sound. For a moment Kate could do nothing but stare blankly at the spot where he had been. Running to the end of the pier, she could see him floundering and gasping for help in the deep water. She fell to her stomach and reached down to him, but he was just beyond her reach. She scrambled to her feet, but there was nothing on the pier that she could throw to him, and the fishermen, absorbed in what they were doing, were too far away to help. She looked frantically at Jimmy, who was bobbing in the water. At the same time she knew she had to help Jimmy. Suddenly she knew she could do it . . . .

1. Underline the things that people walking in the shallow water beside the pier might feel under their bare feet.
   a. sand and pebbles
   b. rough wood planks
   c. smooth cement
   d. sticky mud

2. Which of the following things actually happened? Mark each statement below **T** (true), or **F** (false), or **CT** (can't tell from the description).

   _____ a. Kate vividly recalled her panic in deep water.

   _____ b. Jimmy yelled to Kate.

   _____ c. He turned and fell off the pier.

   _____ d. The pier was too high for Kate to reach down to him.

   _____ e. She climbed into a rowboat.

   _____ f. Jimmy's tin pail was floating near him.

   _____ g. He sank to the bottom.

_____ **h.** Kate jumped up and rapidly glanced all around her.

_____ **i.** She saw the fishermen running toward her.

3. Describe an image that helps you see Jimmy in the water.

_____

4. Give one reason why Kate does not immediately dive in to help Jimmy.

_____

5. Describe how Kate feels as she looks at Jimmy in the deep water.

_____

6. In the last paragraph, Kate's face would most likely show an expression

of _____.
  a. annoyance
  b. total exhaustion
  c. cheerful calmness
  d. fearful determination

Lesson 12
Reviewing the Use of Imagery

Exercise

Try to imagine the sights, sounds, smells, and feelings that are described in the passage below and answer the questions that follow.

from SWIFTWATER
by Paul Annixter

It had been a grim and anxious time in the Calloway cabin, and Bucky could hardly put his mind to anything. Most of the time Cam had lain half asleep, sometimes flushed with fever, sometimes with an ashen pallor, for he had come close to pneumonia. There was little talk in the cabin; even Ma was silent, a bad sign.

It was dusk and Bucky was just bringing in the night's wood, enough short logs to burn till morning and a pile of logs for beside the fireplace that would last the following day if need be. His face and ears burned from laboring in a temperature close to forty below. Coarse gray socks were stuffed into his felt shoes against the cold, and a cap of worn coonskin crowned his shagbark hair that had not been cut in weeks. His face was drawn and pinched, the dark eyes sullen from overwork.

Ma sat darning socks over an egg,[1] rising now and then to stir the mush pot, or turn the cooking rabbit. Cam lay in the cord bunk in the corner of the cabin, his injured leg raised high beneath the blankets. His gaunt, unshaven face still etched with the pain he had endured before Doc Waters had come to reset the bone. His fever was down tonight, and worry showed in the black eyes turned up to the ceiling poles. There was little food left for the family—a few frozen rabbits, a side of bacon, some beans and meal.

Bucky went out for a final log, and the door creaked behind him on its crude hinges. The snow in the clearing was almost knee-deep; the dark ring of the surrounding forest was broken only at one place, where the woods road cut like a tunnel through the pines toward town.

A sudden wind rose with the darkness. Bucky could hear it far off and high, a growing roar above the forest. Abruptly it snatched at the clearing, whirling snow in eddies. Because his impulse was to hurry in again and close the door against it, Bucky stood for several minutes with his face straight into it, letting the cold and darkness and emptiness sink into him.

---

1. *darning socks over an egg,* using an egg or an egg-shaped object to hold cloth in place while a tear or hole is being mended.

1. Write an image from the passage for each of the senses below.
   a. sight:

   _____

   b. sound:

   _____

   c. smell:

   _____

   d. feeling:

   _____

2. Circle the letter of the phrase that best describes Bucky.
   a. busy and talkative
   b. cold and exhausted
   c. tired and warm

3. Circle one of Ma's activities that help you imagine it is dusk.
   a. She is sewing.
   b. She is preparing supper.
   c. She gets up and down.

4. Circle what is the matter with Cam.
   a. He has pneumonia.
   b. He is hungry.
   c. His leg is broken.

5. Which images below could be added to those that Bucky sees, hears, and feels in the last two paragraphs? Write **Y** (yes) or **N** (no) on the space in front of each item.

   _____ a. crunch of snow

   _____ b. sunshine

   _____ c. ax chopping wood

   _____ d. wind blowing through the trees

   _____ e. cold hands and feet

   _____ f. snow-covered tree limbs.

Lesson 13
What Is Figurative Language?

"My grandpa says I'm really bright."

In the sentence above, *bright* is not meant to be understood literally. The sentence does not refer to the boy as being shiny or lit up.

Words, phrases, and sentences that are meant to be understood exactly word-for-word are *literal*. Words, phrases, and sentences that are *not* meant to be understood word-for-word are **figurative**.

Exercise A

The following sentences contain figurative language. Underline the words or phrases in each that are not meant to be understood literally. Then underline the solution that best explains the figurative language.

1. Marissa is such a fast reader that she gulps down novels.
   a. Marissa eats paperback novels.
   b. Marissa reads many novels very quickly.
   c. Marissa is confused by what she reads.

2. Rudy has hands that are like sandpaper.
   a. Rudy's hands have sand glued to them.
   b. Rudy's hands have been rubbed smooth.
   c. Rudy's hands are dry and very rough.

3. Before a big test, Jason is as nervous as a racehorse before a race.
   a. Jason runs very fast.
   b. Jason keeps moving about and can't stay still.
   c. Jason can easily kick and hurt someone.

4. When Sheila is hurt or unhappy, she pulls herself into her shell, like a turtle.
   a. Sheila withdraws from other people when she is upset.
   b. Sheila gets angry and shouts when she is upset.
   c. Sheila moves very slowly when she is upset.

Many figurative expressions, like the one using *bright*, have been used for many years. Their meanings are familiar to many people. Good writers try to create fresh figurative expressions to get their ideas across. These new expressions often require more thought by a reader. For example, underline the figurative expression in the sentence on the next page.

With his long, powerful legs, Luis is a greyhound among beagles when he competes in the 440-yard dash.

Luis, who is a very fast runner, is compared to a greyhound. That dog, which has long, powerful legs, is known for its speed. In fact, it is used as a racing dog. The other runners are described as beagles, dogs with short legs that do not run very fast.

You will sometimes come across words and phrases and even whole sentences that don't make sense when read in a literal way. Sometimes, you can find a particular figurative expression in a dictionary. Other times, you will have to figure out the expression by yourself.

Exercise B

Choose the one sentence in each pair that uses figurative language. Circle the letter of that sentence.

1. **a.** When Howie is in the pool, he's a fish.
   b. When Howie is in the pool, he can swim better than anyone else.

2. **a.** It's so hot outside; the temperature has been over a hundred degrees every day for the last week!
   b. It's so hot outside; I feel like I've been standing under a rocket that has just blasted off!

3. **a.** Richard eats too much, too fast.
   b. Richard cleans up food like a human vacuum cleaner.

4. **a.** When it comes to remembering what other people say, Linda has tape recorders for ears.
   b. When it comes to remembering what other people say, Linda can repeat every word.

5. **a.** As the storm passed, the sky turned a very white color.
   b. As the storm passed, the sky changed color and looked like curdled milk.

Lesson 14
Making Sense of Figurative Language

1. What does it mean to be up with the chickens?

_____

2. Where do you think this expression came from?

_____

"Up with the chickens" is an old, common expression. It means "to be awake very early in the morning." The origins of some figurative expressions, such as this one, are fairly easy to figure out. People who live on farms tend to wake up early—with the farm animals that wake up at sunrise.

Most writers try to avoid old, common expressions. Instead, they try to create new, fresh ones. They expect the reader to figure out the meaning. The reader will need to make sense of the entire expression, not just read the words in a literal way.

Exercise A
Read the title and poem below.

THE TOASTER
by William Jay Smith

A silver-scaled Dragon with jaws flaming red
Sits at my elbow and toasts my bread.
I hand him fat slices, and then, one by one,
He hands them back when he sees they are done.

1. What two things are being compared in the poem?

   _____

2. What are the "jaws flaming red," literally?

   _____

3. When the slices are done, what happens, literally?

   _____

4. Why is a toaster compared to a dragon?

   _____

Why did this poet compare a toaster to a dragon? Think about toasters for a minute. Don't they often have a shiny, silver color? When the toaster is on, don't the openings turn red?

Now think about pictures of dragons that you have seen. Aren't they often pictured with silver scales? Aren't dragons often shown breathing fire?

When you come across a figurative word or phrase that doesn't make literal sense, look at the context in which it is used. Then figure out what the expression could mean that would make sense in that context.

Most figurative expressions involve comparisons. But not all comparisons are figurative. If the things being compared are very much alike, the comparison can probably be understood literally as in the sentence below.

> Liz plays soccer like her brother does.

The things compared above—the way Liz plays and the way her brother plays—are very similar. They are both people who play soccer with a similar style. The comparison is meant to be understood in a literal way.

Exercise B
Each sentence below contains figurative language. After each sentence, there are three phrases or sentences that translate the figurative language into literal language.

Choose the phrase that gives the best literal meaning for the italicized figurative expression. Circle the letter of your choice.

1. Dave doesn't just grow plants—he *mothers them*.
   a. grows them in a nursery
   b. treats them the way a mother treats her children
   c. treats them harshly

2. Bonita can help you in almost any subject; she *is a pocket calculator, a dictionary, and an encyclopedia all rolled into one.*
   a. is good in math and English and knows many facts
   b. owns reference books and other aids for every subject
   c. carries with her anything she may need for schoolwork

3. Daniel doesn't study a textbook thoroughly; instead, *he dips into a chapter here or nibbles at a few pages there*, and enjoys himself.
   a. studies the parts he likes
   b. eats a lot while he's studying
   c. has little appetite for studying

4. The new budget provides more money for the golf and swim teams and for the band, but it leaves the tennis team *out in the cold*.
   a. on the outdoor courts, even in the winter
   b. without warm-up suits
   c. without the necessary support to continue

5. Answering Ms. Helm's questions is *like testifying against yourself*.
   a. tricky because she often asks questions about government and law
   b. dangerous, because whatever you say, it may hurt you
   c. dangerous, because she doesn't like students who fail her tests

Exercise C

Figurative language is often used in poetry. The following poem is about a cat. The qualities of the cat are expressed in figurative comparisons. Read the poem and think about the figurative language. Then, answer the questions that follow.

from THE DEATH OF A CAT
by Louis MacNeice

To begin with he was a beautiful object:
Blue crisp fur with a white collar,
Paws of white velvet, springs of steel,
A Pharaoh's profile, a Krishna's grace,
Tail like a question mark . . .

1. What color were the cat's paws?

   _____

2. Were the cat's paws literally velvet? In your own words, describe how the paws felt.

   _____

3. The cat has "springs of steel." What does this tell you about the cat?

   _____

   _____

4. What do the comparisons to a Pharaoh and to Krishna suggest?

   _____

   _____

5. In your own words, describe the cat's tail.

_____

_____

Exercise D

Not all poems have figurative language. The poem that follows was written by a boy about his cat, named Celestino. Read the poem and underline five things the cat is compared to literally.

A CAT
by John Gittings

Silently licking his gold-white paw
Oh gorgeous Celestino, for
God made lovely things, yet
Our lovely cat surpasses them all.
The gold, the iron, the waterfall,
The nut, the peach, apple, granite
Are lovely things to look at, yet
Our lovely cat surpasses them all.

Lesson 15
Figurative Language in Literature

Figurative language is often used to compare one thing to something else the reader is probably familiar with. For example, read the following sentence.

> Arlene must not be a very good camp counselor since she lets the kids treat her *like a human doormat*.

Arlene is compared to a doormat. You are probably familiar with doormats. What are they used for? What happens to them? Of course, the kids are not literally wiping their feet on Arlene or stepping on her. But the figurative language lets us understand that the campers do not treat their counselor very nicely.

Exercise

Read the following excerpt about a girl who enjoys looking at things through a microscope. As you read, look for examples of figurative language that let you understand what she sees under the microscope. Then, answer the questions that follow.

from A DREAM OF GHOSTS
by Frank Bonham

She flipped a braid back over her shoulder and got to work. With an eyedropper, she placed some pond water on a slide and shielded it with a thin cover-slip. Carefully she fastened the slide in place and bent over the eyepieces. At first all was pearly and blurred, but as she sharpened the focus dozens of tiny wriggling animals materialized. Protozoans! Some were mere blobs *like wriggling ink stains*; but others *were suns with wiggly rays*, or *little worms with whirring propellers*. Many had brilliant ruby eyespots.

Raptly she focused down still further to find the dainty little diatoms, like snowflakes carved from jewels of many colors. She had entered a silent world populated by living things shaped like pieces of Christmas candy, telstars, planets, hourglasses, and pillboxes.

She sighed happily. It was difficult to believe that this magic world was as real as her own! A dishpan was an ocean to a diatom—it might take days to cross. Life-and-death battles were going on in every teaspoonful of water. And some of these little creatures, like the amoeba, could actually enter people's bodies and kill them.

A thought tickled her brain like a small charge of electricity. Her eyes widened in wonder.

In a way, these little creatures were like ghosts. If you could not see them, they did not exist—yet of course they did. The thing was, you had to see them under special conditions.

1. In the first paragraph, three examples of figurative language are italicized. Choose one of these and in your own words describe what that particular protozoan looks like.

   _____

   _____

2. Which of the following best explains the figurative language use in the second paragraph to describe the tiny living things called diatoms? Circle your choice.
   a. Diatoms are very sweet and make the pond water taste good.
   b. Diatoms are delicate, colorful miniature living things in many different shapes.
   c. Diatoms are tiny living things that crowd together in water but that do not speak to each other.

3. Explain what is meant by the phrase "a dishpan was an ocean to a diatom."

   _____

   _____

4. Rewrite the figurative language in the fourth paragraph using either literal language or a different figurative expression.

   _____

   _____

5. In your own words, explain how the "little creatures were like ghosts."

   _____

   _____

Lesson 16
Reviewing Figurative Language

In the following passage, the boy James is sitting by a lake. Down the beach a fence extends out into the lake separating him from a resort on the other side. He's just met a girl who's chased her brother, Jacky, through a hole in the fence. The little boy is playing with his golf ball.

Exercise

Read the passage and answer the questions about figurative language at the end.

from **A FABULOUS CREATURE**
by Zilpha Keatley Snyder

"Wait a minute. He's wearing me out. I've got to get rid of him for a minute." Holding out the golf ball she said, "Look Jacky. Here it is. Here's your ball. Now, go get it." She threw the ball as hard as she could down the beach.

Jacky gave a final angry yelp and trotted off, while the girl watched him go approvingly. "He's a real killer," she said. "Isn't he? I mean for barely two years old?"

Wrapping one of his arms around his neck, James gingerly explored his shoulder blade with the tips of his fingers. "You can say that again," he said grimly.

She glanced at him quickly, as if surprised. "Oh, the golf ball." She shrugged. "Well, don't take it personally. He throws it at everyone."

"Yeah? Why do you let him? I mean, why doesn't someone just take it away from him?"

"Oh, we couldn't do that. He has to have it. My mom did take it away once, but it didn't do any good. All he did was scream the house down until he got it back. Even when he just loses it—look out!" Making pistols of both her hands she shot them off into her temples. "Ka-pow! He drives everybody crazy until he gets it back. Besides my dad doesn't want us to take it away. He thinks Jacky's old golf ball is a real riot."

"Doesn't he ever throw it at him? At your dad?"

"Oh sure. He doesn't mind."

Glancing up, James noticed Jacky stomping purposefully in their direction, golf ball clutched in sandy fist. The girl was crouching slightly preparing to dodge, and he followed her example.

"Look out," she said. "Here it comes." The ball whistled between them, and running after it, she scooped it up and headed toward the fence. "I've got to go," she called. "Come over here and help me get him through the fence."

James followed, wondering how she planned to get Jacky through the hole, which looked as if it would be a tight squeeze, if he didn't want to go. Would she try to stuff him through it, or—he grinned, thinking of a more satisfying possibility—perhaps, throw him over the top? But when he reached the fence the problem had already been partly solved. The girl had thrown the golf ball through the fence, and Jacky was already frantically burrowing after it. Now all that remained for James to do was to make sure he didn't come back while his sister was swimming around the end of the fence in the lake.

It wasn't too difficult. When Jacky tried to crawl back under, James sat down and, instead of vulnerable hands, used a tooth-proof hiking boot to shove him back to the other side. And when the kid gave up on the hole and threatened to golf ball him through the fence, he simply spoke to him firmly. "You throw that thing over here, you little turkey, and you'll never see it again." He wasn't sure how much of that Jacky understood, but it seemed to be enough. He was still clutching his Spaulding torpedo when his sister rose from the lake like a hot-pink mermaid. Grabbing his wrist she towed him, stiff-legged and bellowing, toward the center of The Camp.

1. Underline the figurative expression the sister uses to describe Jacky in the second paragraph. What does she mean by this?

   _____

2. The girl's father calls Jacky's golf ball a "real riot." Is this literal or figurative? What does the father mean?

   _____

   _____

3. Underline the figurative expression James uses in speaking to Jacky.

4. Is Jacky literally holding a torpedo? What is he holding? Why might it be called a torpedo?

   _____

   _____

5. Is the girl literally a mermaid? What does this mean?

   _____

   _____

   _____

Lesson 17
Making Inferences

Exercise A

Read the paragraph and answer the questions.

> As Rebecca turned away from the window, she was frowning deeply. She walked quickly across the room toward the door to the kitchen and to the back stairs. Then she stopped and turned back into the living room. A loud knock sounded at the front door. Hearing it, Rebecca jumped slightly and grabbed the back of a chair. The knock came again. Biting her knuckle, Rebecca glanced toward the kitchen door and then back toward the front door. A third knock sounded. Rebecca could hear her mother calling her name. But still she stood, shifting her weight from foot to foot and holding the back of the chair.

1. Is Rebecca in a hurry to see her mother?

    _____

2. How do you think Rebecca feels?

    _____

3. Underline the words and phrases that helped you figure out what Rebecca's feelings are.

4. What do you think Rebecca would like to do?

    _____

5. Circle the words and phrases you used as clues to answer number 4.

    To answer the questions above you did two things. First you read the words. Then you found clues in the behavior of the character. You were able to conclude—to **infer**—how Rebecca was feeling in the paragraph. Each conclusion was an **inference** based on evidence.

Exercise B

Read each paragraph below. Then answer the questions.

> (A) You ask your sister how she did on her history test. She replies by slamming her books down on a table and snapping, "I don't even want to talk about it!"

1. What would you guess happened?

    _____

(B) Sunday afternoon the back tire of your bike suddenly goes flat. A friend, who says she knows tires, patches the leak and promises that your tire is as good as new. Then, Monday morning, on the way to school, you feel a thumping from the back tire . . . .

2. What can you infer about your tire and your friend?

_____

(C) Your older brother and two friends have been singing together for over a year now. They hope to become big stars some day, but so far they've only appeared in amateur talent shows. Today they were supposed to have a tryout at a major recording studio. You're at home when your brother bursts through the door with a big smile on his face.

3. What can you infer about the tryout?

_____

(D) As you wait in the lobby to get into the theater, people who have just seen the movie are coming out. Almost all of them are silent and have serious expressions. Some even have tears running down their faces . . . .

4. What can you infer about the movie?

_____

(E) When you go to English class on Friday, there is a stranger sitting at your teacher's desk reading the teacher's planbook. She smiles at you as you take your seat . . . .

5. What do you infer about the woman?

_____

Lesson 18
Identifying Clues

As you read, you think like a detective. The writer gives you clues. You must recognize the clues and use them to draw logical conclusions. Occasionally one clue is enough evidence. Most times, however, you need to put many clues together to make a correct inference.

Exercise A

Read the murder mystery that follows. A detective, Dr. Haledjian (he lej'e en), spots clues and makes inferences in order to solve the case. See if you can follow his thinking.

> Death, Dr. Haledjian determined quickly, had been caused by a blunt instrument within the past half hour.
>
> He carefully rolled the body of his old friend, Hugh Clark, on its back. Something glinted within the red carnation in Clark's lapel. Haledjian recognized the object instantly—a gold stater of Croesus—a rare coin.
>
> The detective replaced the coin in the carnation, rolled the body to its original position lying face down on the floor, and looked thoughtfully at the pockets, which were all turned inside out.
>
> He was examining the kitchen of the dead man's three-room bachelor apartment when Clark's nephew, Jim Mimms, entered.
>
> "Uncle Hugh is lying dead in the living room! What happened Dr. Haledjian?" cried the young man.
>
> Haledjian handed Mimms an open canister of flour to hold while he picked out the one marked TEA.
>
> "Your uncle," he said to Mimms, "telephoned me this morning and asked me to come right over. He was planning to take a rare coin downtown for sale and wanted me along. Apparently somebody arrived first—I found the door open—and slugged your uncle to death. The killer searched the body but found nothing, because your uncle didn't put the coin his pocket!"
>
> Haledjian paused to set a kettle of water on the stove. "You might bring the coin to me. It's buried in the flower."
>
> Young Mimms put down the canister he was holding and left the kitchen. In a moment he was back with the coin, taken from the carnation.
>
> "How deeply are you mixed up in this murder?" snapped Haledjian.

1. What did Dr. Haledjian learn from the dead man's pockets being turned inside out?

_____

2. Could Jim Mimms see the flower in Mr. Clark's lapel when he came into the room? Why or why not?

_____

3. When Dr. Haledjian told Mimms that the coin was in the flower, Mimms could have looked in either of two different places. What were these two places?

_____

4. If Mimms knew nothing about the murder, where would you expect him to look for the coin when he heard the word *flower*? Why?

_____

_____

5. When Mimms found the coin, what inference did Haledjian make?

_____

Exercise B

Read the paragraph below and look for clues as to how Sumi feels. Then answer the questions.

Sumi had been studying the letter as she walked rapidly along the sidewalk. Suddenly she was right across from Laurie's building. She glanced up at the second-floor window and saw Laurie looking out at the street. Grinning broadly, Sumi jumped up and down and waved the letter. Laurie saw her, opened her mouth as if to say something, and then disappeared from the window. Immediately Sumi dashed across the street, dodging the traffic, skipped up the front steps, and then ran up the first flight, taking the stairs two at a time . . . .

1. Is Sumi in a hurry to see Laurie?

_____

2. Circle the words and phrases you used as clues.

3. What does she want to see Laurie about?

_____

4. How do you think Sumi feels?

_____

5. Underline the words and phrases in the paragraph that helped you infer Sumi's feelings.

Lesson 19
Inferences About People

When you read, you make many inferences about how characters think and feel. You use the same clues that you use in your daily life. You look for several types of clues. These include (1) a description of a character's appearance and background, (2) what a character says, (3) what others say about the character, and (4) what a character does.

Exercise A

Read the following description of Sue Lee. Look for clues in the way she moves and looks.

As she listened to the conversation between her mother and father, Sue Lee sank back on the sofa. She stretched her legs in front of her, put her feet on the coffee table, and folded her arms. She was neither smiling nor frowning. Her eyes showed no expression at all, as if she were really not seeing anything. Then suddenly she sat up straight. She clasped her hands in front of her knees and looked directly at her father as he spoke. Leaning closer to him, she lifted her hand and began to speak.

Write two phrases that suggest that Sue is bored with the conversation.

1. _____

2. _____

Write two phrases that tell you Sue is becoming interested in the conversation.

3. _____

4. _____

5. What type of clue did the writer use to suggest Sue's feelings—her appearance and background, what she says, what other characters say about her, or her actions?

_____

_____

Exercise B

In this selection Diane Hill—called Di—is talking with her neighbor Bill and his parents and has just mentioned her friend Gia. Bill's father, hearing the name Gia, asks his son a question about Gia. Read the conversation and make inferences about the characters.

"Is Gia coming to your party next Friday?" Dr. Brady asked. Bill looked sharply at Di, and so did his mother.

"I guess so," said Bill, becoming red and flustered. He managed to collect himself. "Di and Gia both," he added with a nervous chuckle.

"Funny, I forgot all about it when I saw you this afternoon. Some of the kids are dropping over next Friday night. You're coming, of course. It wouldn't be the same without you."

"I bet it wouldn't," said Di. She was sure Dr. Brady would hear harsh words later.

"Diane, I'm so glad you're coming," Mrs. Brady purred. She went on, lying smoothly, "Bill was saying just this morning he hoped you could make it, and I was hoping, too. It will be a simple little get-together."

Can you make inferences from what the characters say? Answer these questions:

1. Bill becomes red and flustered because
   a. he forgot to ask Di to his party.
   b. he did not plan to ask Di.
   c. he is afraid Di will refuse his invitation.

2. Di is sure Dr. Brady would hear harsh words later because
   a. he was not supposed to know about the party.
   b. he was not supposed to remind Bill to invite Di.
   c. he was not supposed to mention the party.

3. Mrs. Brady is "lying smoothly" because
   a. she knew all along that Bill hadn't invited Di.
   b. she herself didn't know about the party.
   c. she knows Di cannot come to the party.

4. Do you think that Di believes Bill simply forgot to ask her to the party? What is your evidence?

   _____

   _____

5. What type of clues did the writer use to tell you about the characters?

   _____

Lesson 20
Inferring Time and Place

Exercise A

A writer can give you very exact information about the time and place of a story. For example, a writer may begin a story with the following sentences:

> I will never forget July 10, 1875. In the middle of the afternoon, the sheriff stopped my husband, my mother, and me on Main Street in Santa Fe to tell us about the noontime robbery of the local bank.

1. Underline the words that tell you the time of the story.

2. Circle the words that tell you the place of the story.

This description of the time and place is very specific and easy to find. Often, however, the time and place are not stated. Instead, the writer leaves it up to the reader to infer the time and place. Read the following selection and look for clues about the time and place.

> The beast did not belong here.
> That was Ambassador Jerol Telrig's reaction on seeing it. Telrig blinked and looked again. It was still there. Except for it, he was alone, by choice of the planetary government. Around him stretched the spacious boulevards and plantings and fountains and buildings of Boskavel, the capital. The local sun shone warmly overhead; he no longer noticed its slight excess of orange.
> The beast had appeared from behind a building, padding softly on six heavily clawed feet. It was the size of a large dog; big overlapping plates covering its body made it look like a reptile. But its eyes burned with a brightness more mammal-like than reptilian, and the rest of its head was, with only slight exaggeration, all teeth.
> Possibly—an ambassador from Earth learns to expect surprises on any new world—it was some sort of pet. Nevertheless, Telrig's hand crept to his hidden laser gun—just in case.

3. Where is the story probably taking place—on Earth, on another planet, or on a spaceship?

_____

4. Underline the words in the selection that helped you answer question 6.

5. When does this event take place—in the past, in the present, or in the future?

_____

6. What clues did you use to figure this out?

_____

_____

Exercise B

Read the following selections and look for clues about the time and place of the stories.

(A) He tossed it back, and Bill wound up again. This time the ball came at him as if it had been shot from a cannon, right in the strike zone.

Quacky swung away and again almost fell flat on his face.

"Nice pitch!" he said. In fact, he had never seen such a pitch before.

"Sure was!"

Both Quacky and Bill looked around to see who had said that. It was the mailman, who had stopped to watch while making his rounds.

"Too good to hit." Quacky knew a really good pitch when he saw one.

Bill stared at the mailman and then at Quacky.

"I shouldn't be playing ball," Bill said. "Not on city time. I've got to get back to those hedges."

He dropped the ball and glove at the pitcher's mound and picked up his shears. Quacky couldn't figure him out. One minute he was willing to play; the next he was walking off. He thought it had something to do with the mailman watching, but he didn't know why.

"I'd pitch a few to you, Quacky," said the mailman. "But I'm a little behind this morning."

Quacky gave up. Nobody else was around to pitch to him, and he figured it was almost lunch time anyway. He picked up the bat, ball, and mitt and started for home. . . .

1. Quacky is probably taking his batting practice
   a. on the field of a major- or minor-league baseball park.
   b. in an empty lot or neighborhood park.
   c. in a grade-school or high-school gymnasium.
   d. None of these.

2. The general time of the selection is probably
   a. more than ten years ago.
   b. in the 1980s.
   c. sometime in the future.
   d. All of these choices are possible.

(B) Maureen had often regretted leaving Ireland and her mother behind. She could picture Ma standing before the hearth, her face rosy from the glowing coals.

Little sister Rosheen had died in the spring. After that, Ma had grown weaker, and one day she had spoken to Pa about what must be done. "Sean, take Maureen and the boys to America, before it is too late," she had said. "I will follow when I am able, God willing."

Suddenly the *Star* pitched forward and Maureen gripped the sides of the bunk. She held her breath and waited.

Maureen heard Mrs. Kelly crooning to her son, telling him he'd be well by morning. Maureen shook her head sadly. Timmy had been sick for many days and everyone in the hold knew that he was dying.

Morning came and the storm continued. The rain drummed noisily on the deck overhead while the oil lamps cast their gloomy light into the hold. Maureen sighed. How she dreaded another long day spent in the smelly confines. "At least when I go topside for our rations I can have a breath of air," she told herself, "even if it means getting wet, as well."

3. This selection takes place on the *Star*, (an airplane, a ship, a hot-air balloon), which is probably moving somewhere across (the Pacific Ocean, the Atlantic Ocean, the Gulf of Mexico). Circle the answers.

4. Underline at least four clues in the selection that helped you answer question 3.

5. About when does the story probably take place—before the 1950s, from the 1950s to the present, or in the distant future?

(C) It was almost noon when they heard the first low rumbling sound. It was high above them.

Joby stopped in his tracks to listen. His eyes grew wide. "What was that?"

Reese had stopped, too. His heart was pounding. John had told him about that sound. He knew what it was. "Come on," he said to Joby.

Quickly he reached for the rope. He tied one end around Joby's waist and wrapped the other end around his own hand. "If that sound means what I think it does, we want to keep some distance between us. We do not want to be in the same place. Try to keep a full rope's length between us, okay?"

Joby blinked his eyes hard. "I will try," he said tightly.

The heavy fog hid the sun. Often Reese could not see Joby behind him. Only the tugging on the rope let him know that they were still tied together.

Their progress was slow but steady. Reese had not heard the rumbling sound again. Two hours later, he was beginning to believe they would make it.

Then he felt the earth tremble under him. It was a slow rumble at first. Then it became a loud, grumbling roar high on the slope above. The danger that he had feared would not pass them this time.

He turned to call a warning to Joby.

"Avalanche!" he yelled over the roar of falling, tumbling snow. "Avalanche!"

6. Is this selection taking place on a mountain, on a frozen river, or in a snow-covered forest?

_____

7. Underline at least two clues in the selection that helped you answer question 6.

Lesson 21
Reviewing Inferences

Exercise

Read the following story and make inferences about Jerry and about what is happening. Then answer the questions.

SNAKE DANCE
by Corey Ford

"Hello. That you, Mom?" He glanced at his watch. The game had been over for a half-hour, and the gang would be coming down the street any minute now. "Hello, Mom. This is Jerry. Sure, I'm all right. I'm fine. And you? Mom—" and his voice seemed to falter for a fraction of a second— "How is he? Is there any change?" There was a tiny silence. "Oh."

His voice was a little duller when he spoke again. "I see. Yeah. And that other specialist, he said the same thing? Oh, sure, sure. No, of course there's nothing to worry about. No, I'm not worried; I only just called to find out if there was any change, that was all. Did they say if he could ever—I mean, can he move his arms yet?" He gulped. "Well, that doesn't mean anything, really. All those things take time. Sure, a year, or maybe even less—What? What money? Oh, you mean I sent you last week? Now, Mom, I told you all about that already, didn't I? Sure, it's a scholarship. I got it for playing football. I didn't need all that money you and Pop had been saving up for me to go to college, and so I just thought maybe, with Pop being laid up now for a while and all—Who me? Homesick? Not so you'd notice it." He laughed. "I'm having the time of my life. I know practically everybody here already, and everybody knows me. Every night we all sit around and talk, or else we go down to Semple's Drugstore for a milk shake—"

He opened the folding door a little. In the distance he could hear the sound of a band approaching.

"Well, Mom, I gotta hang up now. The gang'll be here in a minute. We're having a celebration after the game today. Sure, I did, the whole game; you oughta seen me in there. I made two touchdowns. Everybody's going down to Semple's after the game, and they'll all want me to be there, too. Listen, Mom. One other thing before they get here. I'm going to be sending you a little money each week from now on until Pop is better. No, Mom, heck, I got plenty. Here they are now. Hear them?"

The band had halted outside. Someone led a cheer.

"That's for me, Mom. Sure! Didn't I practically win the game for them today? Hear that?" He kicked open the door of the phone booth and held up the receiver. The crowd was calling, "Jerry! Hey, Jerry, come on!"

"Hear that, Mom? Now goodbye. Tell Pop everything's okay, see? Now don't worry. Bye."

He stepped out of the booth, adjusting his white cap with "Semple's" printed in red letters. The crowd was lined along the soda fountain, shouting "Jerry! Milk shake, Jerry!"

1. At the beginning of the story, Jerry has just
   a. arrived home.
   b. started making a phone call.
   c. been surprised by the arrival of his mother at school.

2. The story probably takes place in the
   a. very distant past.
   b. general present.
   c. future.

3. When he asks, "How is he?" Jerry is referring to his
   a. father.
   b. brother.
   c. best friend.

4. When he asks, "Is there any change?" the reply is
   a. "No."
   b. "Yes."
   c. "I don't know."

5. An important event that has occurred in the past is that
   a. Jerry's father has become seriously ill.
   b. Jerry won a football scholarship.
   c. Jerry has become homesick.

6. Jerry says, "Everybody knows me." This statement is
   a. false, but makes him feel important.
   b. true, just as he claims.
   c. true, but for a different reason.

7. The crowd calls, "Hey, Jerry, come on!" because
   a. they want him to go to Semple's.
   b. someone else needs to use the phone.
   c. they want him to wait on them.

8. Jerry really gets the money he sends home from
   a. his football scholarship.
   b. working at the drugstore.
   c. borrowing from friends.

9. An important clue to Jerry's character is that he
   a. lies to his mother.
   b. has taken a job to help his parents.
   c. brags about being a football hero.

10. Based on his actions, Jerry may be described as being
    a. caring.
    b. athletic.
    c. dishonest.

Lesson 22
Finding the Main Idea

The **topic** of a paragraph or other written selection is what the material is about. The main point that is made about the topic is called the **main idea**. It summarizes all of the important details.

Exercise A

Read the paragraph below. The questions following it point to the main idea of the selection.

Today, after forty-five centuries of exposure to the hazards of time, the Great Pyramid rises to a height of 450 feet. At its base the pyramid measures about 756 feet in length along each of the four sides. The pyramid's bulk is enormous. It is made up of 2,300,000 blocks of stone, each averaging two-and-a-half tons in weight; the biggest blocks weigh fifteen tons. If every block were cut into cubes a foot high, wide, and deep, and these were placed side by side along the equator, they would reach two-thirds of the way around the world. The area of the base of the Great Pyramid is so large that the cathedrals of Florence and Milan, as well as St. Peter's in Rome and St. Paul's in London, could all be placed together inside it, with room left for Westminster Abbey.

1. What is the main topic of this paragraph? (Circle one.)
   a. large buildings
   b. stone blocks
   c. the Great Pyramid
   d. cathedrals in Europe

The topic tells the subject of the material. But notice that all the facts given about the Great Pyramid focus on its size.

2. Which of the following statements best expresses the central focus or main idea in this paragraph? (Circle one.)
   a. The Great Pyramid is enormous.
   b. The Great Pyramid is so large it could hold the cathedrals of Florence and Milan, as well as St. Peter's in Rome and St. Paul's in London, with room left for Westminster Abbey.
   c. The world has many very large structures.
   d. The Great Pyramid is one of the Seven Wonders of the World.

Exercise B

Read the following selections and then answer the questions that follow.

Do a shark's wide open jaws filled with razor-sharp teeth make you think of a prehistoric monster? If so, you're right. Members of the shark family have been roaming the seas for 350 million years. Some of the early ones were fifty feet long—that's the size of a school bus. They had teeth to match their size, and used them. In the days of the dinosaurs, sharks ripped into and lashed out at other terrifying sea monsters. Today, those plesiosaurs (plē/sē ə sôrz) and ichthyosaurs (ik/thē ə sôrz) have disappeared. But the sharks haven't. They haven't changed their habits either: modern sea creatures and humans consider sharks as dangerous now as they were then.

1. Circle the letter of the word that best tells the main topic of the above paragraph.
   a. dinosaurs
   b. sea creatures
   c. sharks
   d. monsters

2. The topic tells the subject of the material. The main idea states what is said about the topic. Which of the following statements best expresses the main idea in this paragraph? (Circle one.)
   a. The dangerous shark family has existed for millions of years.
   b. Prehistoric sharks were very large.
   c. In prehistoric times the sea was full of danger.
   d. Sharks and dinosaurs fought until the sharks rid the earth of dinosaurs.

3. Circle the details that help develop and support the main idea.
   a. Some early sharks were the size of a school bus.
   b. Members of the shark family existed in prehistoric times.
   c. Sharks are a danger to animals and humans to this day.

Lesson 23
Direct Statement of Main Idea

Exercise A

(1) The opal miners of Australia have learned that it is cooler to live underground than above ground in the Coober-Pedy region. (2) Almost all of the world's opals are mined in this desert region, but the harsh climate makes it a difficult place in which to live comfortably. (3) So almost half of the 5200 people in Coober-Pedy live underground. (4) These are not crude caves—they boast wall-to-wall carpeting, running water, and electricity. (5) But best of all, these underground dwellers never have to worry about escaping from the heat. (6) The temperature in these homes is almost constantly around 72°F all year round. (7) That's not bad—particularly in an area where the normal summertime temperature ranges from 120° to 140° in the day. (8) Even at night, the thermometer seldom goes below 100°. (9) In such a climate, it's nice not to have to worry about a breakdown in the air-conditioning unit. (10) The thick sandstone walls and roofs of the dugouts provide nature's own protection against the hot desert sun.

1. What is the main topic of this selection? (Circle one.)
   a. opals
   b. opal miners
   c. houses in Australia
   d. housing in Coober-Pedy

2. Which of the following sentences best states the main idea of this paragraph?
   a. The opal miners of Australia have learned that it is cooler to live underground than above ground in the Coober-Pedy region.
   b. These are not crude caves—they boast wall-to-wall carpeting, running water, and electricity.
   c. So almost half of the 5200 people in Coober-Pedy live underground.
   d. Their homes are cut deep into sandstone mounds and go far beneath the surface of the earth.

Notice how sentences 2, 5, 7, 8, 9, and 10 in the paragraph all have something to do with living in the intense heat of this region. Sentence 1 summarizes this idea. It states the main idea of the passage.

You will find that authors sometimes summarize the main idea of their material in a sentence or two. This is called a **direct statement of main idea**. This direct statement is usually, but not always, near the beginning or the end of a selection. It is important to remember that such a sentence does not just tell the main topic. It is a key to the idea behind the whole selection; it does not concentrate on a single detail.

Exercise B
Read the passage and answer the questions.

The M.G. TC is the car that started the sports-car revolution in the United States. When American soldiers came home from World War II in 1945 and 1946, those who had been in England told about a car they had grown to love—the M.G. TC. Many were able to bring one home, and the TC soon became popular in the United States. Designers in Detroit noticed this; as a result, in the early 1950s the Chevrolet Corvette and two-seater Ford Thunderbird were born. American manufacturers also added such things as four-speed transmissions and quick steering to some American cars in an effort to match the performance of European sports cars.

1. What is the main topic of the paragraph? (Circle one.)
   a. English sports cars
   b. Chevrolet Corvettes
   c. influence of the M.G. TC on U.S. sports cars
   d. early sports cars designed in Detroit

2. Underline the sentence that directly states the point that is made about this topic.

Exercise C
Read the passage and underline the direct statement of main idea in the paragraph.

Not only does it seem that everybody is juggling these days, they seem to be tossing around just about anything you can imagine. Street performers, business people, students, professional ice skaters who juggle as they glide, all can be found in increasing numbers practicing how to keep from one to five objects revolving in the air. As to what's up there swirling around—it varies from oranges and apples and juggling clubs to frosted cupcakes, scarves, knives, and even chairs.

Lesson 24
Implied Main Idea

Many writers develop an idea by providing details and examples. They depend on the reader to understand the main point that they are trying to emphasize.

If you pay attention to what the details in a selection emphasize, you should be able to recognize the **implied**, or suggested, **statement of main idea**.

Exercise A

Read the following paragraph and answer the questions.

We often read or talk about things that "man has invented." But maybe "improve" or "apply to human needs" is a better way to say what we mean. Long before people, certain plants and animals were using electricity; birds, bats, and insects had mastered flight; squids and some insects were darting through the water by jet propulsion; chemical warfare was being practiced by various plants and animals; agricultural crops were being cultivated by a number of insects.

1. What is the main topic of the paragraph? (Circle one.)
   a. plants and animals
   b. electricity
   c. nature's achievements
   d. science

2. Which of these statements best summarizes the main idea suggested by the information in the paragraph?
   a. Plants and animals are very complex.
   b. Humans learned how to use electricity by studying plants.
   c. Squids move through water by jet propulsion.
   d. Many human inventions are improvements on things that already existed in nature.

Exercise B

Read the following paragraph and answer the questions.

There seem to be enough stories about the Old West with its cattle drives, round-ups, outlaws, and Indian raids to fill up at least one hundred years of history. In fact, the Old West of the legends didn't start until 1867. In that year, ranchers began rounding up and driving their cattle herds to a newly started shipping center near the railroad in Abilene, Kansas. In the next twenty years alone, ten million longhorns were driven north by the cowboys. But in about thirty years, by 1900, times had changed. The railroad was everywhere; the long cattle drives were no longer necessary. Barbed wire had fenced in the open range. The Old West we see in movies and read about was past history.

1. What is the main topic of this passage? (Circle one.)
   a. cattle drives
   b. the importance of railroads
   c. the Old West
   d. round-ups

2. Which of the following statements best tells the main idea suggested in this passage?
   a. The cowboy was an important part of the Old West.
   b. The Old West really only lasted about thirty years.
   c. Ten million longhorns were driven to northern railroad centers.
   d. Barbed wire caused the end of the cattle drives of the Old West.

Exercise C

Read the following paragraph and answer the question.

In most occupations the number of hours a person can work is limited. The idea seems to be that everybody needs some leisure time—that no one should be worked to the point of exhaustion. In fact, much is written and said about shortening the workweek even more. All this concern about the importance of leisure time makes me wonder what happened to mine. I am a student, and I know a lot of students. The older we get, the harder we have to work. Teachers often heap up enough homework to keep students tied to their desks every evening and all weekend, too.

What is the main idea of this paragraph? (Circle one.)
   a. Students need leisure time just as other workers do.
   b. Workweeks are being shortened.
   c. Leisure time is important.
   d. Students should spend all their time on homework.

Lesson 25
Reviewing Main Idea

Exercise

Read the entire article before you answer the questions.

SNOOPSHOOTERS
by Carl Glassman

(A) If a male spy set out on a mission armed with every type of sneaky camera that has come out in the last one hundred years, he'd be clicking from head to toe. By observing him very carefully, you'd see that his hat and tie are cameras, as well as his ring, revolver, wristwatch, and pocket watch. There are lenses peeking through a buttonhole in his vest, the handle of his cane, and the heel of his shoe.

(B) The first of these snoop shooters were called detective cameras. Despite their name they were used mostly by ordinary people to take ordinary snapshots.

(C) So why these detective cameras? They were popular in the 1880s and '90s when it was considered bad manners to take pictures of strangers. A formal introduction was needed just to ask permission to take someone's picture. Camera makers realized that many people would use cameras if they could snap away secretly.

(D) The detective cameras—designed with tiny plates and often circular images—were indeed popular. They became among the first amateur, or "snapshot," cameras to be put on the market.

(E) The vest camera, which was advertised as being of "great value to artists and detectives," was probably the most popular of the detective cameras—although it's unlikely that either artists *or* detectives used it. When first sold in 1886, this thin, disc-shaped camera came with a false vest that concealed it. The chief disadvantage of the vest camera was that it had no viewfinder. The photographer could only point the camera and hope for the best.

(F) Another remarkable detective camera was the photo revolver, invented in 1883. It is probably the most mysterious of all the detective cameras. It was invented by a Frenchman who somehow had the idea that his camera could be used secretly. This was a peculiar notion, because pointing a pistol in someone's face would surely attract attention. The photographer also risked being shot in self-defense.

(G) The camera had a lens near the end of the barrel and ten tiny plates housed in the chamber. An exposure was made by—you guessed it—pulling the trigger. The photo revolver could "shoot" ten exposures before being reloaded.

(H) But many of these detective cameras were not quite as sneaky as they might appear. It was hard for a photographer to go unnoticed as he focused a book, adjusted the lens on his cane, or pointed a pistol at a stranger.

(I) The undercover camera had plenty of critics too. One writing in an 1890 photography annual, said: "How often has the tourist heard the snap of a shutter and looked up to discover by the satisfied grin on the face of some cub of a boy that he, or she, has been photographed in some embarrassing position. . . ." And, any photographer who would do such a thing, the article said, has "forfeited his title and right to the grand old name of gentleman." For these critics no polite person could use a secret camera.

1. What is the topic of this article?

   _____

2. Underline the main idea in paragraph (A).

3. Circle the letter of the statement that best summarizes the implied main idea of paragraphs (B) and (C).
   a. In the 1880s and '90s it was popular to take snapshots.
   b. People were much more formal in the way they acted towards one another in the 1880s.
   c. In the 1880s and '90s ordinary people used hidden cameras because it was bad manners to take strangers' pictures.
   d. Cameras were used only by detectives in the 1880s and '90s.

4. Underline the main idea in paragraph (D).

5. Underline the main idea in paragraph (H).

6. Circle the letter of the statement that best states the implied main idea of the whole article.
   a. The detective cameras of the 1880s and '90s were cleverly designed, but it was not always practical or polite to use one.
   b. In the early days of photography, there were more kinds of cameras than there are today.
   c. In the 1880s and '90s people had strange ideas about what was proper behavior for photographers.
   d. Cameras have been used for many purposes.

Lesson 26
What Are Judgments?

Good judgments are well-supported opinions. They are based on dependable information, and they agree with common sense.

You make judgments every day. When you read, you are presented with opinions. Sometimes these opinions are supported and sometimes they are not. When you watch television or listen to the radio, you see or hear commercials. Commercials and other forms of advertising are meant to affect your judgments. Before you agree with an opinion or agree to buy a certain product, you should look at all the information you can.

Exercise A
Examine the drawing below. Then write answers to the questions.

1. What judgment has the sports announcer made?

_____

2. How did he arrive at his judgment?

_____

_____

3. What are two of the Grapplers' strengths?

_____

4. What is the Wranglers' only strong point?

_____

5. Do you think the announcer has made a good judgment? Why or why
not?

_____

Exercise B

Read each of the following statements and tell whether you think the person
has made a good judgment or a bad judgment.

1. Paul: I saw my cousin yesterday, and today my mom told me he has the
flu. I don't feel bad, but I think I should go see the doctor anyway.
    good judgment   bad judgment

2. Carmen: I want to buy an outfit I saw at the mall. I wrote my
grandmother and told her I needed a uniform for band. She sent me the
money. She lives far away, so she'll never know how I really spent it.
    good judgment   bad judgment

3. Nick: I want to go to college when I graduate. I've been mowing lawns all
summer, and I'm going to keep my grades up so maybe I can get a
scholarship.
    good judgment   bad judgment

4. Carla: I heard an ad on the radio for a great stereo. The announcer said
it's the best one in town. Even though it's expensive, I'm going to buy one
tomorrow.
    good judgment   bad judgment

5. Jasmine: My little brother wants a dog for his birthday. I saw an ad for
free puppies in the newspaper, so I'm going to get one for him. We live in
an apartment that doesn't allow pets, but I'm sure we can keep it a secret.
    good judgment   bad judgment

Lesson 27

Fact and Opinion

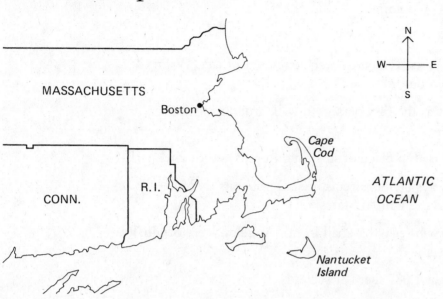

Read the following sentences and check those that you think are facts.

1. Nantucket Island is east of the Massachusetts coastline and a little south of Cape Cod.

2. Nantucket is the best summertime vacation spot because of its great coves and beaches.

3. Nantucket was once a center for the whaling industry.

4. Visitors will always be able to admire Nantucket's quaint homes and beautiful scenery.

5. Herman Melville used Nantucket as the hometown for some of the characters in his novel *Moby Dick*.

A **fact** can be proved true or false. **Opinions** give personal beliefs, and they cannot be proved true or false. Even if many or most people agree with an opinion, it can't be proved right or wrong.

Sentence 1 above is a statement of fact. You can prove whether Nantucket is or isn't east of Massachusetts and south of Cape Cod. You could prove the statement by looking at a map or going there.

Sentence 3 is also a statement of fact. You could look in history books, in old diaries or newspapers, or at paintings of Nantucket long ago and prove whether it was a whaling center.

The last sentence is also a statement of fact. You could prove whether or not the author Herman Melville used Nantucket as the home of his characters in *Moby Dick* by reading the novel.

But sentences 2 and 4 are opinions. Sentence 2 is a personal feeling about Nantucket and its coves and beaches. Many people may agree with the opinion, but there is no way to prove that the island is the "best summertime vacation spot" or that its coves and beaches are "great." Sentence 4 is about the future. Since no one can prove something that hasn't yet happened, any statement about the future is an opinion.

Exercise

Read each statement below. Write **F** next to each statement of fact. Write **O** next to each statement of opinion.

_____ 1. David Kunst was the first person to walk around the entire world.

_____ 2. Aluminum is used in place of steel in different automobile parts.

_____ 3. There will always be more registered Democrats that Republicans in the United States.

_____ 4. The Dodgers, who play baseball in Los Angeles, were originally a New York team.

_____ 5. Sound travels at 1,087 feet per second.

_____ 6. Wool is the best material to use if you are going to make a sweater.

_____ 7. Golf was invented in Scotland and played by the royal family of that country.

_____ 8. The African elephant has larger ears than the Indian elephant.

_____ 9. The Eagles are sure to win the Super Bowl next year.

_____ 10. The great white shark is the most terrifying of all the sea creatures.

Lesson 28
Mixed Statements

Read the following paragraph and then answer the questions.

Walt Disney will always be known for his cartoons and animated films. Several other artists who are less well-known have also worked at the Disney studios. Frank Thomas and Ollie Johnston worked on many animated movies, including *Pinocchio, Snow White*, and *The Fox and the Hound*.

1. Does the paragraph contain facts, opinions, or both?

_____

2. Why is the first sentence an opinion?

_____

3. The second sentence has both fact and opinion. Write the part of the sentence that is a fact.

_____

_____

4. Is the third sentence a fact or an opinion?

_____

_____

You will seldom read any writing that is either all fact or all opinion. Usually, there will be both facts and opinions in a single sentence.

The first sentence in the paragraph above is an opinion because it is about the future. The third sentence is a statement of fact. You could prove whether Frank Thomas and Ollie Johnston were artists who worked on those movies. But the second sentence contains both fact and opinion. You could prove whether "Several other artists . . . have also worked at the Disney studios." The middle part of the sentence, however, is an opinion. You could not prove "who are less well-known" to be true or false.

Such **mixed statements** can be misleading. You need to read them carefully and sort out the facts from the opinions.

Exercise

The sentences below are examples of all three types of statements. On the blanks, write **F** if the sentence is a statement of fact that can be proved true or false. Write **O** if the sentence is an opinion. If the sentence is a mixed statement, write **M** on the blank and underline the part that is opinion.

_____ **1.** *Pinocchio* was made in 1937, and *Snow White* in 1940; those were called the "golden years of animated movies."

_____ **2.** *Pinocchio* cost 2.8 million dollars to make, which was a great deal of money to spend on a motion picture in those days.

_____ **3.** One thousand people worked on the film, and the artists made 2.5 million drawings.

_____ **4.** Walt Disney was devoted to the quality of the films made at his studio, and he did everything possible to improve them.

_____ **5.** Disney built a zoo at his studio, and his artists studied the animals raised there.

_____ **6.** The main character in *Bambi* was a baby deer; the character was based on a real fawn raised at the zoo.

_____ **7.** For the *Fox and the Hound*, which is one of the best Disney films, the artist used his own pet fox for a model.

_____ **8.** Disney artists also act out the movements of animals, even though they look foolish to studio visitors.

_____ **9.** Walt Disney himself once demonstrated how a dancing bear would look.

_____ **10.** So that their films will always be lifelike, Disney artists will continue to jump up from their desks, flap their arms, and quack like a duck.

Lesson 29
Valid Opinions

No one's opinion can be proved true or false. But some opinions are better than others. **Valid opinions** are supported by facts. These opinions are reached when people think objectively. You are being objective when you try to see things as they are, not as you feel they should be. People who are unobjective, or subjective, allow their personal feelings to influence their opinions.

When you read or hear an opinion, you should consider whether it is valid. If facts are given to support the opinion, it probably is valid. But remember that facts can be proved to be wrong.

Exercise A

The paragraphs that follow contain facts and opinions. Read the sentences, and write **F** for facts or **O** for the opinion on the blanks. Then, decide if the paragraph presents a valid or an invalid opinion. Circle the correct choice.

(A)

_____ 1. Tropical rain forests are the most fragile and spectacular of any forest type.

_____ 2. An estimated 50 percent of all plant and animal species live in tropical rains forests.

_____ 3. Little Panama's forests alone contain as many plant species as all of Europe.

_____ 4. Most tropical rain forest destruction is caused by land-hungry farmers who first clear the land and then burn what they have cut down.

_____ 5. This paragraph is: Valid/Invalid

(B)

_____ 1. Many people the world over are concerned about the rapid rate of destruction of the planet's tropical rain forests.

_____ 2. Scientists are concerned because so little is known about how a tropical forest works, what makes the forests so fragile, and just how important they are in our lives.

_____ 3. Tropical rain forest ecology is an important new area of scientific study.

_____ 4. Several institutions are now doing research to find out just how big a tropical rain forest has to be in order to maintain its rich diversity.

_____ 5. This paragraph is: Valid/Invalid

Exercise B

In the left-hand column, there are statements of opinion. In the right-hand column, there are statements of fact. On the blank, write the letter of the statement of fact that directly supports the opinion.

_____ 1. If we keep losing rain forests in America, the whole world will be in trouble.

_____ 2. A basic threat to rain forests is the number of people who want to get rich.

_____ 3. Many countries are concerned about the loss of rain forests.

_____ 4. Most scientists see the rain forests as vital protectors of the planet.

_____ 5. The quickest and worst destruction of rain forests is by farmers.

a. In 1989 more than 75% of those surveyed in Latin America, Asia, and Africa voiced concern about the loss of trees in their homelands.

b. Prospectors are removing 70 tons of gold a year from rain forests.

c. Rain forests are known to be major regulators of local climate.

d. Rain forests are a source of numerous drugs used to fight disease.

e. Farmers use a slash-and-burn agriculture that is responsible for the ruin of 50 acres of rain forests every hour.

Exercise C

Some of the opinions below are presented by authorities in the field. Some of the opinions are also backed up with facts. Some of the opinions are those of people who have some personal interest or something to gain.

Check the opinions you think are valid. On the blank below each item, write why you checked or did not check an opinion. Write "authority" (or "no authority") and/or "fact" (or "no fact") or "personal interest."

Example: News reporter: "The best place in the world to take a vacation is South Carolina."
<u>no authority, no fact</u>

1. Lawyer: "Your low water pressure probably means you have a blockage in your pipes."

_____

2. Doctor: "If you're having trouble with your knee, you should see an orthopedist, a doctor who specializes in joint diseases."

_____

3. Camera store owner: "The best camera for your needs is this 35 millimeter with the telephoto lens. Even though it's more expensive than that other brand, I'm sure you'll be happier."

_____

4. Chemist: "Our water supply is becoming so polluted with chemical wastes that in another ten years we won't be able to drink it."

_____

5. Forest ranger: "I've been fishing this stream for twenty years, and I can assure you that this is the best spot for catching trout."

_____

6. Banker: "Racquetball is the best sport for sharpening your reflexes."

_____

7. Electrician: "In light of the high amount of energy used and the cost to you, you'd be better off putting in a gas clothes dryer rather than an electric one."

_____

8. Editor: "I've eaten pecan pies all across the country, and I say that Mother Folsom's pecan pies are the best you can find north or south of the Mason-Dixon line."

_____

9. Nutrition counselor: "It's important not to eat too many foods with artificial colorings or preservatives if you want to stay in good health."

_____

10. Carpenter: "My car is in excellent condition, and at the price I'm asking, it's really a bargain."

_____

11. Music critic: "The orchestra's sound was dazzling, fully capturing the cheerful, sunny mood of the evening's three symphonic works."

_____

12. Furniture dealer: "Even if you don't like the color of this chair, you should consider buying it because it's made well and the price is right."

_____

13. Watchmaker: "Aerojet Airlines offers the fastest, safest, smoothest rides for the money."

_____

14. Lawyer: "I've had cases before this judge many times. I can assure you she is fair and honest."

_____

15. Doctor: "The EX 540 is the best car on the road. I wouldn't buy anything else."

_____

16. Movie director: "*The Creature* is the greatest movie I've ever made. I've seen it three times, and it gets better every time. See it and I guarantee you'll love it."

_____

17. Coach: "Good Sport sports equipment is a good deal. My teams have worn this gear for years, and it still looks new."

_____

18. Dentist: "As someone who works with my hands all day, I recommend Sparkle jewelry. Their rings will make your hands feel like they're on vacation."

_____

Lesson 30
Emotional Effect of Words

Words do more than communicate information and ideas. They can also affect people's emotions. Some words have a positive effect because their basic meaning, or *denotation* (dē/nō tā/shən), is positive: love, happiness, peace. Some words have a negative denotation: hate, sadness, war.

Many words also have *connotations* (kon/ə tā/shənz), shades of meaning that affect different people in different ways. The word *snowmobile* is a good example. The basic meaning has neither a positive nor a negative effect. A snowmobile is a vehicle, usually equipped with runners, for traveling across snow. But different people may have different emotional reactions to the word *snowmobile*. People who enjoy riding snowmobiles for recreation would probably have a positive emotional reaction. So would those who depend on snowmobiles for transportation in winter. But some conservationists, who object to the damage snowmobiles cause in natural areas, would be likely to react negatively.

Exercise A
One of the headlines in each pair below uses words to appeal to readers' emotions. The other headline does not. Check the headline in each pair that does *not* make a strong emotional appeal.

1. _____ **a.** Eastern High Explodes in Fourth Quarter, Stuns Central

   _____ **b.** Eastern High Defeats Central with Strong Fourth Quarter

2. _____ **a.** New Oil Pipeline Causes Concern About Nature Area

   _____ **b.** Will New Oil Pipeline Ruin Natural Paradise?

3. _____ **a.** Cutbacks in Work Force Hit Women Hardest

   _____ **b.** Trends Show Reductions in Female Workers

4. _____ **a.** A Mystery of the Deep: Sea Swallows Ship

   _____ **b.** Ship Reported Lost in Southwest Atlantic

5. _____ **a.** Unfavorable Climate May Lead to Food Shortages

   _____ **b.** Severe Weather Raises Fears of Famine

6. _____ **a.** City on Fire: Downtown Blazes Out of Control

   _____ **b.** Firefighters Battle Downtown Fire

7. _____ **a.** Prisoner Escapes from Local Jail

   _____ **b.** Escaped Convict Terrifies Small Town

8. _____ **a.** Officials Meet on Government Budget

     _____ **b.** Government Shuts Down Tonight

9. _____ **a.** New Mall Costs Millions Too Much

     _____ **b.** Building Costs for New Mall Reported

10. _____ **a.** Flood Wipes Out Homes

     _____ **b.** Rising Waters Fill Houses

Exercise B

In the speech below, a politician wants to create bad feelings toward his opponent. He describes people he claims support his opponent in very negative words. He describes his own supporters and his own rights and privileges in very positive words. Underline ten examples of words used to create a negative effect. Circle five words used to create a positive reaction.

"Last night we saw a terrible, frightening picture of the type of people who support my opponent. Screaming, cursing students invaded the Civic Center to rage against me and ruin a lovely evening for my dear family and loyal friends. These spoiled brats sneaked into a dinner held in my honor, stuffed their bellies, and then tried to shout me down. They had the nerve to call me a tyrant. They showed all fair-minded people that they were the true tyrants, trying to deny me my freedom of speech."

Lesson 1
Main Idea in a Paragraph

A paragraph is a group of sentences that develops one main idea. In a narrative paragraph the main idea is usually not directly stated.

Most paragraphs focus on one **main idea**, the one idea that the paragraph is about. A narrative paragraph tells about something that happened; its main idea is not usually directly stated. The reader may have to draw a conclusion as to what the main idea is by examining the details in the paragraph.

Read the paragraph below from the novel *The Yearling*, set about a century ago in Florida. Jody Baxter has raised a fawn named Flag for nearly a year. One day his mother is preparing dinner; Jody has brought the young deer into the house and leaves it alone for a moment. Use your ability to draw conclusions to decide what the main idea of the paragraph is.

> She set the dish of shelled dried peas on the table and went to the hearth. Jody went to his room to look for a piece of rawhide. There was a clatter and commotion and then Ma Baxter's storm of fury. Flag had leaped onto the table, seized a mouthful of the peas and sent the pan sprawling, the peas scattered from one end of the kitchen to the other. Jody came running. His mother threw the door open and drove Flag out with the broom. He seemed to enjoy the fracas. He kicked up his heels, flicked his white flag of a tail, shook his head as though threatening to attack with imaginary antlers, sailed over the fence and galloped away to the woods.
> —*from* **The Yearling** by Marjorie Kinnan Rawlings

The unstated main idea of the paragraph is that Flag is now too wild and big to be allowed in the house any longer.

Exercise A
Answer these questions about the paragraph.

1. If the main idea of the paragraph were to be stated, where do you think it would fit best—at the beginning, in the middle somewhere, or at the end?

   _____

   _____

2. What details support the idea that Flag is too wild and big to be allowed in the house any longer?

   _____

   _____

Excercise B
Read a later paragraph from *The Yearling* on the next page and underline the answers to the questions. Jody has discovered that Flag can jump the fence he built and has been eating the farm's corn plants.

Jody clung to the fence. He was numb. He could neither feel nor think. Flag scented him, lifted his head, and came bounding to him. Jody climbed down into the yard. He did not want to see him. As he stood, Flag cleared, as lightly as a mockingbird in flight, the high fence on which he had labored. Jody turned his back on him and went into the house. He went to his room and threw himself on his bed and buried his face in his pillow.

1. Which of these three statements expresses the main idea?
   a. Jody decided immediately to get rid of Flag.
   b. Jody was shocked and upset by Flag's behavior.
   c. Jody was too young to understand what was happening.

2. Add a third detail, labeled **c**, that supports the main idea.
   a. Jody buried his face in his pillow.
   b. Jody turned his back on Flag.

   c. _____

Excercise C

Underline the main idea once and three supporting details twice for each of these paragraphs. The main idea for the second paragraph is unstated; write the main idea in the space provided.

1. Melissa wanted to prove that she could do her share on the camping trip with her dad. She rushed to unpack the tent and camping gear while her dad removed stones from their site. She helped put up the tent and set out the necessary items for dinner. Melissa then insisted that she do all the cooking as well as build the fire. After sunset she even contributed a number of scary stories as they sat by the dying fire.

2. Beth and Luisa first met in kindergarten. During fourth grade they joined Girl Scouts and did projects together. In the fifth grade, they both started guitar lessons. Last year they had fun in the park-district softball program. Now, in seventh grade, they are taking swimming lessons together.

   _____

   _____

Lesson 2
Topic Sentences

A topic sentence is a statement of the main idea of a paragraph.

You have already learned about the main idea in a paragraph. Often this main idea is stated in a single sentence. A **topic** is what a paragraph is all about. A sentence that tells what a paragraph is about is called a **topic sentence**. The other sentences in a paragraph support the topic sentence by providing additional details.

When a topic sentence is used, it usually appears first in the paragraph. However, a writer may choose to put the topic sentence at the end of a paragraph, or in the middle.

Read the following descriptive paragraphs. Note that the descriptive details in each paragraph support the topic sentence.

Not all sharks have the streamlined shapes we usually visualize when we hear the word *shark*. One common kind of shark, for example, has a head shaped like a double hammer. This strange horizontal head is about three feet long. The carpet, or woebegone, shark is a squat fish with a round head. From around its mouth dangle seaweed-like tassels of skin, which look like a mustache.

For a long stretch, dark gray rocks with sharp edges protruded out of the green water. White-headed waves rolled slowly toward the land, gathered speed, and then crashed violently against the jagged rocks. Ribbons of water shot erratically into the air and then disappeared with a splash into the sea. There was something restlessly beautiful about this side of the island.

Red, pink, and white coral dot the white ocean floor. A school of small silver fish swim behind a red-speckled rock. A dazzling orange-striped fish is swimming near the dark green seaweed. The seas around us are filled with wonderful colors. Here comes a bright yellow fish. Look at that unusual purple plant.

Exercise A
Answer the following questions on the lines provided.

1. Which paragraph starts with a topic sentence?

_____

2. Which paragraph has its topic sentence in the middle?

_____

3. Which paragraph ends with a topic sentence?

_____

Excercise B

In each group of sentences underline the topic sentence.

> **Example:** Small children dug with new shovels into the damp sand.
> <u>The seashore that day was a bustle of activity</u>.
> Swimmers crowded into the water.

1. Herons circled the marsh to search out nesting places.
   The ducks began to establish their territories as well.
   In spring, the marsh echoed with the cries of wild birds.

2. On that misty morning, the lake was quiet.
   Two men were fishing silently from an old wooden rowboat.
   The ducks floated noiselessly around the bank.

3. Just beneath the surface, tadpoles wiggled and darted.
   Odd, winged creatures skimmed the surface.
   The pond seemed empty of life until we looked closely.

Excercise C

Read the following descriptive paragraph.

> Some of my earliest memories are of the storms, the hot rain lashing
> down and lightning running on the sky—and the storm cellar into which
> my mother and I descended so many times when I was very young. For me
> that little room in the earth is an unforgettable place. Across the years I see
> my mother reading there on the low, narrow bench, the lamplight
> flickering on her face and the earthen walls; I smell the dank odor of that
> room; and I hear the great weather raging at the door.
> —*from* **The Names** by N. Scott Momaday

1. Where does the topic sentence occur in the paragraph?

   _____

2. In the other sentences, what supporting details refer to sight, smell, and
   sound?

   _____

   _____

Exercise D

Do this exercise on your own paper. Think about your favorite place. As you
think about this place, list details that tell about it—where it is, why you
remember it, how you get there, what it looks like, and so on. Then, write a
topic sentence that expresses a main idea about the place you are describing.
Read your notes again and cross out all the details that do not support your
topic sentence. Write at least three sentences, using the details in your list.

Lesson 3

Writing a Narrative Paragraph

Write a narrative paragraph when you want to tell a story about events that have happened over a period of time.

A **narrative paragraph** tells a story or a part of a story. The person telling the story is the narrator and can be someone in the story or an outside observer. A narrative paragraph presents a series of events in time order and often uses words and phrases such as *first*, *then*, and *after that* to make the order clearer. Such words and phrases are called **transition words and phrases**.

> ### Transition Words and Phrases
> after
> at first
> eventually
> finally
> later
> meanwhile
> next
> second
> soon
> then

Read the narrative paragraphs below. Notice the transition words and phrases. In the first paragraph, the narrator is an outside observer. Three friends—Paris, Pee Wee, and Big Dog—are walking near a river when Big Dog falls in. As Paris leans out to help Big Dog, Pee Wee holds on to Paris's legs.

> "Tread water," Paris called. "Tread the water like I showed you last summer." Big Dog started treading the water. "Your hand," Paris called out. Big Dog reached up. At first Paris couldn't catch it. Then he did. He pulled. But instead of Big Dog coming up, Big Dog started pulling him over. He felt himself slipping through Pee Wee's little arms.
> —*from* **Paris, Pee Wee, and Big Dog** by Rosa Guy

In this second paragraph, the narrator is a character. He and his family move quite often, and they are in the process of moving again.

> Papa parked the car out in front and left the motor running. "Ready," he yelled. Without saying a word, Roberto and I began to carry the boxes out to the car. Roberto carried the two big boxes and I carried the two smaller ones. Papa then threw the mattress on top of the car roof and tied it with ropes to the front and rear bumpers.
> —*from* **"The Circuit"** by Francisco Jimenez

Exercise A

Answer these questions about the paragraphs.

1. What transition words and phrases are used in the first paragraph?

   _____

2. Draw a conclusion to tell the main idea of the second paragraph.

   _____

   _____

Exercise B

As you read the paragraph on the next page, fill in each blank with a transition word or phrase that makes the sequence of events clear. Use the words in the box on this page.

Noni grabbed his warmest boots and sealskin hat. 1. _____ he put on his heaviest coat, because the trip ahead would be a long one. Outside his two faithful dogs, Nikki and Rikki, greeted him. The dogs were 2. _____ hitched to the sled and they all set off. However, 3. _____ traveling only a short distance, the sled overturned on a steep slope. Noni tumbled down the snowy slope and was shaken but not hurt. 4. _____ he wanted to continue the trip, but 5. _____ he decided to put it off a day. 6. _____ the dogs barked loudly, wanting to be unhooked from the sled. 7. _____ they were freed and ran on ahead of Noni back to home, happy the journey was over so soon.

Exercise C

Read the sentences below. Then rearrange them in time order. Use the transition words and phrases and other clues to help you. Finally, rewrite the sentences as a narrative paragraph on the lines provided. When you have finished, use the Narrative Paragraph Revision Checklist to improve your work.

1. Immediately he rushed past the dogs and stormed into the cabin.

2. Then, as Noni came close to the cabin he panicked.

3. At last, he rushed out the front door with them, flinging them into the snow.

4. After a while, Noni neared home, dragging the sled.

5. Smoke was coming from a side window near the stove.

6. Even before he arrived, he could hear the sled dogs barking.

7. Then he ripped flaming curtains from the wall.

Narrative Paragraph Revision Checklist

√ Does my paragraph have a main idea ?
√ Does my paragraph tell a story, with emphasis on events?
√ Have I told the actions in order, first to last?
√ Have I used words that clearly show the sequence of events?
√ Have I avoided sentence fragments and run-ons?

_____

_____

_____

_____

_____

Lesson 4
Conflict in Story Plots

A story's plot is a series of events creating a conflict that is eventually resolved.

Most good stories follow a similar pattern. In the beginning, characters are introduced. Soon these characters become involved in events that center on a problem, or **conflict**. The conflict may be between one character and another, between a character and some outside force, or between a character and himself or herself. As the characters deal with more and more events, tension often rises. The conflict reaches a critical level, or **climax**. At this point, the course of events changes. The conflict is resolved in some way, and the story comes to an end, or **resolution**. In some stories, the resolution is not directly stated and the reader must draw a conclusion about it.

The diagram below shows the usual pattern of a story's plot line.

beginning ⟶ conflict ⟶ climax ⟶ resolution

Read the following summary of the plot of "The Circuit." Try to fit the summary to the plot pattern shown in the diagram.

> Francisco hates the idea of moving again. He and his family are immigrant workers and move often. This time they find work in a vineyard and move into an old garage with no windows and a dirt floor. Francisco works long and hard. His muscles ache after a day's work. When the grape season ends in November, Francisco goes to school. He is very nervous the first day. Everyone has books and friends; Francisco has neither and has trouble remembering English. When asked to read in class, he becomes dizzy. Francisco asks his teacher for help, and for a month the two work on English during lunch. One day Francisco's teacher offers to teach him how to play the trumpet. When Francisco comes home from school, excited about his teacher's offer, he finds everything is packed up in cardboard boxes.

Exercise A
Use the plot summary of "The Circuit" to answer these questions.

1. What conflict or problem is evident early in the story?

_____

_____

2. Give three details from the summary that contribute to the conflict.

_____

_____

3. What type of conflict does the summary present?

_____

4. What is the story's climax?

_____

_____

5. What information is given to draw a conclusion about the resolution?

_____

_____

6. What is the resolution?

_____

_____

Exercise B

On your own paper, write a plot summary of one of the following items. Identify the plot's conflict, climax, and resolution. Then state whether you think the resolution could have been predicted and whether it was believable.

1. a movie or play you have seen recently

2. a short story you have read recently

Exercise C

Divide into groups of four or five. Read the following beginning of a plot summary and discuss possible developments, climax, and resolution. When group members agree on how to finish the plot summary, have a volunteer write it down to present to the class. As you work, consider questions like these: What three things must Tom do to accomplish his goal? How might others respond to his actions? Does he accomplish what he sets out to do?

> Tom is a class leader. A new student, Jerry, arrives. Jerry is a talented athlete and math student. His good nature wins friends. Tom is unhappy because he is no longer the center of attention. He schemes to regain his role as class leader.

Lesson 5
Characters and Dialogue

Dialogue helps make story characters come alive.

Readers get to know characters in a story in a number of ways. One way is through the narrator's description of their appearance, actions, and feelings. Another way is through **dialogue**, the exact words of characters. In the following excerpt from Paul Darcy Boles's "Lucas and Jake," the author uses all of these methods. Pay attention to things you learn about the characters.

> Lucas waited for their first smidge of smart talk. But the bigger boy's voice sounded thoughtful, not smart talking at all. "Wonder how come they keep him here, Paddy? Not back with all the others?"
>
> The smaller boy shrugged. He went on making his Yo-Yo climb up and roll down. "Maybe he *likes* it here."
>
> That was as good an answer as Lucas had ever heard from a layman who couldn't know anything solid about lions. Most people thought they were lion experts.
>
> The bigger boy's eyes widened toward Lucas. "Sir, how come he's here? Not messing around with the other lions up at the moat?"
>
> Paddy let his Yo-Yo spin to a stop. He wanted to know too.
>
> Lucas cleared his throat. But before he could say word one, information fountained out of the taller boy: "My name's Ridefield Tarrant. This is Patrick McGoll. Call him Paddy, sir. We came out on the bus. We each had two bits for Saturday. I didn't like the baboons; they make me nervous barking. But I sure like the lions and the tigers. Especially lions." He drew fresh breath. "We could have gone seen *Dancers in the Dark Night of Time*, adults only, we know how to sneak in. But it felt like a better day for animals."

Before you begin writing dialogue, decide how you want your characters to come across. If you want to portray a character as confident, curious, or angry, create dialogue that is appropriate for this type of person. For example, if Paul Darcy Boles had wanted to portray Lucas as an angry person, he might have written dialogue like this: "You boys just get away from here. Don't bother me. And don't go near that lion!" However, if he had wanted Lucas to come across as curious, he might have written dialogue like this: "What are you boys doing here? Are you lost? Have you been to this zoo before?"

Guidelines for Writing and Punctuating Dialogue

1. Enclose a speaker's exact words in quotation marks.
2. Begin a new paragraph each time the speaker changes.
3. Begin a direct quotation with a capital letter.
4. Set off a direct quotation with a comma when it is preceded or followed by a phrase such as *he said* or *she replied*.
5. Avoid overusing the word *said*. The Word Bank contains examples of more descriptive words.

Word Bank
bellowed
whimpered
retorted
whispered
insisted
shouted
repeated
pleaded

Exercise A
Answer these questions on the lines provided.

1. When the boys first stop at Jake's cage, how is Ridefield's voice described? What does this tell you about him?

    _____

    _____

2. Paddy stops playing with his Yo-Yo to hear Lucas's answer to Ridefield's question. What does this action tell you about Paddy?

    _____

    _____

3. What details of Ridefield's long speech to Lucas suggest that he is friendly, adventuresome, and interested in animals?

    _____

    _____

Exercise B
Write two sentences that tell more about each character described below. In one, tell something he or she says. In the other, describe something he or she does.

1. Josita was happy when she won the swimming event.

    _____

    _____

2. Morgan became curious about a strange shadow in the hall.

    _____

    _____

3. Allison was upset when she heard Pam was moving.

    _____

    _____

4. David was surprised to see a deer in the yard.

    _____

    _____

Lesson 6
Classifying

To classify information, arrange it into similar groups.

When you gather information, you need to organize it so that it makes sense. You must **classify** your information, which means you arrange it into similar groups. As you prepare to write a composition, take time to classify the details.

Suppose you are planning to write a description of the Fourth of July celebration in your town. You would think of all the things that people will be doing to celebrate the Fourth of July. You might make a list of descriptive details, and then put these details into categories. The following chart classifies details according to the senses of sound, taste, and sight.

Sound	Taste	Sight
bangs and whistles of fireworks	grilled chicken	sparkling fireworks
oohs and ahs of viewers	sweet lemonade	crowds of people
sizzling hamburgers	buttery corn on the cob	smoke from grills
laughter	juicy watermelon	picnic tables
cheers at baseball game	creamy coleslaw	someone napping under tree

There are many other ways to classify details. The details in the chart above, for example, might be organized with categories such as these: **People, Food, Fireworks**. As you write down details during prewriting, think of categories that will help you organize your material.

Exercise A
Answer the following questions, based on the chart.

1. Under what classification do you find *smoke from grills*?

_____

2. Under which headings might you add *whining children? apple pie? red, white, and blue banners?*

_____

3. What other detail can you think of for each classification?

4. What other senses could be added to the chart? Give two details for each.

_____

_____

Exercise B

The words below are grouped according to something they have in common. Underline the word that does not fit the classification. You may need to use a dictionary.

Example: woe, despair, joy, gloom
Answer: woe, despair, joy, gloom

1. orange, broccoli, apple, banana

2. Detroit, Miami, Utah, Chicago

3. poverty, early, late, middle

4. hammer, saw, tulip, chisel

5. quiet, honest, glasses, shy

6. eel, whale, cat, clam

7. mad, angry, furious, calm

8. talk, walk, speak, shout

9. dress, shirt, teeth, shoe

10. break, repair, fix, mend

Exercise C

Each of the following groups have one or more characteristics in common. Write the common characteristic or characteristics that make each group a class.

Example: dime, nickel, quarter
Answer: American coins; round

1. fear, glee, sorrow

_____

2. French, German, Latin

_____

3. clank, ring, roar

_____

4. finger, knuckle, nail

_____

5. football, soccer, golf

_____

6. lake, river, creek

_____

7. sour, bitter, sweet

_____

8. poem, novel, essay

_____

9. comet, meteor, star

_____

10. sent, tent, went

_____

Lesson 7

Arranging Details in Spatial Order

You can use spatial order to help readers visualize details.

When you write you can use **spatial order** to describe what you want your readers to see. For example, you use spatial order when you describe a room from top to bottom or right to left. Spatial order helps your readers visualize the scene accurately. Be sure to stick to whatever spatial order you select so that your readers' mental image moves smoothly along with your words.

The chart below contains some words that can help you express spatial relationships. You can also use phrases such as *off to the side* or *as far as the eye can see* to give your readers a sense of direction and distance. The passage below describes what twelve-year-old Maria Luisa and her cousin Mike experience while on a walk. Note the words and phrases that indicate spatial order.

Spatial Order	
above	near
away	over
back	right
down	left
up	beyond
toward	through
far	bottom
in	distance
under	closer
ahead	farther

They stopped to watch the waves. Every now and then an enormous one would roll up to a huge crest as far along the coast as the eye could see, and then would burst into a long line of churning white foam which grew smaller and gentler as it came toward the shore. Little flocks of sandpipers walked rapidly up and down the edge of the water in hopes of finding food in each wave. In the distance another wave began to rise to a huge green crest.

—*from* **Maria Luisa** by Winifred Madison

Exercise A

Answer the following questions about the paragraph above.

1. Which phrase helps you see how large the beach is?

2. What other words and phrases indicating spatial order are used in this paragraph?

_____

3. Reread the first three sentences of the description. What kind of spatial order is used in these sentences—left to right, far to near, or top to bottom?

_____

Exercise B
Read the paragraph below and answer the questions.

> Sarah and Bob were excited as they adjusted their air tanks and jumped into the water. Each kick sent them closer to the ocean floor. A large school of brightly colored fish swam a few feet below Sarah. The two divers kicked harder and headed farther down into the darkening water, hoping to locate the submerged coral reef they thought was straight ahead.

1. What words and phrases indicating spatial order are used?

_____

2. Are details presented from far to near, left to right, or top to bottom?

_____

3. Which words help tell you direction? distance?

_____

Exercise C
Imagine that you are walking through a dense forest and find a clearing that you never knew existed. What you see makes you stop and stare. Write three sentences to describe what is in the clearing. Use the spatial-order words from the chart on the preceding page.

_____

_____

_____

_____

_____

Lesson 8
Writing a Descriptive Paragraph

A descriptive paragraph creates a vivid image of a person, thing, or place.

A **descriptive paragraph** paints pictures with words. In a good description, the reader will be able to do more than see the scene, however. He or she will be able to hear, taste, smell, and feel it as well. Your choice of words helps create the picture you want the reader to visualize. That is why it is important to use a thesaurus and to classify your details so they can be presented in an organized way. Good descriptive paragraphs create very vivid impressions but do not try to describe too much in one paragraph.

Notice the way Nicholasa Mohr paints a picture of Mr. Mendelsohn. Her choice of words helps you visualize this character. Pay special attention to the spatial order presented in the paragraph and to the adjectives that appeal to the senses.

> "Good morning to you all!" He had just shaved and trimmed his large black mustache. As he smiled broadly, one could see that most of his teeth were missing. His large bald head was partially covered by his small black skullcap. Thick dark gray hair grew in abundance at the lower back of his head, coming around the front above his ears into short sideburns. He wore a clean white shirt, frayed at the cuffs. His worn-out pinstripe trousers were held up by a pair of dark suspenders. Mr. Mendelsohn leaned on his brown shiny cane and carried a small brown paper bag.
> —*from* **Mr. Mendelsohn** by Nicholasa Mohr

Exercise A
Answer these questions.

1. To what sense do the details in the paragraph about Mr. Mendelsohn appeal?

   _____

2. What are some words used by Nicholasa Mohr that help you visualize Mr. Mendelsohn?

   _____

   _____

3. What spatial order is used to describe Mr. Mendelsohn?

   _____

Exercise B
Complete this exercise on your own paper. List six or seven details that describe a place. Include details that appeal to at least three senses. Some of the details

should also reflect your feelings about the place. Choose one of the subjects below or think of another place that is special to you.

1. a room in a house

2. a landscape through which you have traveled by plane, car, train, or boat

3. a place associated with a holiday

4. an imaginary place you would like to visit

5. the inside of a closet

Exercise C

Complete the following activities as preparation for writing a descriptive paragraph. Use the place you chose in Exercise B.

1. Classify the details so that you will be able to present them in a clear and organized way.

2. Add appropriate adjectives and adverbs to your details.

3. Write down your feelings about this place. Try to reflect these feelings with vivid adverbs and adjectives.

4. Write two possible topic sentences that could be supported by your details.

5. Decide on a spatial order for your description. For example, will you order your details from near to far? outside to inside? left to right?

Exercise D

Use the work you have done in this lesson and in previous lessons to write a descriptive paragraph. Review the following checklist.

Descriptive Paragraph Revision Checklist

√   Have I classified my details in groups that make sense?
√   Have I used words and phrases to help the reader visualize my description?
√   Have I written a topic sentence?
√   Have I used the same spatial order throughout my description?
√   Have I included precise adjectives?
√   Have I used the correct forms of adjectives and adverbs that compare?

Lesson 9
Comparing and Contrasting

To compare means to identify likenesses among things. To contrast means to identify differences.

You have learned that when you **classify** you group things into similar categories. Comparing and contrasting takes two such groups and looks at their similarities or differences. When you see how something is like something else, you are **comparing**. When you see how two objects are different, you are **contrasting**. When you compare or contrast two things, you use words and phrases like the following.

For Comparisons	For Contrasts
both . . . and	but
the same as	unlike
just as	however

Sometimes, you can even compare and contrast things with themselves. The caterpillar and the adult butterfly are both stages in the life cycle of a butterfly. Caterpillars and adult butterflies both have three pairs of legs and a head with eyes and a mouth. However, the caterpillar and the butterfly look very different. Look at the picture below. You can compare and contrast the appearance of a butterfly at the larva (caterpillar) stage and at the adult (butterfly) stage.

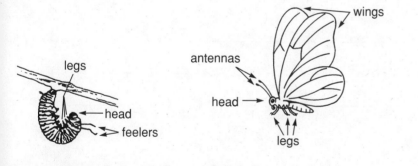

Exercise A
Answer these questions.

1. What is the shape of the caterpillar? _____

2. What does the adult butterfly have on its body that the caterpillar does

   not have? _____

3. Would the shape of the caterpillar and the butterfly be a feature for

   comparison or contrast?_____

Exercise B

One way to make comparisons and contrasts is to create a chart. The items compared and contrasted are written in the far left column, and points to compare and contrast are written at the top of each of the other columns. Fill in all of the blank boxes in the chart. Note the comparisons and contrasts.

	Shape	Eyes	Stage of Life Cycle
Caterpillar		detect only light and dark	larva
Butterfly		compound, detect motion	

Exercise C

For each pair of items below, write a sentence that compares the items and a sentence that contrasts them on the lines provided. Use words and phrases that signal comparisons and contrasts.

Example: caterpillar, butterfly
Answers: The caterpillar and the butterfly are both stages in the life cycle of a butterfly. Both the caterpillar and the butterfly have three body parts—head, chest, abdomen. The caterpillar has a long body with many pairs of legs, but the butterfly has wings and only a few pairs of legs.

1. aquarium, zoo

_____

_____

_____

2. encyclopedia, dictionary

_____

_____

_____

3. television, radio

_____

_____

_____

Lesson 10
Writing a Comparison/Contrast Description

A comparison/contrast description explains how two things are alike and how they are different.

In Lesson 9 you learned about comparing and contrasting. This skill can be used when you write descriptions. You may want to describe things or make a point by showing how objects are alike and how they are different. This technique is called **comparison and contrast**. In the following description, the writer compares and contrasts ballet dancers and football players.

Ballet dancers and football players differ in physical size and appearance. Yet both are highly trained athletes. Classical ballet and pro football both demand years of training, great strength, and agility. It takes endurance and speed to run for a touchdown. Likewise, these same qualities are used by a ballerina performing a series of turns in *Swan Lake*. As the football player practices plays, the dancer rehearses steps.

Physical skills, however, are used quite differently on a ballet stage and on a football field. Football players must react quickly to moves by their opponents. Ballet dancers, in contrast, follow precise steps designed by choreographers. Planned movements do not change during a ballet the way plays change during a football game. While football players use strength to overpower opponents, dancers express emotions or tell a story by using graceful movements.

Here are some ways to develop comparison/contrast descriptions:

- Clearly identify the two items being compared and contrasted.
- Give examples of how the two items are alike and different.
- Classify the characteristics being compared into clear patterns. Decide whether you will discuss each item fully in a separate paragraph or compare both items point by point within the same sentences or paragraph.
- Use words and phrases such as *both* and *just as* to indicate comparisons. Use words and phrases such as *however*, *differ*, and *on the other hand* to signal contrasts. (See the list in the box.)
- Summarize or restate the point of the description for the reader.

Comparison or Contrast Words and Phrases
as
both
just as
like
likewise
similarly
the same as
differ
different
however
in contrast
on the other hand
unlike

Exercise A
Answer the following questions on the lines provided.

1. What two items are compared and contrasted in the description?

   _____

2. What are the points of comparison and contrast?

   _____

3. What words or phrases indicate comparisons or contrasts?

_____

4. What pattern of comparisons and contrasts does the writer use?

_____

Exercise B

Old-fashioned porches and new-styled decks on houses both offer places for people to sit outside in good weather. Yet porches often are found at the front door, while decks most often are built in the backyard. Read the descriptive details below. Write **D** or **P** next to each one for *Deck* or *Porch*. Some details may fit under both headings.

- has porch roof to block sun
- lets you see front sidewalk
- private place in backyard
- family gathering place

- place to sit and talk
- no porch roof to block sun
- lets you see backyard
- attached to or near house

Exercise C

Choose one of the following pairs of items to compare and contrast. List at least six similarities and/or differences between the two items. Use the lines provided.

snakes and birds
pencils and pens
movies and TV shows

hockey and soccer
photographers and painters
singers and dancers

_____

_____

_____

_____

_____

Exercise D

On your own paper, write a description comparing and contrasting the two items that you considered in Exercise C. Use what you have learned to develop clear and vivid comparisons and contrasts. Review the checklist below.

Comparison/Contrast Description Revision Checklist

√ Have I clearly identified the two items being compared and contrasted?
√ Have I included examples of how the two items are alike and different?
√ Have I used comparison and contrast words and phrases?
√ Have I summarized the point of the description?
√ Have I included precise adverbs?

Lesson 11
Transitions in Paragraphs

Transitions are words and phrases that show the order and relationship of ideas.

Transition words and phrases can show time order in narratives and spatial order in descriptions. Transition words are also used to show various relationships in explanatory writing. Study these charts.

Spatial	Time	Cause and Effect
above	after	as a result
behind	before	because of
below	finally	due to
far	later	for this reason
inside	meanwhile	it is evident
left	next	therefore
right	then	thus

Comparison and Contrast	Example or Classification
instead of	for example
just as	for instance
like	in fact
more than	in other words
on the one hand	in this case
similarly	to illustrate

Read the paragraph that follows. Study the underlined transition words and phrases in the sentences within the paragraph.

Jason set his goal and <u>then</u> decided how to reach it. <u>More than</u> anything, he wanted that aquarium! <u>First</u>, he was going to save his allowance. <u>Next</u>, he was going to find out everything he could about tropical fish. <u>For example</u>, he planned to spend hours in the library and in the pet shop downtown. <u>Finally</u>, he would clear a space in his bedroom to hold the aquarium. The aquarium would fit perfectly <u>next</u> to his desk. <u>Because of</u> his planning, his parents would be convinced that he was responsible enough to buy and maintain an aquarium.

Exercise A
Answer the following questions.

1. Which transition words signal time relationships?

_____

2. Which transition phrase signals a cause-effect relationship? a spatial relationship?

_____

_____

3. Which transition phrase signals a comparison and contrast? an example?

_____

_____

Exercise B

Fill in each blank in the paragraphs with one of the transition words or phrases given below each paragraph.

1. The doctor looked at the X-ray and still felt uncertain about Tony's

injuries. _____ his uncertainty, Tony's doctor ordered

more tests and X-rays. _____, severe injuries were found.

_____ that Tony needed an operation.

It was evident   Because of   As a result

2. Planning your route for a long trip is a good investment of time.

_____, buy a good, up-to-date map.

_____, mark your starting point and your end point.

_____, with a brightly colored marker, trace the route you

prefer. Whether you choose the scenic drive or the most direct route,

your preparation will result in a more pleasant trip.

Finally   Then   First

3. The road sign was a real surprise. _____ the cornfield it

loomed, bright blue and tall. _____ the metal rectangular

face were printed the words: Enter at your own risk. _____

the sign we saw rows of corn that extended to the horizon. Perhaps, we

thought, the sign was meant to be a joke.

Under   On   Above

Lesson 12
Writing an Explanatory Paragraph

An explanatory paragraph uses facts to explain something.

You can make a topic clear to someone when you write an **explanatory paragraph**. Explanatory paragraphs define, illustrate, analyze, or explain something. You can write about what a mammal is, how to take a photograph, why one football team is better than another, or why animals hibernate. In each case, you give information that helps someone understand something.

You should always be familiar with a topic that you write about in an explanatory paragraph. Remember that transition words and phrases like *therefore*, *because of*, and *for example* show how ideas are connected. Use transitions when you write an explanatory paragraph to help a reader understand your ideas.

Read the following paragraph.

> Ravens are known for their intelligence as well as for their playfulness. While most other birds act mainly by instinct, ravens show curiosity, learn quickly from experience, and even use this experience to solve problems in new situations. For example, after watching its parents, a young raven puts nearly everything new into its mouth to find out if it's edible. But later it learns many different food-gathering skills. Like gulls, it drops shellfish from high in the air to break them open. A scientist observed one pair of ravens working together to take food from a cat. While one bird swooped low to make the cat drop the mouse it had caught, the second bird grabbed the dinner. This was not habit or instinct on the ravens' part—the birds had figured out how to solve a problem.
> —*from* **"One Smart Bird"** by Katherine Hauth

Exercise A
Answer the following questions.

1. What topic is being explained?

   _____

2. What details does the author give you to help you understand the topic?

   _____

   _____

3. Underline the transition words and phrases used in the paragraph.

Exercise B
Read the explanatory paragraph on the next page. Underline the transition words and phrases used in the paragraph.

To most people, bees seem to fly aimlessly from place to place. However, to other bees, the pattern and speed of their flight communicate very important information. For example, to tell other bees that food is within a hundred yards of the hive, a scout bee will fly in a circle. On the other hand, if the food is farther away, the bee will move in a figure-eight formation. In addition to telling the distance to the food, the scout will cross from one loop of the figure eight to the other to indicate the direction of the food. The speed with which the bee flies also tells the distance to the food. As a result, if a bee sees another bee flying very fast in a circle, it knows that food is very close.

Exercise C

Complete the following activities as preparation for writing an explanatory paragraph. Use your own paper.

1. Choose one of these suggested topics: how to cook chili, why dinosaurs are extinct, what a comet is, how a cell divides, how to play your favorite sport, how to choose and care for a pet. You may also choose your own topic.

2. Write a topic sentence for your paragraph.

3. List the details that you will include in your explanation.

4. List transition words and phrases that you will use.

5. Find or create a photograph or drawing that illustrates the subject you are explaining.

Exercise D

Use the work you have done in this lesson to write an explanatory paragraph. Use the following checklist to evaluate your paragraph. Write your paragraph on your own paper.

Explanatory Paragraph Revision Checklist

√ Have I included enough details so that the explanation is clear to the reader?

√ Have I used transitions such as *first*, *behind*, *similarly* and *for instance* to connect the ideas in my paragraph?

√ Have I included a graphic aid that enhances my explanation?

√ Have I combined subjects and predicates where appropriate?

Lesson 13
Cause and Effect

Understanding cause-and-effect relationships will help you improve your reading, writing, and study skills.

You probably know that when a parachutist pulls the ripcord, the parachute opens. A parachute slows down because the air trapped inside the umbrella resists the weight of the falling parachutist. These are both examples of **cause and effect**.

A **cause** is what makes something happen. An **effect** is what happens as a result of the cause. Pulling the ripcord causes the parachute to open; the parachute's opening is the effect of pulling the ripcord. Air trapped inside the umbrella, which resists the weight of the parachutist, causes the parachute to slow down; the parachute slowing down is the effect of air trapped inside the umbrella, which resists the weight of the parachutist. Understanding cause-and-effect relationships helps you understand what you read. Transition words such as *because* and *since* signal cause. Transition words such as *so* and *thus* signal effect.

One effect can have more than one cause, and one cause can produce more than one effect. For instance, you might have a stomachache because of two causes—overeating and the stomach flu, both at the same time. One cause—too much sun—can bring about more than one effect, as shown below.

Exercise A
Identify the causes and effects in the following sentences. Underline the causes once and underline the effects twice.

   Example: Because of the rain, our basement flooded
   Answer: <u>Because of the rain</u>, <u><u>our basement flooded</u></u>.

1. Jake broke his leg; therefore, he couldn't play in the game and had to use crutches to walk.

2. As a result of last night's power shortage, we ate a cold dinner by candlelight.

3. Jane forgot to put the top on the grasshopper's box; consequently, the insect escaped.

4. Since it has not rained in several days and because it has been cold, the new seedlings have died.

5. Joe's dad left his car's headlights on last night; hence, the car won't start.

6. The farmland meant everything to the Hutchisons because it had been in the family for generations.

7. Rosemary overslept this morning, and as a result, she didn't have time to eat breakfast and was late for work.

Exercise B

Read the following paragraph. Then answer the questions that follow.

> Yet in spite of the savagery and the ruthlessness of the Mongol conquest, some good was accomplished. Roads were built between Europe and Asia, and peoples of different cultures met each other and began to trade goods and knowledge. Oriental delicacies in foods and also fine fabrics were introduced. The Chinese areas of papermaking, woodblock printing, and painting were shared with the West.
> —*from* **All About Horses** by Marguerite Henry

1. What caused roads to be built between Europe and Asia?

_____

_____

2. What other effects came about because of this?

_____

_____

Lesson 14
Writing a Cause-Effect Paragraph

A paragraph of cause and effect clearly states how one person, thing, idea, or action influences another.

Some explanatory paragraphs tell how one action causes another or prove that a certain belief or action will lead to a certain behavior. This is a **cause-effect paragraph**. Cause-effect paragraphs rely on logical argument and clear thinking. To indicate the relationship between causes and effects you can use transition words and phrases.

Read the following paragraphs. Note the cause (why something happened) and effects (what happened).

> The decision to keep a pet can cause a major change in a family's lifestyle. Since pets require attention, family members have to be willing to give up some of their free time to care for them. Pets depend on people to keep them clean, well fed, and healthy. Therefore, families must arrange to have someone care for the animal when they go away on vacation, and, if the animal is sick, take it to the vet. If a dog is selected as a pet, time has to be set aside for walking and exercising it. Pets are fun but helpless, and consequently, are a big responsibility to a family.
>
> Cats were not always as popular as they are today. During the Middle Ages, some people in certain parts of the world thought cats were evil. As a result, cats were feared and persecuted. Consequently, the population of rats and mice grew in the cities because there were not enough cats to hunt them. Today, cats are sometimes kept because they hunt mice, but mostly because they are good company.

Think about the answers to the following questions about the cause-effect relationships in the paragraph.

1. What is the effect of the decision to keep a pet?
2. What causes a family to arrange for pet care when they go on vacation?
3. What was the cause of cats being feared and persecuted during the Middle Ages?
4. What was the effect of not having enough cats to hunt rats and mice?

Exercise A
Read the following cause-effect paragraph.

> Presenting information in a graph is an effective way to help people understand information. When, for example, you put data you have collected as part of a science project into graph form, people notice and remember what you did. A colorful, clear graph makes people pay attention and, as a result, helps them understand your research.

1. What will be the effect of a colorful, clear graph? Underline the answer once in the paragraph.

2. What will cause people to notice and remember what you did? Underline the answer twice in the paragraph.

Exercise B

Underline the transition words and phrases that are in the following paragraph.

Our school needs more plants. First, plants are beautiful to look at; consequently, the school would be a more visually pleasing place. Their presence would encourage student attendance. Finally, all plants could be labeled and presented with descriptions and care instructions. As a result, they would have educational value. Plants would be appreciated by our eyes, noses, and brains.

Exercise C

Fill in the blanks to complete each statement.

1. Our air conditioner is broken; as a result, _____

_____ .

2. If public transportation were cheaper, _____

_____ .

3. _____ ; therefore,

I'm not going to the party.

4. _____ ; consequently, I

couldn't complete my homework.

5. I fell and twisted my ankle because of _____

_____ .

Exercise D

Write a cause-effect paragraph. For a topic, use an idea from Exercise C of this lesson or think of your own. Write your paragraph on your own paper.

Cause-Effect Paragraph Revision Checklist

√   Have I clearly explained the effects and the causes?

√   Have I used transition words and phrases such as *consequently*, *because of*, and *as a result* to signal cause-effect relationships?

√   Have I set off appositives with commas?

Lesson 15

Writing a Persuasive Paragraph

A persuasive paragraph tries to convince others to accept an opinion by giving strong reasons in support of that opinion.

You read persuasive writing every day in advertisements, movie reviews, editorials, and letters to editors. You usually begin a **persuasive paragraph** with a topic sentence that states your opinion about a subject. The rest of the paragraph gives supporting reasons, including facts, to support your opinion. These reasons should be ordered from least convincing to most convincing.

Topic sentence: School athletes should participate in school sports but should not be excused from taking a full schedule of other subjects.

Reasons:
1. Athletes should not base all their hopes on having sports careers.
2. "Dr. B," the famous basketball star, urges all school athletes to prepare for an alternative career.
3. A well-rounded student makes a better, more confident athlete.
4. Students are better prepared for life when they take part in the whole program.

Use the following guidelines to help you write a persuasive argument.

1. Express your opinion clearly in a topic sentence.
2. Give relevant, accurate reasons or facts as evidence.
3. Give specific examples from your personal observations or experience.
4. Quote statements of authority, such as the comments of experts or the results of public-opinion polls.
5. Order reasons from least convincing to most convincing.
6. Use transition words and phrases that signal your supporting evidence. These include *first, next, finally, because, since, more important, furthermore,* and *therefore.*
7. Present a balanced argument. Avoid loaded words or faulty generalizations.

Think about the answers to these questions about school athletes. Use the information from the topic sentence and reasons given above.

1. What will the effect be on students who take part in a whole school program?
2. What transition words and phrases could be added to each of the reasons given?
3. Do you consider the final reason the most convincing? Why or why not?

Exercise A

Read the topics listed on the next page, and choose five topics about which you have an opinion. Write a topic sentence that expresses your opinion for each.

1. homework

2. city recreation centers

3. choosing friends

4. unusual pets

5. grades

Exercise B

Choose a topic sentence from those you have written in Exercise A. List three reasons that support your opinion, from least convincing to most convincing.

Exercise C

Use the work you have done in Exercise B to write a persuasive paragraph. Choose one of your topics from Exercise B for your paragraph. Use the following checklist to evaluate your work. Write your paragraph on your own paper.

Persuasive Paragraph Revision Checklist

√   Have I stated my opinion clearly in a topic sentence?
√   Did I support my opinions with good reasons, including facts?
√   Are my reasons organized from least convincing to most convincing?
√   Have I used transition words in ordering my reasons?
√   Have I used the correct forms of the verbs *be*, *have*, and *do*?
√   Did I present a balanced argument? Have I avoided loaded words and faulty generalizations?

Lesson 16

Writing a Summary Paragraph

A summary tells main ideas and omits irrelevant details.

In a **summary paragraph**, only the most important ideas are stated. A summary is always much shorter than the original. When you write a review of a novel, a short story, or film, you use the skill of summarizing. Follow these guidelines.

Guidelines for Summarizing
1. After you read something ask yourself, "What is this about?"
2. Find the main idea. If this idea is not directly stated, you must infer it.
3. Begin your summary with a topic sentence that states the main idea. Add sentences that supply supporting details.
4. Avoid unnecessary details.
5. To summarize lists of things or actions, find a category that covers what is on the list. For example, do not say a character coughed, sneezed, felt dizzy, had the chills, and felt weak. Instead, say the character had the flu.

Exercise A

Read the following summary of "Cinderella."

    This is the story of patience and virtue being rewarded. The kind and sweet-tempered Cinderella was constantly mistreated by her stepmother and stepsisters. When she was forbidden to accompany her stepsisters to a magnificent ball, she wept. Suddenly, a fairy godmother appeared, dressed her in splendid clothes, and transported her to the ball in a magic coach. The unknown beauty dazzled everyone, including a prince. She quickly departed just before midnight, leaving a glass slipper in her haste. In the following weeks, the love-struck prince searched everywhere for the beautiful woman whose foot would fit the slipper. Finally, he found Cinderella and made her his princess.

Answer the questions about the summary.

1. What is the main idea stated in the topic sentence?

2. Has any unnecessary information been provided?

Exercise B

Read the following summaries of an excerpt from Betsy Byars's novel *A Midnight Fox*. Then answer the questions.

(A) Tom's father tries to persuade his son to go to the farm so that he and Tom's mother can take a trip to Europe. One thing Tom's father mentions is that Tom will be able to go swimming each day. Tom resists his father's reasoning. Finally, Tom's father recalls a time that Tom's mother sacrificed a trip because Tom got sick. If Tom doesn't go to the farm, he could ruin this trip for his mother because she would worry about him.

(B) First, Tom's father tells his son there's a pond at the farm. He says that Tom can go swimming every day. Tom reminds his father that he isn't much of a swimmer. Then Tom's father says that Tom can learn. He also says that two months on a farm could make a mental and physical difference in Tom. Tom responds that he likes the way he is and continues working on his model. Tom's father asks him to put the model down. Finally, Tom's father says that this trip means a lot to his mother. He reminds Tom that she didn't go to the Smokies, stayed home, nursed Tom when he got the measles, and never complained. Tom's father wants her to go to Europe and see everything she's wanted to see her whole life. If Tom does not go to the farm, she will worry.

1. Which summary has a main idea? What is the topic sentence that expresses this main idea?

   _____

   _____

2. Identify a detail that supports the main idea.

   _____

3. Find a sentence in both summaries that tells what Tom's father reminds Tom of. Which summary states this more briefly?

   _____

4. Which summary contains unnecessary details? _____. Identify three by underlining them.

Exercise C

On your own paper, write a summary paragraph about a short story you have read. Use the checklist below to decide whether your summary accurately and briefly reflects the content of the story.

Summary Paragraph Revision Checklist

√ Have I included a topic sentence that states the main idea?
√ Have I added the details that support the main idea?
√ Have I avoided unnecessary details?
√ Have I used one or two words to cover lists of things or actions?
√ Have I used irregular verbs correctly?

Lesson 17
Research: Choosing a Topic

When you write a research report, choose a topic that interests you. Then take time to narrow your topic.

The first step in preparing to write a research report is choosing your topic. Begin by making an **interest inventory**, a list of topics that interest you.

The next step is to check that each topic on your list is narrow enough to handle in six to eight paragraphs. Try webbing or clustering each topic that needs to be narrowed. Here is an example of a web in which the broad topic Animals is narrowed to the more manageable topic Working Dogs.

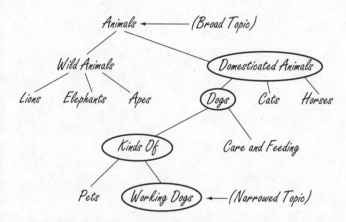

Next, write a list of five to eight questions that you would like your report to answer. With these questions in hand, you will know exactly what to look for when you do your research. The following is a list of questions on the topic of Working Dogs.

1. What work did dogs do long ago?
2. What work do they do now?
3. How do dogs help people who are handicapped?
4. How do dogs herd animals?
5. How are sled dogs trained?

Exercise A
Narrow each topic to one that could be covered in a research report of six to eight paragraphs. Draw webs if you think they will help you.

Example: Photography
Answer: Early Cameras

1. South America

_____

2. Great Inventors

_____

3. Jungle Animals

_____

4. Weather

_____

5. Athletics

_____

6. Texas

_____

7. Careers in Medicine

_____

8. Bees

_____

9. Bicycles

_____

10. Mirrors

_____

Exercise B

Choose five of the topics below. On your own paper, write three good
questions to use in researching each of the following topics.

> **Example:** Early Airplanes
> **Answer:** Who built the first engine-driven airplane?
>   How do the first planes compare with modern planes?
>   What were early airplanes used for?

1. Martin Luther King, Jr.   **6.** Marie Curie

2. The Civil War   **7.** Education in China

3. Life in a Mexican Village   **8.** African Art

4. Japanese Poetry   **9.** Death Valley

5. Ocean Tides   **10.** Careers in Law Enforcement

Exercise C

On your own paper, make an interest inventory of topics you might use for a
research report. Narrow each topic that seems too broad. Choose the one you
would most like to write about. Then write five to eight questions that you
would like your report to answer.

Lesson 18
Research: Using Reference Sources

Reference books help you find specific information.

When you want to find out about a topic—for a school research project or simply for your own information—there are many books that can help you. **Reference sources** such as dictionaries, encyclopedias, atlases, and almanacs are located in a reference section of the library. The key to using reference sources is knowing which one to use for the information you want.

Encyclopedia   Because an encyclopedia contains articles on a wide range of subjects, it usually is a good place to start looking for information. If your topic is *Working Dogs*, for instance, you will find background information by reading a general article about dogs. Cross-references at the end of the article may point out related articles in the encyclopedia.

    Articles in the encyclopedia are organized in alphabetical order. If the encyclopedia consists of more than one volume, find the volume that includes the key word in the name of your topic. The key word for an article about Libby Riddles is *Riddles*. Most encyclopedias also present an index of subject titles in the last volume.

Almanac   An almanac is a source to use when you want to find a few facts or statistics. Consult an almanac to answer questions like this: How large is the Statue of Liberty? Who won the gymnastics gold medal for men and women in the most recent summer Olympic games? In an almanac, facts are organized in an index under headings such as *Olympics* or *U.S. Government*. Because many almanacs are revised each year, use the current edition for the most up-to-date information.

Atlas   An atlas is a book of maps. You can use an atlas to find the location of a place, information about the geographical features of an area of land, the populations of cities, and the distance from one place to another. World atlases contain maps of countries and continents all over the globe. Road atlases contain highway maps of states, countries, or regions within countries.

The Readers' Guide to Periodical Literature   This is an index that will help you find magazine articles. It lists articles from about two hundred periodicals—publications that appear regularly but not daily. The articles are indexed by name of the author and by subject. Here is part of an entry for the subject *Dogs*.

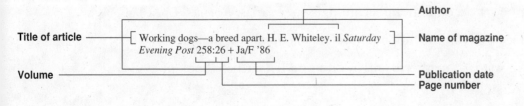

Books of Quotations   Books such as *Familiar Quotations* and *The Home Book of Quotations* list famous quotations. The quotations may be arranged by subject or author. Quotations may be indexed at the back of the book by authors and key words.

The Vertical File   This is a file of such materials as pamphlets, charts, newspaper clippings, and magazine articles about topics of current interest. Information is arranged alphabetically according to subject.

Nonprint Media   Reference sources are not limited to the printed materials described thus far. Nonprint media can include collections of CDs, films, filmstrips, records, tape cassettes, microfilm, and microfiche.

Exercise A
Answer the questions below.

1. Which reference source would you consult if you wanted to know who was the winner of the Rose Bowl in 1983?

   _____

2. Which reference source would include an article on spacecraft?

   _____

3. Which reference source would you consult if you wanted to find a map of Alaska?

   _____

4. Which reference source would help you find a magazine article that was published last year?

   _____

Exercise B
Underline the reference source in parentheses that would be best to consult for the following information.

   Example: a list of sunrise times for 1996 (atlas, almanac)
   Answer: almanac

1. a map of Alberta, Canada (atlas, encyclopedia)

2. information about the history of motion pictures (encyclopedia, nonprint media)

3. a 1959 magazine article on Hawaii becoming a state (atlas, *Readers' Guide*)

4. a film of the first walk on the moon (encyclopedia, nonprint media)

5. the author who wrote, "Neither a borrower, nor a lender be" (book of quotations, encyclopedia)

6. the final standings of the East Division American League in 1986 (*Readers' Guide*, almanac)

Lesson 19
Research: Taking Notes

Summarize information in your own words as you take notes.

The second step in preparing your research report is to find information on your topic and take notes. Read the following passage from a book. Then notice how the information from this passage has been recorded on the note card that follows.

Good sheep dogs have both "eye" and "style." The style allows the dog to approach a flock without scaring them. The dog moves in a crouched position rather than rushing and causing the sheep to scatter. When the dog is close, its "eye" comes into play, for a good dog can stare so intently at the sheep that they are literally hypnotized and will not move.

4
<u>Working Dogs</u>
by George S. Fichter, p. 10
Good sheep dogs need "style" and "eye."
1. <u>Style</u> = approach flock in crouch so won't scare sheep.
2. <u>Eye</u> = close to flock, dog stares at sheep—can hypnotize.

The note is written on an index card. Use index cards so that your notes will be easy to sort. The number at the top tells which question the information relates to. The title, author, and page of the source follow. Book and magazine titles are underlined. Titles of articles are enclosed in quotation marks. Include this information on each note card above the note.

The information on the note card is a summary of the information in the passage. When you summarize you use your own words to note main ideas and details. Summarize when you take notes for your research report. When you do, take note only of information that will help to answer the question.

The sample note card shown above was made from information in a nonfiction book. Examples of cards made from other kinds of sources can be found on the following page.

5
National Wildlife, "Dogging It Through the Wilderness,"
by the editors. Feb. - Mar., 1986, p. 44
Sled dogs need qualities:
1. mentally tough
2. leadership
3. "a mixture of hardy old native strains
   and modern breeds"

2
"Dog," World Book Encyclopedia,
1986, Vol. 5, p. 224
19 breeds of working dogs
1. Dobermans and mastiffs—police dogs
2. Malamutes, Siberian huskies pull sleds
3. St. Bernards—rescue work

Notice that the facts on each card are broken down and numbered. Number the facts on each card so you will not confuse them later. When you use the exact words of a source, be sure to put them in quotation marks.

As you do your research, you can add or drop questions to change the focus of your report. Remember, do not make your topic too broad or too narrow.

Think Back: Summarizing
When you write a summary, give only the main points of something. Use the skill of summarizing when you take notes for your research report.

Answer these questions about the note cards in this lesson.

1. What abbreviations and symbols were used on the cards?

_____

2. What are some other abbreviations and symbols you might use to make note taking easier?

_____

Exercise A

Read each question and passage below. On your own paper, follow the form shown on the note cards in this lesson and write the source of the information. Then summarize only the information that will help to answer the question given.

1. Question: How do dogs help people who are handicapped? From the entry "Guide Dog" on pages 784-785 of Volume 4 of *The New Encyclopaedia Britannica*, 1982.

   At the age of approximately one year, the dog is trained for three to four months to mold the animal's behavior to its owner's handicap. The dog learns to adjust to a harness, stop at curbs, gauge its owner's height when traveling in low or obstructed places, and disobey a command when obedience will endanger its master. Although several breeds, including Doberman pinschers, retrievers, and boxers, have been successfully educated as guide dogs, German shepherds are the most used.

2. Question: What work did dogs do long ago? From pages 42-43 of the book *All About Dogs* by Carl Burger.

   As the centuries went by, early men discovered new ways to make life more comfortable and secure. They advanced beyond being mere hunters of wild game and gatherers of wild vegetables and fruits. Animals other than the dog were domesticated: herds of cattle and horses, flocks of sheep, and various kinds of fowl. People began to cultivate food crops: different sorts of vegetables and grain to feed themselves and their domestic animals.

   Men found that dogs could be trained to guard and herd flocks. New weapons, such as the bow and arrow, led to new hunting methods. For all these purposes dogs were increasingly useful. Among tribes that followed their flocks from one grazing ground to another, dogs drove the herds and guarded them from thieves and wild beasts. In addition, they were set at new and more menial tasks. They became bearers of burdens and haulers of loads. When the tribe moved, the dogs were pressed into service to help carry the household goods.

Exercise B

Research the questions you have for your research paper. Note the question and source at the top of each index card. Then summarize the important information.

Lesson 20
Research: Organizing Information

Use classifying skills to organize your information.

Begin to organize the information you have gathered for your research paper by deciding which note cards you will actually use. Review each card and ask yourself: Does this information really help answer the question? Is it important and interesting enough to include in my report? Keep in mind that you have only six to eight paragraphs in which to present your information. Remove any cards that don't measure up. Aim for a total of no fewer than ten and no more than thirty cards.

Next, decide on the order in which you will present your information. Your notes are already sorted into piles, one for each question. Look through each pile and decide on the order in which you plan to deal with the questions. The writer who researched Working Dogs decided to present the questions in this order. Notice that a question was added to the original list from Lesson 17.

1. What work did dogs do long ago?
2. What work do they do now?
3. How do dogs help save people's lives?
4. How do dogs help people who are handicapped?
5. How do dogs herd animals?
6. How are sled dogs trained?

The first two items are in **time order**. Reports on the lives of famous people, on historical events, and on how-to projects often use time order.

The writer decided to present the last four items in **order of importance**, with the most important ideas presented first, and less important ideas following. This order is often used for research reports that present a series of examples.

Problem and solution reports begin by presenting a problem and go on to suggest possible solutions. A report on air pollution, for example, might use this kind of order.

Cause-and-effect reports explain why an event happened, or what happened as a result of some event. A report on the Civil War might focus on its causes. A report on automobiles might focus on what effects automobiles have had on our lives.

Think Back: Classifying

Remember what you already know about classifying—how to sort things into groups according to what they have in common. Use your classifying skills when you organize your research information.

Exercise A

The following notes were collected for a research report. Rearrange them in the order you think they should be presented in the report. Write what kind of order you used. List first the item that gives the topic of the research report.

1. Ban cars entirely from certain areas of the inner city

2. The problem of noise pollution in large cities

3. Make laws on auto mufflers stricter

4. Pass laws against playing portable radios on buses

5. Move airplane flight paths farther from populated areas

_____

_____

_____

_____

_____

Exercise B

For each report topic below, decide on a good method of organization. Write *Time order*, *Order of importance*, *Problem and solution*, or *Cause and effect* to tell which method you chose.

1. Preventing Fires in the Home _____

2. How a Caterpillar Becomes a Butterfly _____

3. The Birth of a Hurricane _____

4. Ways to Improve Your Memory _____

5. Life in a Mexican Village _____

6. The Development of the Bicycle _____

7. How Clouds Form _____

8. The Beliefs of Martin Luther King, Jr. _____

9. The Sinking of the *Titanic* _____

10. Birds of Northern California _____

Exercise C

Now go over your own notes. Pick the cards you will use in your report. You may want to use one of the four kinds of order presented in this lesson for your report.

Lesson 21
Research: Outlining

Use sequencing skills to organize your information into an outline.

Once you have organized the information for your report, it is time to make an **outline**—a general plan for your report. Study the outline for a report on Working Dogs. Notice that the writer used the questions from Lesson 20 as the basis for the outline. Then read the guidelines for outlining.

Title ————————→ Working Dogs

Main Topic ————→ I. Introduction

Subtopics ————→ A. More than mere pets
 B. Served us since long ago

Main Topic ————→ II. Long ago

Subtopics ————→ A. First domesticated animal
 B. Helped in hunting
 C. Hauled heavy loads
 D. Herded other animals

Main Topic ————→ III. Modern times

Subtopics ————→ A. Rescue work
 B. Help handicapped

Details ————→ 1. Guide dogs
 2. Companions for disabled

Subtopics ————→ C. Herd sheep
 D. Pull sleds

Main Topic ————→ IV. Conclusion

Guidelines for Outlining
1. Capitalize the first word of each line.
2. Write each main topic with a roman numeral and a period.
3. Write each subtopic with a capital letter and a period.
4. Write each detail with a number and a period.
5. Indent each subtopic and detail.
6. Make sure subtopics support main topics and that details support subtopics.
7. Each time you list subtopics or details, list at least two.

Exercise A

Look over the outline for a report and the information in the box. Copy the outline on your own paper, filling in the blanks with the information in the box. One blank has been filled in for you.

1. Disney World in Florida
2. Made first cartoons at 19
3. Born in Chicago
4. Donald Duck
5. Showed animals in nature
6. At 16 studied art
7. Minnie Mouse
8. Rare scenes of animal life
9. Disneyland in California
10. Moved to Missouri when a child
11. Mickey Mouse

Walt Disney
I. Introduction
II. Early life
   A. _____
   B. _____
   C. _____
   D. _____
III. Motion Pictures
   A. Cartoon
      Characters
      1. _____
      2. Minnie Mouse
      3. _____
   B. Nature Films
      1. _____
      2. _____
IV. Amusement Parks
   A. _____
   B. _____
V. Conclusion

Exercise B

Make an outline from the notes you took for your research topic. Make the first main topic *Introduction* and the last *Conclusion*. Be sure to use correct outline form.

Lesson 1
Kinds of Sentences

A sentence may be declarative, interrogative, exclamatory, or imperative.

A sentence begins with a capital letter, expresses a complete thought, and ends with a punctuation mark. There are four kinds of sentences. The paragraph below has an example of each.

> Firecrackers banged! What was going on? A family in the sleepy town of Rich Square, North Carolina, was battling some annoying birds. Read on to find out more about what happened.

The first sentence is an **exclamatory sentence**. It is a statement or command that expresses surprise or strong feeling. The next sentence is an **interrogative sentence**. It asks a question. The third sentence is a **declarative sentence**. It is a statement that tells something. The last sentence is an **imperative sentence**. It is a command or request in which the subject *you* is understood.

Now study the chart below.

Kind	Purpose	Example	Punctuation
declarative	telling	The family had troubles.	period
interrogative	asking	Can they solve the problem?	question mark
exclamatory	showing strong emotion	Birds love their town!	exclamation mark
imperative	ordering or requesting	Don't do that! Think about it.	exclamation mark or period

Exercise A
Read these sentences and write what kind each one is.

Example: Families face many challenges.
Answer: Declarative

1. Listen to this story. _____

2. It's fantastic! _____

3. One family had a problem. _____

4. They lived in a small town. _____

5. It was filled with birds. _____

6. The birds roosted all over. _____

7. Would you like to live there? _____

8. Think of the problems! _____

9. First, the family just complained. _____

10. Things got worse. _____

11. Other families began to worry, too. _____

12. Could they scare the birds? _____

13. No, but they tried! _____

14. They honked their horns. _____

15. They banged pots and pans. _____

16. They set off firecrackers. _____

17. Nothing worked. _____

18. What else could they do? _____

19. The birds weren't scared. _____

20. Think of a possible solution. _____

Example B

Add the correct end punctuation to each sentence.

Example: What a problem these birds were
Answer: What a problem these birds were_!_

1. Soon the town asked for help from outside _____

2. Please send some helicopters right away _____

3. Do you suppose that worked _____

4. The birds scattered at first but returned again, later _____

5. Whew, were the townspeople disappointed _____

6. The whole town was awakened at sunrise by the birds _____

7. What did the people try next _____

8. Experts arrived with special loudspeakers _____

9. They aimed loud, high-pitched sounds at the birds _____

10. How frustrated the people were by yet another failure _____

11. Guess what happened next _____

12. Someone tried playing loud music on very large speakers _____

13. It took a while, but it actually worked _____

14. What a happy day it was when the birds left _____

Lesson 2
Subjects and Predicates

A sentence has a simple and complete subject and predicate.

Every sentence has two parts—the **complete subject** and the **complete predicate**.

Many colorful tulips / are grown in Holland.

In the sentence above the complete subject is *Many colorful tulips.* The complete subject tells whom or what the sentence is about. The complete predicate is *are grown in Holland.* The complete predicate tells what the subject is or does.

The most important word in the complete subject is the **simple subject.** It names whom or what the sentence is about. The simple subject can be a noun or a pronoun.

My brother **Ed** | visited Holland early last May.
He | was a tourist in a group of tulip lovers.
Several **passengers** on his flight | are going on other tours.

The simple subject can be the same as the complete subject, as in the second example. The simple subject may also have various modifiers, such as prepositional phrases. Note that in the third example *passengers*, not *flight*, is the simple subject.

The most important word in the complete predicate is the **simple predicate**, usually called the **verb.** The verb tells what the subject does or is. It may be a one-word verb or a verb phrase.

In a sentence the subject, predicate, or both may be compound. A **compound subject** is made up of two or more subjects, usually joined by *and* or *or.* A **compound predicate** is two or more predicates joined by *and, but,* or *or.*

Ed and his **wife** | **flew** to Amsterdam but **took** trains after that.

Exercise A
Rewrite each sentence. Draw a vertical line between the complete subject and the complete predicate.

   Example: The motorcycle was invented by Gottlieb Daimler in 1885.
   Answer: The motorcycle | was invented by Gottlieb Daimler in 1885.

1. It was made of wood and traveled at only twelve miles per hour.

2. The first double-decker buses appeared in London in the 1850s.

3. Horses of great size pulled them on tracks.

4. The first true submarine was used in 1776.

_____

5. No American President rode in one until Harry Truman.

_____

6. Alexander Graham Bell invented the telephone in 1876.

_____

7. Telephone service from coast to coast began in 1914.

_____

8. The invention of the radio by Marconi in 1895 revolutionized communications almost overnight.

_____

9. Boats at sea could send messages and distress signals.

_____

Exercise B

Underline the simple subject once and underline the simple verb twice in each sentence below.

> **Example:** Either a Greek or an Egyptian invented the first pipe organ.
> **Answer:** Either <u>a Greek or an Egyptian</u> <u>invented</u> the first pipe organ.

1. Both Greece and Egypt claim credit for its invention.

2. A man from Greece became the first organist.

3. Egyptian inventors further developed the instrument.

4. Their instrument had a keyboard and ran on water power.

5. Historians and researchers have studied the origins of the first pipe organ and have discovered these ancient models.

6. Someone built and played a wind-powered organ in the tenth century.

7. Innovators and musicians produced later improvements.

8. Handel and Bach were great organ composers.

9. Gottfried Silbermann improved the organ's sound and added more voices.

Lesson 3

Sentences with Modifiers

The subject or predicate in a sentence may contain other words that modify, or add to, their meaning.

The sentence *Families moved* has only two words—a subject and a predicate. Few sentences are that short. Usually writers add a few well-chosen words to the subject and the predicate to make their sentences clearer. Study these examples.

Families | moved.

Several families | moved.

Several old families | suddenly moved.

Several old families from our town | suddenly moved into the city.

The first sentence has only a subject—*Families*—and a verb—*moved*. In the second sentence, the adjective *Several* was added. It modifies *families* by telling how many families moved.

In the third sentence, the adjective *old* was added. It tells what kind of families moved. The adverb *suddenly* was also added, before the verb. It tells how they moved. Adjective and adverb modifiers may come before or after the words they modify.

In the last sentence, the prepositional phrases *from our town* and *into the city* were added. *From our town* modifies the noun *families* by telling which families—families from our town. Prepositional phrases that modify nouns always come after the nouns they modify. *Into the city* modifies the verb *moved* by telling where the families moved. Prepositional phrases modifying verbs may come anywhere in a sentence.

Remember that most sentences contain modifiers. They give more exact meaning to simple subjects and predicates.

Exercise A

Write the words which modify each subject and predicate. Do not count *a*, *an*, or *the*.

1. Two nervous teams headed for the baseball field. _____

2. The wooden bleachers quickly filled with noisy fans. _____

3. The ball burst into pieces from the impact of the bat. _____

4. People in the bleachers laughed loudly. _____

Exercise B

In the sentences on the next page, underline the simple subject once. Draw two lines under the adjectives or prepositional phrases that modify each subject. Do not count *a*, *an*, or *the*.

Example: A severe snowstorm from Canada hit our city.
Answer: A <u>severe</u> <u>snowstorm</u> <u>from Canada</u> hit our city.

1. A small wooden house on our street was on fire.

2. The electric heater in the living room had exploded.

3. Some flimsy lace curtains had caught fire.

4. An alert neighbor called the police.

5. Ten firefighters from various stations answered the alarm.

6. Deep, blowing snow hindered their job.

7. A large family trapped in the house was saved.

8. Many residents in adjoining houses fled to safety.

9. The terrible fire could have cost many lives.

10. The brave firefighters should receive medals.

Exercise C

In each sentence below, underline the verb once and underline the adverbs or prepositional phrases that modify it twice. Two sentences have compound predicates.

Example: Spring moved gradually into the area.
Answer: Spring <u>moved</u> <u>gradually</u> <u>into the area</u>.

1. The dirty wet snow melted slowly.

2. Birds chirped noisily in the budding trees.

3. The sun rose earlier on each new morning.

4. People often smiled now.

5. The grass grew quickly in people's yards.

6. Storms sometimes blew in from the west.

7. Trees bent and swayed in the heavy rains.

8. Telephone lines sometimes broke.

9. Schools closed occasionally.

10. On sunny days, children ran outside into the warmth and played excitedly.

Lesson 4
Inverted Order in Sentences

In some sentences, the complete subject does not come before the complete predicate.

In most sentences the subject comes before the predicate. Sometimes, as in interrogative sentences, part or all of the verb comes before the subject. This kind of sentence is said to be in **inverted order.** Study these examples.

> Has the detective solved the case?
> Is he an employee of the store?

One helpful way to find the subject in sentences like these is to turn the question into a statement.

> The **detective** *has solved* the case.
> **He** *is* an employee of the store.

Other kinds of inverted sentences begin with the complete predicate and end with the complete subject. These sentences can also be put into natural order to find their subjects.

> On a shelf above my desk are several models.
> Several **models** *are* on a shelf above my desk.

> Nearby is my dictionary.
> My **dictionary** *is* nearby.

Sentences that begin with *Here* or *There* are often in inverted order. To find the subject, first find the verb. Then ask who or what is doing the action.

> Here comes my train. (What comes? train)
> There goes my allowance for the next month. (What goes? allowance)

Exercise A
Circle the simple subject in each sentence.

1. Near the stream in our pasture stands a huge tree.

2. Have you noticed its golden branches in the springtime?

3. There was mud all around it after the recent heavy rains.

4. Was Tom in the basement during that last storm?

Exercise B
Underline the simple subject once and the verb or verb phrase twice.

> **Example:** Did you see today's assignment?
> **Answer:** <u>Did</u> <u>you</u> <u>see</u> today's assignment?

1. Is your homework on the desk?

2. Did you get the assignment from Dan?

3. Is it difficult work?

4. Will you help me?

5. Do you want a snack?

6. Are the apples sweet and juicy?

7. Are they studying hard?

8. Can you discuss the assignment?

9. Have you finished already?

10. Have the others left?

Exercise C

Write **S** above the subject and **V** above the verb in each sentence below.

   Example: There are my grandparents.

                    V   S

   Answer: There are my grandparents.

1. Here is Uncle Chet in his sports car.

2. Here is a birthday present.

3. There are many other great gifts as well.

4. Here is my favorite one.

5. There is my second choice.

6. Here is my new baseball glove from Mom and Dad.

7. There is the baseball.

8. Here is the camera.

9. There are several pictures of the guests.

10. Here is the best one.

Exercise D

Underline the subject once and the verb twice in each sentence below.

   Example: Into the hole jumped the rabbit.
   Answer: Into the hole <u>jumped</u> the <u>rabbit</u>.

1. Into the hall went my two cousins with their dog.

2. Under the shade trees sat my aunts and uncles.

3. Above them floated fat, puffy clouds.

4. Beyond the tree flowed the river.

5. Over the rocks gushed cool, clear water.

Lesson 5
Sentence Fragments

A group of words punctuated like a sentence but not expressing a complete thought is called a sentence fragment.

A sentence contains a subject and a predicate and expresses a complete thought. A **sentence fragment** is a group of words punctuated like a sentence but not expressing a complete thought.

> **Sentence:** The outfielder ran to the fence.
> **Fragment:** Caught the ball with ease.

Some fragments can be corrected by adding words. Remember that a complete sentence must have a subject and a verb.

> **Fragment:** Arrived early this morning.
>   V
>
> **Corrected:** The builder arrived early this morning.
>   S   V

Some fragments are parts broken off from complete sentences. To correct these, attach them to the sentences they belong with. You must also correct capitalization and punctuation.

> **Sentence and fragment:** Luis felt energized. After his workout.
> **Corrected:** Luis felt energized after his workout.

Some fragments are more difficult to spot because they do contain a subject and verb. Fragments like these must also be corrected by attaching them to the sentences they belong with.

> **Sentence and fragment:** Emma received the vase. That Hal sent.
> **Corrected:** Emma received the vase that Hal sent.

Exercise A
Write how you would correct each fragment below.

> **Example:** Left the tools out at the end of the day.
> **Answer:** Add a subject.

1. No one touched the electrical tools. Because they had warned us not to.

_____

2. Work on the kitchen went fast. Once the cabinets arrived. _____

3. Carpenters measure things carefully. To avoid mistakes. _____

4. Will be done by the end of next week. _____

Exercise B
Correct the sentence fragments on the next page. Attach each one to the sentence next to it. Change capitalization and punctuation as necessary.

Example: Tigers have a bad reputation. For fierceness.
Answer: Tigers have a bad reputation for fierceness.

1. They are often feared. Because they attack people.

   _____

2. Most tigers are really shy. And avoid contact with people if possible.

   _____

3. Tigers sometimes attack people. After being cornered.

   _____

4. Tigers can live almost anywhere. Needing only food and water to survive.

   _____

5. They do not run well. For long distances.

   _____

6. Nowadays tigers are no longer captured for zoos. Since enough are born in captivity.

   _____

7. Some zoos have special areas. That are magnificent.

   _____

Exercise C

Correct each fragment by using one of the methods you have learned. If an item is correct, write *Correct*.

1. My dad often has scraps of wood lying around the basement.

   _____

2. My sister, who knows carpentry.

   _____

3. She built my brother a bookshelf for his room.

   _____

4. For her next project for her class at school.

   _____

5. And requires precise measuring and cutting.

   _____

6. A secret surprise for Mom and Dad!

   _____

7. The family will be surprised. By the creation.

   _____

Lesson 6
Run-On Sentences

A run-on sentence contains two or more sentences written together without the proper punctuation between them.

Sometimes you may be in a hurry to put your thoughts down on paper. Be sure not to write two or more sentences and improperly join them with no punctuation or with just a comma. Sentences that run together without the proper punctuation between them are called **run-on sentences.** Read this pair of example sentences.

> Juan writes music he does not write stories.
> Kelly is a mechanic, she repairs her own car.

The first example has no punctuation between the two sentences. The second example has only a comma. Both are run-on sentences. The chart below shows three ways to correct run-on sentences.

Guidelines for Correcting Run-On Sentences
1. Separate the two sentences in a run-on with a period. Use a capital letter to begin the second sentence. Juan writes music. He does not write stories. Kelly is a mechanic. She repairs her own car.
2. If two ideas in a run-on sentence are closely related, join them with a comma and a conjunction such as *and, but, or,* or *so.* Juan writes music, but he does not write stories. Kelly is a mechanic, so she repairs her own car.
3. Join two closely related ideas with a semicolon. Juan writes music; he does not write stories. Kelly is a mechanic; she repairs her own car.

Exercise A
Show three different ways to correct the following run-on sentence.

Jean is an artist she paints children's portraits.

1. _____

2. _____

3. _____

Exercise B
Use one of the guidelines above to correctly rewrite each of the run-on sentences in the exercise on the next page. If an item is not a run-on, write *Correct.*

Example: Karen writes music she is a fine pianist.
Answer: Karen writes music. She is a fine pianist.

1. Wolfgang Amadeus Mozart was born in Austria his father was a musician.

2. Mozart never attended school his father taught him about music.

3. By age fourteen Mozart had composed many musical works.

4. He wrote several operas and forty-one symphonies almost all of his works are still performed today.

5. Mozart had severe hardships and disappointments his music is cheerful and vigorous.

6. During his lifetime Mozart's works were well-known.

7. He died in poverty at the age of thirty-five.

Exercise C

On a separate piece of paper, rewrite the paragraph below, correcting all run-on sentences. Your paragraph should have between seven and ten sentences.

Rock and roll is a form of contemporary music, it is especially popular among young people. This music grew out of the blues it also has its roots in gospel music. Chuck Berry is often considered a founder of rock music, he is a composer and a performer. Rock songs often speak about current problems some people consider rock to be a way people communicate with each other. There are many rock 'n' roll performers, Elvis Presley is regarded by some people as the most popular artist ever.

Lesson 7
Appositives

An appositive is a noun or phrase that follows a noun and identifies or explains it. Appositives can be used to combine sentences.

A noun or pronoun that follows another noun and identifies or explains it is called an **appositive**. An appositive and its modifiers make up an **appositive phrase**.

> Lea's older brother, **Gavin**, is a lawyer.
> Lea wants to be a doctor like Shawn, **her other brother**.

The appositive *Gavin* in the first sentence identifies Lea's older brother. The appositive phrase *her other brother* explains who Shawn is. Notice that the appositive in the middle of the sentence is set off by two commas. The appositive phrase at the end of the sentence is set off by only one comma.

You can use appositives to combine short, choppy sentences into longer, smoother sentences. Read the examples below.

Sentences: Chicago is the Windy City.
                 We left Chicago at five o'clock.
Combined: We left Chicago, **the Windy City**, at five o'clock.

Sentences: By ten o'clock we were on Catalina.
                 Catalina is a lovely island.
Combined: By ten o'clock we were on Catalina, **a lovely island.**

Exercise A
Underline the appositive or appositive phrase in each sentence.

(1) My best friend, Linda, always gets lost. (2) Once I was supposed to meet her at Pages, a bookstore in our neighborhood. (3) She was thirty minutes late because she turned onto Grover, the wrong street.

Exercise B
Rewrite the following sentences. Set off the appositives and appositive phrases with commas.

Example: Chinatown a home for thousands is a lively area.
Answer: Chinatown, a home for thousands, is a lively area.

1. Chinatown a part of San Francisco has about 35,000 people.

_____

2. Some shoppers look for porcelain a fine china.

_____

3. Grant Avenue the main street is filled with Chinese shops.

_____

4. Chinatown is near Union Square the city's main shopping area.

5. Shoppers can ride a special trolley the cable car.

6. Some people like squid a common Chinese seafood.

7. I often eat with chopsticks a pair of small, slender sticks.

8. Much of the cooking is done in a wok a special kind of pot.

9. Visitors especially enjoy one holiday the Chinese New Year.

Exercise C

Use appositives to combine the following sentences. Remember to use a comma or commas to set off each appositive.

Example: I bought my cousin a tie in Chinatown. My cousin is Lee.
Answer: I bought my cousin, Lee, a tie in Chinatown.

1. Many ties are made of silk. Silk is a cloth that originated in China.

2. Lee practices Kung Fu. Kung Fu is a form of self-defense.

3. Our friend, Ling, taught us how to make chow mein. Chow mein is a tasty dish made with fried noodles.

4. She stirred in cloud ears and soy sauce. Cloud ears are a kind of mushroom.

Lesson 8
Combining Subjects and Predicates

Sentences with the same predicate or with the same subject can often be combined into one sentence.

Sentences with the same predicate can be combined by joining the subjects to create a **compound subject**. With more than two subjects, use commas and a conjunction.

The coyote **howled all night**.
The wolves **howled all night**.
The coyote and the wolves howled all night.

The bride **is in the church**.
The groom **is in the church**.
The best man **is in the church**.
The bride, groom, and best man are in the church.

The common predicate in the first group is *howled all night*. The compound subject in the second group is *bride, groom, and best man*.

Keep in mind when combining sentences that the verb must always agree with its subject. Notice that the verb *is* was changed to *are* to agree with the plural compound subject.

To combine sentences with the same subject, join the predicates to create a **compound predicate**. With more than two predicates, use commas and a conjunction.

The cook tossed the salad.
The cook stirred the soup.
The cook tossed the salad and stirred the soup.

Deer bounded across the road.
Deer jumped over the fence.
Deer fled into the woods.
Deer bounded across the road, jumped over the fence, and fled into the woods.

Exercise A
Rewrite the following sentences. Combine the subjects in the sentences. Be sure to make each verb agree with its subject.

Example: Angelo plays the guitar. Rita plays the guitar.
Answer: Angelo and Rita play the guitar.

1. The teachers want to organize a band. Their students want to organize a band.

2. Cara writes music. Mitch writes music. Bo writes music.

_____

3. Allison studies the clarinet. Monty studies the clarinet.

_____

4. Lisa is late for practice. Barbara is late for practice.

_____

5. Robert set up the chairs and instruments. Luis set up the chairs and instruments.

_____

6. The oboe sounds lovely. The piano sounds lovely.

_____

Exercise B

Rewrite the sentences below. Combine the predicates in each sentence.

   Example: Gorillas travel by day. Gorillas make camp at night.
   Answer: Gorillas travel by day and make camp at night.

1. These apes eat fruits. These apes also like vegetables.

_____

2. Gorillas eat in the morning. Gorillas sleep in the afternoon.

_____

3. Gorillas travel in groups. Gorillas never stay in the same place for more than one night.

_____

4. Group leaders signal the time to awaken. Group leaders decide the time to rest.

_____

5. Young adult gorillas like to wrestle with each other. Young adult gorillas enjoy playing games.

_____

6. Gorillas live in zoos. Gorillas perform in circuses.

_____

Lesson 9

Direct Objects and Subject Complements

A direct object is a noun or pronoun that follows an action verb. A subject complement is a noun, pronoun, or adjective that follows a linking verb and refers to the subject.

A **direct object** is a noun or pronoun that follows an action verb and tells who or what receives the action of the verb. Look at these examples.

> Marvin collects baseball **cards.**
> He trades and sells **them** to his friends.
> He owns **boxes** and **boxes** of cards.

In the first sentence the direct object *cards* tells what Marvin collects. The direct object *them* in the second sentence tells what Marvin trades and sells. The third sentence has a compound direct object: *boxes and boxes.*

A **subject complement** is a noun, a pronoun, or an adjective that follows a linking verb and identifies or describes the subject. Study these examples.

> Louise is an **actress** in New York.
> The starring role in that play is **hers.**
> Her costume looked **regal** and **beautiful.**

In the first sentence the noun *actress* is the subject complement. It identifies the subject *Louise.* A noun used as a subject complement is called a **predicate noun.** The subject complement in the second sentence is a pronoun: *hers.* An adjective used as a subject complement is called a **predicate adjective.** *Regal and beautiful* is the compound predicate adjective in the third sentence. The adjectives describe *costume.*

Exercise A

In each sentence below, underline the direct object or the subject complement. Write **DO** above each direct object and **SC** above each subject complement.

> **Example:** She won the leading role.
>
>   **DO**
> **Answer:** She won the leading <u>role</u>.

1. She is a good actress.

2. The audience applauded her.

3. She appeared quite young.

Exercise B

Write **S** over each subject, **V** over each verb, and **DO** over each direct object in the sentences on the next page.

> **Example:** Hobbies offer pleasure to many people.
>
>   **S**   **V**   **DO**
> **Answer:** Hobbies offer pleasure to many people.

1. Baseball cards give many statistics about players.

2. Young hobbyists trade the cards among themselves.

3. Some people file their collections by teams.

4. One collector owned twenty thousand cards.

5. Old cards bring the most money.

6. Mistakes on the cards increase their value tremendously.

7. Collectors love any errors in printing.

Exercise C

Write **S** over the subject and **LV** over the linking verb. Write **PN, PP,** or **PA** over the subject complement to tell if it is a predicate noun, a predicate pronoun, or a predicate adjective.

Example: Amusement parks are major locations for haunted houses at Halloween.

Answer:
          S   **LV**   **PN**

Amusement parks are major locations for haunted houses at Halloween.

1. My friend became an expert on monster costumes.

2. My friend's talent is rare.

3. His creatures grow scarier all the time.

4. His elaborate costumes look unearthly.

5. Rubber masks are the heads.

6. My friend's work appears real.

7. He is helpful to people giving parties.

8. His dreadful outfits are works of art.

9. It is he underneath those fake scars and bandages.

10. I feel sure about his future success.

Lesson 10
Indirect Objects

An indirect object is a noun or pronoun that tells to whom or for whom the action of the verb is done.

Many times a sentence that contains an action verb and a direct object also contains a noun or pronoun that acts as an indirect object. An **indirect object** tells to whom or for whom the action of the verb is done. Look at the following sentences.

The judge gave the signal.
The judge gave **Sam** the signal.

Both sentences contain an action verb, *gave*, and a direct object, *signal*. The second sentence also contains an indirect object, *Sam*. The indirect object tells to whom the signal was given. Now look at these sentences.

The audience made **Sam** a path.
The audience made a path for **Sam**.

In the first sentence, the word *Sam* is an indirect object. In the second sentence, the word *Sam* is the object of the preposition *for*. An indirect object cannot be the object of a preposition. The indirect object always comes before the direct object. If a word is preceded by *to*, *for*, or another preposition, it is not an indirect object.

Pronouns can also be used as indirect objects, as in the following sentences.

The audience made **him** a path.
The judge gave **them** ballots.

In these sentences, the pronouns *him* and *them* are indirect objects.

Exercise A
Check the sentences that have indirect objects.

_____ **1.** Sam sang a song for us.

_____ **2.** He sang us a new song.

_____ **3.** Sam entered his song in a contest.

_____ **4.** The judge quickly gave Sam an entry.

Exercise B
Rewrite each sentence, changing the prepositional phrase to an indirect object.

Example: Shari gave a sheet of music to Joe.
Answer: Shari gave Joe a sheet of music.

1. The guitarist showed the music to Sam.

2. The guitarist hummed some notes for the pianist.

_____

3. Ushers found seats for people.

_____

4. The ushers could not offer seats to some spectators.

_____

5. Other workers handed programs to people.

_____

6. Sam gave a nod to the leader of the band.

_____

7. Then Sam sang his song for the audience.

_____

8. Everyone gave their full attention to the performance.

_____

9. The audience gave a big hand to Sam.

_____

10. Sam sang two more songs for the crowd.

_____

Exercise C

In each sentence, label the subject **S**, the verb **V**, the indirect object **IO**, and the direct object **DO**.

                  S   **V**   **IO**   **DO**

    Example: The contest offered people some fun.

1. The whistlers gave the listeners some surprises.

2. The contest gave everyone a chance.

3. Different categories offered contestants many opportunities.

4. Senior citizens taught the youngsters old tunes.

5. This unusual event brought Carson City recognition.

6. The judges promised each entrant an award.

Lesson 11
Simple and Compound Sentences

A simple sentence has a complete subject and complete predicate. A compound sentence consists of two or more simple sentences.

A **simple sentence** has a complete subject and a complete predicate. Either the subject or predicate or both may be compound. Study these subjects and predicates.

       S   **V**
The detective | chased the thief.
       S   **V**   **V**
The detective | chased and caught the thief.
       S   **S**   **V**   **V**
The detective and his partner | chased and caught the thief.

To make a **compound sentence**, join simple sentences. A coordinating conjunction such as *and*, *but*, or *or* may be used to join them. The conjunction is usually preceded by a comma.

      The detective and his partner chased the thief, but only the detective actually caught him.

Two parts of a compound sentence may also be joined by a semicolon instead of a comma and coordinating conjunction.

      The chief congratulated the detective; he was a hero.

Exercise A
Write **S** if the sentence is simple or **C** if it is compound.

1. The detective got a medal; the thief got ten years. _____

2. Tom and Jill read about it in the newspaper. _____

3. Tom reads the paper every day, and Jill does too. _____

Exercise B
Write **S** above each subject and **V** above each verb in the following sentences. Then write **CS** if the sentence has a compound subject or **CV** if it has a compound verb.

   Example: The wind and the rain blew viciously.
               S   **S** **V**
   Answer: The wind and the rain blew viciously. **CS**

1. The ducks and geese flew south. _____

2. Some birds swam or hunted for grain. _____

3. Many flocks landed and ate in a bird refuge. _____

4. Loud honks and quacks filled the air. _____

5. The hunters and bird watchers followed the birds' flight. _____

6. Occasional fog and heavy snow slowed their flying speed. _____

7. The birds glided and drifted on the air currents. _____

8. The weather warmed and mellowed in the south. _____

9. Quiet lakes and active rivers awaited them. _____

10. Familiar sights and sounds welcomed their arrival. _____

Exercise C

Write **C** if the sentence is compound and **S** if the sentence is simple.

    Example: The parrot spoke, but the child didn't answer.
    Answer: The parrot spoke, but the child didn't answer. **C**

1. Mr. Gleason runs a pet store, and his two children help him. _____

2. Eric and Lida feed, groom, and train the animals. _____

3. Eric prefers grooming animals, but Lida likes feeding them. _____

4. Sometimes Eric assists his father; sometimes Lida does. _____

5. Lida feeds the parrot, and Eric teaches it words. _____

6. Parrots and mynas can imitate human speech. _____

7. Fish, dogs, and cats sell very well. _____

8. Puppies are the best sellers, but they are fairly expensive. _____

9. Fish and birds are less expensive pets. _____

10. Two cats live permanently in the store. _____

11. The cats are playmates, and both are good mouse hunters. _____

12. The store is closed on Sundays, Mondays, and holidays. _____

13. Then Mr. Gleason visits the store twice during the day. _____

14. Eric may become a zoo keeper, or he may become a veterinarian. _____

15. Lida would like to be an animal trainer. _____

Lesson 12
Independent Clauses

A part of a sentence that has a subject and a verb and makes sense by itself is called an independent clause.

Remember that a compound sentence is made up of two or more simple sentences, usually joined by a comma and a coordinating conjunction. When a simple sentence becomes a part of a compound sentence, it is called an **independent clause**. An independent clause has a subject and verb and makes sense by itself. It can be taken from the compound sentence and stand alone as a simple sentence.

       S   V   S   V
The dog | was weary, and he | panted.

The *dog was weary* and *he panted* are two independent clauses. Each makes sense by itself and can stand alone as a simple sentence. Each has a subject and a verb.

Independent clauses are usually joined by a comma and a coordinating conjunction, such as *and*, *but*, and *or*. They may also be joined by a semicolon.

I called to him; he was sleeping.

Exercise A
Write **S** above the subject and **V** above the verb in each independent clause.

    Example: Jeff purchased a book about dogs, and I bought one about cats.
                  S   V   S   V
    Answer: Jeff <u>purchased</u> a book about dogs, and I <u>bought</u> one about cats.

1. My book has many pictures, but only the photos are in color.

2. That cat is a Siamese; mine is an Abyssinian.

3. Cats see well in daylight, but their eyes also adjust.

4. Wild cats often hunt at night, but some prefer dusk or dawn.

5. Angora cats have long hair; Siamese cats have short hair.

Exercise B
Underline each independent clause once. Underline the comma and coordinating conjunction, or the semicolon, twice.

    Example: Cats vary in size, and many have wild colorings.
    Answer: <u>Cats vary in size, and</u> <u>many have wild colorings</u>.

1. Wild cats often hunt at night, but some prefer dusk or dawn.

2. Cats may meow softly, or they may shrill loudly.

3. Grassland leopards are tan with black spots; forest leopards are much darker.

4. Lions live in Africa, but most of them are in national parks.

5. Tigers are good swimmers, and they may cross rivers for food.

6. Most cats can extend their claws, but the cheetah cannot.

7. Domesticated cats do well as house pets, and wild cats fare best in their natural habitats or in zoos.

8. A cat's rough tongue is suited to eating, but it is equally useful for grooming the cat's fur.

9. Most cats have tails, but a Manx cat does not.

10. Angora cats have long hair; Siamese cats have short hair.

11. Tabbies may have stripes, or they may be just black and white.

12. Most cats like catnip, but some do not.

13. Cats purr when happy, but they spit and hiss when angry.

14. A cat's hearing is good, and its sense of smell is excellent.

15. Cats hate baths, but they keep themselves clean.

Exercise C

In each independent clause, label the subject **S** and the verb **V**. Place a comma before each conjunction that joins an independent clause.

    Example: Dan shops at the plaza but Cindy shops at the mall.
                  S   **V**   **S**   **V**
    Answer: Dan shops at the plaza, but Cindy shops at the mall.

1. Dan's father works at Benton's and Dan buys his clothes there.

2. His father sells shoes but he prefers the suit department.

3. Dan may become a salesman but he likes recreational sports.

4. He admires professional athletes and he likes most coaches.

5. Dan skis well and he plays basketball with equal skill.

Lesson 13
Dependent Clauses

A dependent clause has a subject and a predicate but does not make sense by itself.

A **dependent clause** has a subject and a verb, but cannot stand alone. All of the following word groups are capitalized and punctuated as sentences, but not all of them make sense by themselves.

> We gathered wood for a fire.
> The fire was lit, and the food was unpacked.
> After we ate.

The first group of words is a simple sentence. It makes sense by itself. The second group of words is a compound sentence. Each of its independent clauses can stand alone and make sense by itself. The third word group is a dependent clause. It cannot stand alone as a sentence. It needs to be attached to an independent clause in order to make sense.

> **After we ate,** we put out the fire.

Dependent clauses begin with words like *which, who, that, before, after,* and *since*. A dependent clause may come at the beginning of a sentence, in the middle, or at the end.

> **Before we started,** we checked our backpacks.
> The person **who told us about a good campsite** was a ranger.
> We set up out tents **when we arrived there**.
> Some other campers **whom we met** shared their campsite with us.

A dependent clause at the beginning of a sentence is usually followed by a comma, as in the first sentence.

Exercise A
Underline each dependent clause once and each independent clause twice.

> **Example:** Laura was in charge because she is an expert camper.
> **Answer:**   <u>Laura was in charge</u> <u>because she is an expert camper.</u>

1. Although she was in charge, she was not bossy.

2. We found the stack of firewood that the ranger had mentioned.

3. My cousin Jan was the one camper who recognized the poison ivy.

Exercise B
Write **SS** if the group of words on the next page is a simple sentence or **DC** if it is a dependent clause.

> **Example:** Light gleamed through the trees.
> **Answer:** <u>SS</u>

1. Because the owls were awake in the forest. _____

2. Every sound in the distance frightened us. _____

3. The wind brushed our cheeks. _____

4. After a gentle rain fell over the area. _____

5. That glimmered darkly on the leaves. _____

6. We dashed through the dark woods on our way home. _____

7. Dry branches cracked beneath our feet. _____

8. Though we didn't notice at first. _____

9. Lightning flashed when least expected. _____

10. Which illuminated eerie, looming shapes in the shadows. _____

11. A frightened rabbit hopped before us through the bushes. _____

12. After someone accidentally stumbled over its burrow. _____

13. Because we were very noisy during the rainstorm. _____

14. Fluttering birds chirped in alarm. _____

15. Since it was getting light in the east. _____

16. Someone saw smoke rising from a chimney in the distance. _____

17. Before an hour had passed. _____

18. The cabin to the left of us was in view. _____

19. Though we were very tired and hungry. _____

20. Everyone ate a hearty breakfast before nine o'clock. _____

Exercise C

Write **DC** if the underlined part of each sentence is a dependent clause or **IC** if it is an independent clause.

Example: Everyone rose early <u>because the alarm went off</u>.
Answer: **DC**

1. It was time to leave, but <u>the bus had not arrived</u>. _____

2. A group leader whistled <u>because he wanted everyone's attention</u>. _____

3. People could rest, or <u>they could take a short walk</u>. _____

4. All the people chose to walk <u>since they could nap on the bus</u>. _____

5. A red bus came up the drive, and <u>everyone rushed back</u>. _____

Lesson 14
Complex Sentences

A sentence that has one independent clause and one or more dependent clauses is a complex sentence.

Though a dependent clause has a subject and a verb, it cannot stand alone. It has to be joined with an independent clause to make a sentence. A sentence with one independent clause and one or more dependent clauses is called a **complex sentence.** Look for the dependent clauses in these sentences.

1. The locket **that Ted found in the desk** was his grandmother's.
2. **Before he could examine it,** his candle, **which had been flickering,** dimmed and went out.
3. **While he searched for his matches,** Ted heard strange noises.
4. He lit the candle **after he made several tries**.
5. **Although he searched carefully,** the locket, **which had been on the desk,** was nowhere in sight.

Exercise A
Answer these questions about the example sentences above.

1. Write the dependent clauses in the first two sentences.

_____

_____

_____

2. Write the dependent clause that comes within the independent clause in the second sentence.

_____

3. Write the dependent clause in the third sentence.

_____

4. Write the dependent clause in the fourth sentence.

_____

5. Write one of the dependent clauses in the fifth sentence.

_____

Exercise B
Rewrite each sentence on the next page by adding a dependent clause to form a complex sentence. Use the word in parentheses to introduce the dependent clause.

Example: Ted had to find the locket. (because)
Answer: Ted had to find the locket because it was valuable.

1. Ted could find the locket. (if)

_____

2. He heard strange noises. (before)

_____

3. The locket could have been stolen. (although)

_____

4. Ted might have to call the police. (if)

_____

5. Ted found the culprit in the closet. (after)

_____

6. It was a squirrel. (that)

_____

Exercise C

Read each sentence below. If the sentence is complex, underline the dependent clause.

Example: Flying squirrels, which are nocturnal, come out only at night.
Answer: Flying squirrels, <u>which are nocturnal</u>, come out only at night.

1. Although the tree squirrel is a wonderful acrobat, it sometimes misses its mark.

2. If a squirrel should fall, its tail will fan out and function as a parachute.

3. Some squirrels have a permanent home and a temporary one.

4. A temporary nest, which is a loose pile of twigs and leaves, is cool enough for hot weather.

5. Because temporary nests fall apart easily, squirrels build several during the summer.

6. Squirrels prefer nests in tree holes, but sometimes there aren't enough around for all of them.

7. An outside nest is called a "dray."

8. Although tree squirrels do not hibernate in the winter, they may stay in their nests for several days at a time.

9. Tree squirrels, who are omnivorous, can eat almost anything.

10. The seeds and nuts that squirrels bury in the fall are used for food all winter.

11. Squirrels are great foresters because many of these seeds and nuts grow into new trees.

Lesson 15
Adjective and Adverb Clauses

An adjective clause is a dependent clause that modifies a noun or pronoun. An adverb clause is a dependent clause that modifies a verb.

A dependent clause can do the work of an adjective by describing a noun or pronoun. Such a clause is called an **adjective clause**. Adjective clauses usually begin with words such as *that, which, who, whom,* or *whose,* called **relative pronouns**. Read these sentences.

This is the bicycle **that I bought**.
The tires, **which were flat**, had to be repaired.
It was I **who repaired the tires**.

In the first sentence the clause *that I bought* modifies *bicycle*. The clause is necessary to the basic meaning of the sentence because it tells which bicycle. Notice that the clause is not set off by a comma. In the second sentence the clause *which were flat* modifies *tires*. This clause is set off by commas because it is not necessary to the basic meaning of the sentence, which is *The tires had to be repaired*. What word does *who repaired the tires* modify in the third sentence?

A dependent clause can act as an adverb by modifying a verb. Such a clause is called an **adverb clause**. Adverb clauses tell how, when, where, or why an action happened.

I rode my bicycle [**before I ate breakfast**].

I stopped [**where there was a good view of the sunrise**].

I hurried home [**because I was hungry**].

Adverb clauses begin with **subordinating conjunctions**. Some of these are listed below.

Subordinating Conjunctions				
after	because	since	until	where
although	before	though	when	wherever
as	if	unless	whenever	whether

An adverb clause that begins a sentence is followed by a comma. If the adverb clause comes at the end of the sentence, no comma is used.

When I ride my bicycle, I always use hand signals.
I always use hand signals **when I ride my bicycle**.

Exercise A

Write the adjective or adverb clause in each sentence. Tell what kind of clause
it is.

    Example: Pete Durgan lived alone until one snowy night in December.
    Answer: until one snowy night in December   Adverb

1. Pete opened his back door because he heard a cat crying.

   _____

2. The cat, which was shoulder-deep in snow, looked miserable.

   _____

3. Before Pete could blink, the cat was in his kitchen.

   _____

4. The cat purred gratefully when Pete offered it some leftovers.

   _____

5. Pete put an ad in *The Express*, which was the local newspaper.

   _____

Exercise B

Turn each simple sentence into a complex sentence by adding an adjective or
adverb clause. Begin each clause with the relative pronoun or subordinating
conjunction in parentheses. Be sure to punctuate the clause correctly.

    Example: Les closed the window. (because)
    Answer: Les closed the window because the room was cold.

1. Jeff took a walk in the woods. (after)

   _____

2. He will return soon. (if)

   _____

3. We don't know. (where)

   _____

4. Kevin has a compass. (who)

   _____

5. Try the trail to the lake. (that)

   _____

Lesson 16
Combining Sentences

Sometimes two sentences with related ideas can be combined into a compound sentence.

A comma and a coordinating conjunction such as *and*, *but*, or *or* can be used to combine sentences with closely related ideas. The new sentence is called a **compound sentence**.

Congress passed a bill. The President vetoed it.	Congress passed a bill, **but** the President vetoed it.
Congress passed a bill. The President signed it.	Congress passed a bill, **and** the President signed it.
Will he sign the bill? Will he veto it?	Will he sign the bill, **or** will he veto it?

Notice that *but* shows contrast in the first sentence. The conjunction *and* shows addition in the second sentence, and *or* shows choice in the third sentence. The comma is placed before the coordinating conjunction in each combined sentence above.

Be sure that the ideas in the sentences you combine are closely related. You cannot combine the ideas in the following sentences. The price of the tickets has nothing to do with the band's leaving the hall.

The band left the hall.	The tickets were expensive.

You *can* combine these two closely related ideas.

The band left the hall. The fans went home.	The band left the hall, **and** the fans went home.

Exercise A
Write the coordinating conjunction you would use to combine each pair of sentences. If they cannot be combined in a way that makes sense, write **Can't Combine**.

1. Rover chased the mail carrier. He didn't bite him.

_____

2. The carrier dropped some mail. We helped him pick it up.

_____

3. He continued on his route. I need to buy some stamps.

_____

4. The incident didn't bother the carrier. He would have said so.

_____

5. Our usual carrier didn't come today. It was Dad's day off.

_____

6. Mr. Hill is our carrier. I need to write my cousin.

_____

Excerise B

Combine each pair of related sentences. Use a comma and the conjunction
and, *but*, or *or* as indicated.

    Example: I am proud of my senator. She often upsets me. (but)
    Answer: I am proud of my senator, but she often upsets me.

1. The Senate has one hundred members. The House of Representatives has
more than four hundred. (and)

_____

_____

2. Congress has a great deal of power. The power is balanced by other
branches of government. (but)

_____

_____

3. Congress makes laws. The President carries them out. (and)

_____

_____

4. Congress can cooperate with the President. Sometimes it does not. (but)

_____

_____

5. Cooperation is usually best. This is not always true. (but)

_____

_____

6. The President can sign a bill. He can veto it. (or)

_____

_____

Lesson 17
Combining Sentences with Modifiers

Short sentences that have adjectives, adverbs, and prepositional phrases can sometimes be combined into a single, more interesting sentence.

Combining sentences can make your writing more interesting and your sentences more forceful. Study the three ways to combine the sentences that describe the lion. Notice where the adjectives are placed.

The lion was old.
The lion was toothless.
The lion was weary.

The lion was **old, toothless,** and **weary.**
The **weary old** lion was **toothless.**
The **toothless old** lion was **weary.**

Each combined sentence has a different emphasis. The first sentence presents the lion's traits equally. The second sentence emphasizes that the lion was toothless. The third sentence emphasizes that the lion was weary. What you wish to emphasize should determine the way you combine sentences.

Sentences can also be combined when they contain adverbs that describe the same verb. Study the following example. Notice the commas that separate the adverbs in the fourth sentence.

Andrea worked swiftly.   Andrea worked **swiftly, carefully,** and
Andrea worked carefully.   **accurately.**
Andrea worked accurately.

Prepositional phrases in sentences can also often be combined.

The convict ran down the street.
The convict ran across the bridge.

The convict ran **down the street and across the bridge.**

Exercise A
Combine the following sentence groups.

Example: The boy was short. The boy was blond. The boy was freckled.
Answer: The boy was short, blond, and freckled.

1. He leaped high over the fence. He leaped onto the trampoline.

_____

2. He jumped vigorously. He jumped expertly. He jumped intensely.

_____

Exercise B

Combine each group of sentences below in two different ways.

> **Example:** The iron fence was rusty. The iron fence was broken.
> **Answer:** The iron fence was rusty and broken.
> The rusty iron fence was broken.

1. The house was old. The house was empty. The house was on a hill.

_____

_____

2. The windows were dirty. They were cracked. They were partially open.

_____

_____

3. The living room was chilly. The living room was empty.

_____

_____

4. The noise he heard was dreadful. The noise was mysterious.

_____

_____

5. Dennard left without looking back. He left immediately. He left through the window.

_____

_____

Excerise C

Read the paragraph below carefully. Decide which sentences should be combined. Rewrite the paragraph with combined sentences on a separate sheet of paper.

Jan walked across the campus. She walked swiftly. She walked confidently. Her black hair shone in the sunlight. Her hair was curly. She walked up the steps. She walked into the principal's office. She placed her books on the counter. The secretary greeted Jan quickly. She greeted Jan cheerfully. Jan glanced thoughtfully at the principal's door. "Is Mrs. Ortez here?" Jan inquired.

Lesson 18
Improving Sentences

Make your sentences clear, smooth, and concise.

In writing sentences, keep modifiers close to the words that they modify, use balanced structures, and avoid wordiness. Here are some ways to improve your sentences.

1. Be careful not to use **misplaced modifiers**. Look at these sentence pairs. Each first sentence contains a modifier that seems to modify the wrong word because it is misplaced in the sentence. The modifier is placed correctly in each second sentence.

> They could see the road **barely** ahead of them.
> They could **barely** see the road ahead of them.

> The shark swam in front of us **in the aquarium**.
> The shark **in the aquarium** swam in front of us.

2. Make items of equal importance in a sentence balanced. This is called **parallel structure**. Compare these pairs of sentences.

> His explanation was **clear, concise, and gave much information**.
> His explanation was **clear, concise, and informative**.

> She made her point **carefully, precisely, and with force**.
> She made her point **carefully, precisely, and forcefully**.

3. Check your sentences for **wordiness**—the use of more words than necessary to express ideas clearly and accurately.

> The statue seemed enormous **in size**.
> Sue was often tardy **and not on time**.
> **In the event that** it rains, the picnic will be rescheduled.

The words in dark type in the first two sentences should be deleted. The word *if* could replace the words in dark type in the third sentence.

Exercise A
Rewrite the following sentences. Improve the sentences by making words parallel, by eliminating wordiness, or by repositioning misplaced modifiers.

> **Example:** Last fall in October Uncle Phil took Art and me with him to the zoo.
> **Answer:** Last October Uncle Phil took Art and me to the zoo.

1. We drove in my uncle's new car there.

2. We arrived at exactly 10:30 A.M. in the morning.

_____

3. The day was sunny, warm and it was also windy.

_____

4. One zoo visitor was studying the monkeys, with binoculars.

_____

5. One monkey entertained its audience of onlookers with its antics.

_____

6. We thought the large birds were beautiful at the lagoon.

_____

7. Just as we passed, a gorilla screamed loudly and in a menacing manner.

_____

8. The polar bears were sunning by their pool in the sun.

_____

9. The giraffes moved slowly and with grace.

_____

10. All the animals in the zoo fascinate me in one way or another.

_____

Excerise B

Rewrite the following paragraph, correcting misplaced modifiers, making words parallel, and deleting wordiness. Use your own paper.

The house was old, shabby, and a desolate place. The original color of the house was recognizable hardly. Now the paint was faded and gray in color. The front porch sagged and slanted downward. The steps were wobbly and cracked on the side of the house. We entered the house slowly, hesitatingly, and in a reluctant way. Inside, we found the house needed even more work and repair.

Lesson 19

Identifying Nouns

A noun is a word that names a person, place, thing, or idea.

Words used to name people, places, things, or ideas are called **nouns.** Here are some examples.

snow	kindness	music	apple
teacher	neighborhood	odor	grief

The following clues can help you identify nouns in sentences.

1. Many nouns in sentences are preceded by the articles *a*, *an*, and *the*. If you see one of these words in a sentence, you know that a noun will soon follow. One or more words may come between the article and the noun.

> **The** fierce storm blew down **a** portion of **an** old, empty barn.

2. Most nouns have a singular and a plural form.

Singular	**Plural**
guard	guards
radio	radios
toy	toys
grief	griefs

3. Some nouns end with one of these suffixes: *-hood, -dom, -ment, -ance, -ness, -er, -or.* Study the examples below.

Word Root	**+**	**Suffix**	**=**	**Noun**
happy		-ness		happiness
free		-dom		freedom
amuse		-ment		amusement
insure		-ance		insurance

Exercise A

Begin each group of words with *a* or *an* and then write a sentence using each group of words.

> **Example:** lively discussion
> **Answer:** The class held a lively discussion about the comet.

1. good idea

_____

2. firm promise

_____

3. angry, loud voice

_____

4. intense debate

_____

5. sincere apology

_____

6. merry laugh

_____

7. offhand comment

_____

8. brief order

_____

9. silly, unwise remark

_____

10. intelligent choice

_____

Excerise B

Write the nouns in each sentence below.

    Example: The children discussed a legend popular in their town.
    Answer: children, legend, town

1. The tale explained that a pirate had his base there.

_____

2. Searchers never found the golden coins and the bars of silver.

_____

3. This boy led the group down a path to the deserted beach.

_____

4. With great excitement, they scrambled to the end of the pier.

_____

5. They felt a weight on the end of the line and hauled it up.

_____

6. The "treasure" was only a crab in a bad mood.

_____

Excerise C

Change the words below into nouns by adding one of these suffixes: *-hood*,
-dom, *-ment*, *-ance*, *-ness*, *-er*, *-or*. Use a dictionary to check your spelling.

1. strange _____   2. wise _____

3. false _____   4. observe _____

Lesson 20

Kinds of Nouns

**Nouns that name particular persons, places, or things are proper nouns.
All other nouns are common nouns. Nouns may also be categorized as
concrete or abstract.**

Nouns that name something general—*person, city,* and *day*—are **common
nouns.** Nouns that name particular persons, places, or things—*Roy Evans, San
Diego,* and *Friday*—are **proper nouns.** A proper noun begins with a capital
letter. A common noun does not, unless it begins a sentence. In the following
sentences, the common nouns are underlined once, and the proper nouns are
underlined twice.

> <u>Teresa Rojas</u> rode a <u>bicycle</u> from <u>San Francisco</u> to <u>Oakland</u>.
> <u>Artists</u> live in <u>Monterey</u>, a <u>town</u> in <u>California</u> near the <u>Pacific</u>.

Nouns can also be categorized as concrete or abstract. A noun is a
concrete noun if it names someone or something that can be heard, seen,
touched, smelled, or tasted.

> **Mr. James** parked his **car** in his **driveway**.

You can see Mr. James, his car, and the driveway.

An **abstract noun** names an idea, quality, or state of mind. Abstract nouns
often end with such suffixes as *-ty, -ism, -ment, -hood, -ness, -ion, -tion, -dom,
-ance,* and *-ence.*

> Her **freedom** is of **importance** to the **government.**

Freedom, importance, and government are real, but they do not exist in
the physical world. They exist in our minds as ideas. They cannot be seen or
touched. These words are abstract nouns.

Exercise A

Identify whether each noun is *proper* or *common.* Then tell whether it is *concrete*
or *abstract.*

> **Example:** Miss Simmons
> **Answer:** proper, concrete

1. honesty _____

2. poem _____

3. confidence _____

4. St. Louis _____

5. prize _____

Exercise B

Underline the common nouns once and the proper nouns twice.

Example: Mr. Leo Ferencik had his dream come true.
Answer: Mr. <u>Leo</u> <u>Ferencik</u> had his <u>dream</u> come true.

1. Mr. Ferencik, my neighbor, came to America from Europe.

2. This brave man wanted freedom from persecution.

3. He arrived in New York City on a freighter.

4. The Statue of Liberty appeared in the distance.

5. Tears of joy and anticipation welled up in his eyes.

6. His loneliness for his country turned to happiness.

7. Mr. Ferencik wanted the advantages of a democracy.

8. America had a tradition of liberty and justice.

9. The new immigrant would be free from unjust treatment here.

10. The Constitution guaranteed Mr. Ferencik equality.

Exercise C

Circle the concrete nouns and underline the abstract nouns.

Example: The joys and sorrow of the artist were reflected on the canvas.

Answer: The <u>joys</u> and <u>sorrows</u> of the (artist) were reflected on the (canvas.)

1. He drew his sketches from his thoughts.

2. Using his creativity, he imagined two characters.

3. He painted them with dark colors for a mood of sadness.

4. The faces of these people were partly in shadows and darkness.

5. Their shabby clothes and bundles showed great poverty.

Lesson 21
Plural Nouns

Most plural nouns are formed by just adding -s or -es to the singular. Some nouns require a spelling change to form plurals.

There are several ways singular nouns are made plural. Study the chart to review the most common ways. If you have a question about the spelling of a plural form, check a dictionary.

Plural Nouns	
Most nouns: add **-s**.	boat—boats; computer—computers
Nouns ending in **s, x, ch, z, sh, ss**: add **-es**.	fox—foxes; brush—brushes; lass—lasses; lunch—lunches
Nouns ending in **y**: change **y** to **i** and add **-es** unless a vowel precedes **y**.	diary—diaries; body—bodies; monkey—monkeys; toy—toys
Nouns ending in **f** or **fe**: change **f** to **v** and add **-es** for some; add just **-s** for others; use either form for a few. See dictionary.	loaf—loaves; wife—wives half—halves; thief—thieves; roof—roofs; safe—safes; hoof—hoofs or hooves
Nouns ending in **ff**; add **-s**.	tariff—tariffs
Nouns ending in **o**: if **o** is preceded by a vowel, add **-s**. If **o** is preceded by a consonant, add **-s** for some and **-es** for others; add either **-s** or **-es** for a few. See dictionary.	video—videos solo—solos; piano—pianos echo—echoes; tomato—tomatoes zero—zeros or zeroes cargo—cargoes or cargos
Compound nouns of more than one word: make only the most important word plural.	father-in-law—fathers-in-law; double play—double plays; great-grandson—great-grandsons
Nouns that change spelling.	mouse—mice; tooth—teeth; man—men; alumnus—alumni; basis—bases
Nouns that do not change.	moose—moose; species—species

Exercise A
Write the plurals of these nouns.

Example: maid of honor
Answer: maids of honor

1. potato _____
2. chief _____
3. branch _____
4. valley _____
5. box _____

Exercise B
Write the plural of each noun below.

Example: penny
Answer: pennies

1. book _____
2. bunch _____
3. foot _____
4. allergy _____
5. thief _____
6. aluminum _____
7. half _____
8. spaghetti _____
9. lunchbox _____
10. hero _____

Exercise C
Rewrite the sentences, changing the nouns in parentheses to their plural forms.

Example: Unusual (creature) are seldom found in (city).
Answer: Unusual creatures are seldom found in cities.

1. (Zoo) give people in (city) a chance to see wild (animal).

_____

2. (Fox) lie by their dens, and (monkey) play on (rope).

_____

3. (Sea lion) and (seal) frolic and splash in two (pool).

_____

4. (Rhino) and (hippo) rest in separate (enclosure).

_____

5. (Child) and (adult) can see what (farm) are like.

_____

Lesson 22
Personal Pronouns

A personal pronoun takes the place of one or more nouns. An antecedent is the word or words to which the pronoun refers.

Personal pronouns take the place of nouns and other pronouns. The word (or words) a pronoun refers to is called its **antecedent.** Pronouns and their antecedents are shown below.

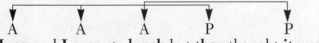

A   A   A   P   P
Juan and **Laura** ate **lunch** but **they** thought **it** was too salty.

Below is a chart of personal pronouns arranged according to person; first person (referring to the speaker), second person (the one spoken to), and third person (the one spoken about).

Personal Pronouns		
Person	Singular	Plural
First person	I, me	we, us
Second person	you	you
Third person	he, she, it, him, her	they, them

Other personal pronouns take the place of possessive nouns. They are called **possessive pronouns**. Study the example and the chart.

If Sue has forgotten **her** sweater, will Donna lend Sue **hers**?

Possessive Forms of Personal Pronouns		
Person	Used Before Nouns	Used Alone
First person	my, our	mine, ours
Second person	your	yours
Third person	his, her, their, its	his, hers, theirs, its

Exercise A
Underline the personal pronouns in each of these sentences.

Example: I lost the pocket calculator that Julio let me borrow.
Answer: I lost the pocket calculator that Julio let <u>me</u> borrow.

1. I asked my friends, "Have you found the calculator today?"

2. "Oh, so the strange object we found is yours?" Ben kidded me.

3. "Why isn't your name on the back?" his brother Jack said.

4. I said it was not mine; my brother Julio owned the calculator.

5. "You should feel lucky it was found by us," Mara said.

6. "Its case is ripped, but I bet your father could repair it."

7. Later, she and we boys discussed our summer plans.

8. "Are you going to try out for our community play?" Ben asked.

9. "Yes, I would like the hero's role. Are you two trying out?" I asked him and his brother.

10. They said they would rather try their luck as villains.

11. Mara complained, "Jana told me the part of the heroine was already hers and I shouldn't waste my time trying for it."

12. "We will all be lucky if they choose us," I commented.

Exercise B

Write all of the personal pronouns and their antecedents contained in the following sentences.

Example: Denise told friends she would entertain them with magic.
Answer: she—Denise; them—friends

1. They saw Denise do her first magic trick.

_____

2. She started it by borrowing Carmen's straw hat.

_____

3. "What are you going to do with my hat?" she asked.

_____

4. Denise took off the ribbon and cut it into several pieces.

_____

5. She told Carmen to put them into the hat and shake it.

_____

6. Then she told Carmen to jump up and down with her.

_____

7. The crowd was amazed when Denise pulled the ribbon out of her hat and it was whole again.

_____

8. They applauded her magic, and Carmen waved her hat.

_____

Lesson 23
Interrogative and Relative Pronouns

Interrogative pronouns introduce questions. Relative pronouns introduce groups of words that act as adjectives.

We often begin questions with pronouns. The most common of these pronouns are *who, whom, whose, which,* and *what.* They are called **interrogative pronouns**. Read the examples and notice where the interrogative pronouns are located.

Who is that scientist?
Which is your book?
Whom did the author choose?
What is its main idea?
Whose is that book?

The pronouns *who, whom, whose,* and *which* can also be used to introduce a group of words that acts as an adjective. When used for this purpose, they are called **relative pronouns**. Another relative pronoun is the word *that.* Read these sentences.

The scientist **who** wrote the book on dinosaurs is Joan Riley.

The book, **which** is a best seller, was made into a movie.

Joan gave a talk **that** explained the great Ice Age.

In the sentences above, each relative pronoun introduces a word group that acts as an adjective. Each word group modifies a noun. In the first sentence, *who wrote the book on dinosaurs* modifies *scientist* by telling which one. In the second sentence, *which is a best seller* modifies *book* by telling what kind. What modifies *talk* in the third sentence?

Exercise A
Underline the interrogative pronoun in each question.

Example: Which is the horse you bought?
Answer: <u>Which</u> is the horse you bought?

1. Who owned the horse?

2. What is the horse's name?

3. Which is the best saddle?

4. Whom did you ask?

5. What is the price of the harness?

6. Whose are these boots?

7. Whom did you pay?

8. Which of the trails is best?

9. What is calf roping?

10. Which is Gail's farm?

Exercise B
Underline the relative pronoun in each sentence.

> **Example:** The principal thanked the photographers, who are students.
> **Answer:** The principal thanked the photographers, <u>who</u> are students.

1. One photographer whom she congratulated won first prize.

2. Each photo that was selected pictured a person or landscape.

3. One man who was photographed wore overalls.

4. The man whom Harvey photographed was a veteran.

5. The photographer who won second prize is a good friend of mine.

6. She lives in Golden Gate Park, which is nearby.

7. The photograph that won third prize was taken on a boat.

8. The best photo, which took fourth prize, was of a farm.

9. A barn that is very old can be quite lovely.

10. One photographer, whom I didn't know, is on the school paper.

Exercise C
Identify the underlined pronouns in the following sentences as *interrogative* or *relative*.

> **Example:** <u>Who</u> is the youngest senator in Congress?
> **Answer:** Interrogative

1. The bill, <u>which</u> you supported, did not pass. _____

2. <u>Who</u> are the female senators in Congress now? _____

3. <u>What</u> is the best day to tour the Senate Office Building? _____

4. The tour, <u>which</u> is given at noon, is quite informative. _____

5. The senator <u>whom</u> the President applauded is from Iowa. _____

Lesson 24
Possessive Nouns

Possessive nouns show ownership. They are formed with an apostrophe and the letter _s_ ('s) or with an apostrophe alone (').

Possessive nouns are used to tell who or what owns something. They are formed with an apostrophe and _s_ or with only an apostrophe.

    Possessive nouns name someone or something, as all nouns do. But they are also like adjectives because they modify, or limit, other nouns. Read these sentences.

> The **boy's** dog was brown.
> The **collie's** collar was red.
> Our **class's** picnic will be next week.

    The possessive noun _boy's_ modifies the noun _dog_. The possessive noun tells which dog or whose it is—the dog belonging to the boy. You will recall that nouns have singular and plural forms. Possessive nouns also have singular and plural forms. The chart shows how to form singular and plural possessive nouns.

Singular Possessive Nouns			
If the noun is singular, add **'s**.			
cousin	**cousin's** book	Chris	**Chris's** honesty
dish	**dish's** design	Mike Jones	**Mike Jones's** car
Plural Possessive Nouns			
If the noun is plural and ends in s, add only an apostrophe.			
citizens	**citizens'** rights	cities	**cities'** mayors
classes	**classes'** schedules	Joneses	the **Joneses'** car
If the noun is plural and does not end in s, add **'s**.			
women	**women's** votes	children	**children's** games

Exercise A
Add an apostrophe or an apostrophe and _s_ to make each noun possessive.

    Example: lasses
    Answer: lasses'

1. father _____

2. thieves _____

3. jockey _____

4. men _____

Exercise B

Rewrite the paragraph below. Use a possessive noun for each underlined group of words.

(1) Every soldier praised the courage <u>that belonged to Washington</u>. (2) The army <u>of Cornwallis</u> met Washington and his men in battle. (3) The hopes <u>of the soldiers</u> soared when they saw Washington. (4) His leadership encouraged the men, and the bravery <u>that belonged to the army</u> returned.

_____

_____

_____

_____

_____

Exercise C

Write the singular possessive form and the plural possessive form of each noun in parentheses.

Example: the (dog) home
Answer: singular—the dog's home; plural—the dogs' home

1. my (teacher) pupils _____

2. the (fisherman) catch _____

3. the (plumber) jobs _____

4. the (artist) work _____

5. the (dancer) shoes _____

6. the (glass) cracks _____

7. the (doctor) patients _____

8. the (woman) education _____

9. the (country) people _____

10. the (baby) toys _____

Lesson 25
Plural or Possessive

An apostrophe is used to form the possessive of a noun. It is not ordinarily used to form the plural of a noun.

Plural forms and possessive forms sound the same but are formed differently. Notice the sentences below. An apostrophe is used only with the possessive forms of the nouns.

> **Singular possessive form:** A **walrus's** tusks are used like tongs.
> **Plural form:** Some populations of **walruses** have been hunted almost to extinction.
> **Plural possessive form:** Eskimos sometimes use **walruses'** skins for tents and boats.

The plural form *walruses* and the plural possessive form *walruses'* are used to show more than one. The singular possessive form *walrus's* and the plural possessive form *walruses'* are used to show ownership.

Read the sentences below. Notice which words in dark type need apostrophes.

> **Icebergs** float slowly.   **Ships** sail to the Arctic.
> An **iceberg**'s size varies.   A **ship**'s strength is tested in a storm.

Remember, when you write plural possessives, follow two steps. First, write the plural form. Then add just an apostrophe if the plural ends in *s*. If the plural doesn't end in *s*, add an apostrophe and an *s*.

Exercise A
Replace each word in parentheses with a plural or possessive form.

> **Example:** In 1899 (Alaska) _____ gold attracted many
>   (prospector) _____ .
> **Answer:** In 1899 <u>Alaska's</u> gold attracted many <u>prospectors</u>.

1. For many (year) _____ gold was (Alaska)

   _____ most important product.

2. Most (mine) _____ yields were not as great as (miner)

   _____ expected.

3. However, many (miner) _____ stayed to become

   permanent (inhabitant) _____ of Alaska, and the

   (territory) _____ population doubled in a ten-year period.

4. Alaska was one of the last two (state) _____ to join the

   Union.

Exercise B

Underline the correct form of the noun for each sentence.

>   **Example:** The (towns, town's) boundaries extend into the country.
>   **Answer:**   <u>town's</u>

1. The (oceans, ocean's) waters became choppy.

2. Then (wave's, waves) washed over the deck.

3. Deck (chairs, chair's) were blown about.

4. The (passengers, passengers') faces showed worry.

5. The (ships, ship's) captain wasn't alarmed.

6. He asked people to go to their (cabins, cabin's).

7. Everyone followed Captain (Jones, Jones's) orders.

8. The (engine's, engines) hummed through the night.

9. The (navigators, navigator's) kept the ship on course.

10. By dawn the (sun's, suns) rays began to shine through clouds.

Exercise C

Read this report about Thomas Edison's inventions. Add apostrophes where needed. You will find eight words to correct.

>   **(1)** Thomas Alva Edisons first patented invention was an electronic
>
>   vote recorder. **(2)** This invention improved the method of totaling voters
>
>   ballots. **(3)** Later, Edison improved the financial worlds communication by
>
>   designing a better stock ticker. **(4)** In time, Edison set up this countrys first
>
>   industrial research laboratory. **(5)** Using the labs equipment, he developed
>
>   a telephone transmitter and the phonograph. **(6)** He also developed the
>
>   worlds first commercially successful electric light bulb. **(7)** The publics
>
>   response to his inventions was tremendous. **(8)** Edisons ideas have made
>
>   possible many electronic devices.

Lesson 26
Pronoun Homophones

Homophones are words that sound alike. They have different meanings and are usually spelled differently.

Some possessive pronouns and contractions are homophones. **Homophones** are words that are pronounced the same, but are spelled differently and have different meanings.

Read the following sentence groups and explanations. Notice how the words that sound alike are formed differently.

Can you judge a book by **its** cover?
It's an important part of a book.

Its is the possessive form of the pronoun *it* and does not have an apostrophe. *It's* is a contraction for *it is* or *it has*.

Where is **your** science book?
You're assigned two chapters.

Your is the possessive form of the pronoun *you* and does not have an apostrophe. *You're* is a contraction for *you are*.

These are **their** art books.
They're all books about surfing.
The books are **there** on the table.

Their is the possessive form of the pronoun *they* and does not have an apostrophe. *They're* is a contraction for *they are*. *There* is an adverb which answers the question "Where?" and does not have an apostrophe.

Whose books are these?
Who's the author of this story?

Whose is the possessive form of the pronoun *who* and does not have an apostrophe. *Who's* is a contraction for *who is* or *who has*.

Exercise A
Complete each sentence with a possessive pronoun or a contraction.

1. The cat hurt _____ paw.

2. _____ at the door?

3. _____ going, aren't you?

4. Have them sign _____ names.

5. _____ idea was that?

6. _____ raining again.

Exercise B

Circle the correct word for each sentence.

> **Example:** (Its, It's) unusual for a mother to have twins.
> **Answer:** (It's)

1. You and (you're, your) family may use special words.

2. (Its, It's) not unusual for twins to have a private language.

3. Sometimes twins (who's, whose) lives have been isolated know how to talk only with each other.

4. When people are (their, there), the twins ignore them.

5. (Their, There) private vocabulary is called "twin talk."

6. (It's, Its) special sounds can make it sound foreign.

7. The specialist records the twins when (their, they're) talking to each other.

8. The specialist will learn each word and (it's, its) meaning.

9. Twin talk fascinates anyone (who's, whose) studying language.

10. Many times (there, they're) hard to understand.

11. (It's, Its) not known exactly how twin talk develops.

12. Both fraternal and identical twins were (there, their) at the conference.

13. (Its, It's) harder to tell identical twins apart.

14. Joy is a friend of mine (whose, who's) mother is a twin.

15. I asked Joy's mother and aunt if (its, it's) fun being twins.

16. They said that (their, they're) relationship is very special.

Lesson 27

Reflexive and Intensive Pronouns

A reflexive pronoun reflects the action of the verb back to the subject. An intensive pronoun adds intensity to the noun or pronoun just named.

Reflexive and intensive pronouns end in *-self* or *-selves*. Study the chart below showing the forms of these pronouns.

Person	Singular	Plural
1st person:	myself	ourselves
2nd person:	yourself	yourselves
3rd person:	herself, himself, itself	themselves

Reflexive pronouns serve as reflectors, as their name suggests. They reflect back to the subject. Read these examples.

The children taught **themselves** Italian.

I forced **myself** to sit still.

Sometimes we use a pronoun ending in *-self* or *-selves* to intensify, or emphasize, the noun or pronoun it refers to. This pronoun is called an **intensive pronoun**. Look at these examples.

Did you lift that **yourself**?
The President **himself** will address the meeting.

Remember these facts about reflexive and intensive pronouns.

• There are only eight correct reflexive and intensive pronouns. Never use incorrect forms like *hisself*, *ourself*, or *theirselves*.

• Reflexive and intensive pronouns should not be used in place of personal pronouns.

Henry went with John and **me**. (Not: John and myself)
Lois and **he** were early. (Not: Lois and himself)

Exercise A

Write **R** above each reflexive pronoun and **I** above each intensive pronoun in the sentences below.

Example: Have you ever seen yourself on television?

                              R
Answer: Have you ever seen yourself on television?

1. In media class, the teacher had us videotape ourselves.

2. She herself gave each one of us an event to pantomime.

3. Some people can apparently discover themselves through mime.

4. Several in the group had seen themselves on TV before.

5. Jerry had never watched himself on TV.

6. The teacher told Jerry he would do fine if he would be himself.

7. Jerry himself did not share in her confidence.

8. We then prepared ourselves for the taping.

9. Some students allowed themselves several days to practice.

10. The students themselves were eager to begin.

11. I myself practiced for one week.

12. Many of us did not act like ourselves, but like other pupils.

13. You often find yourself amused when someone imitates you.

Exercise B
Circle the correct pronoun form in each sentence.

Example: Ted (hisself, himself) painted the picture.
Answer: (himself)

1. Has Larry ever had a portrait of (himself, hisself) painted?

2. Our family enjoyed the portrait of (ourself, ourselves).

3. Some people like to do portraits of (themselves, theirselves).

4. Ted and (I, myself), for example, painted self-portraits last year.

5. We (ourselfs, ourselves) thought we did well.

6. Some famous artists have painted (theirself, themselves).

7. Van Gogh painted several portraits of (hisself, himself).

8. Some artists have drawn caricatures of (theirselves, themselves).

9. A new artist painted Ted and (me, myself).

10. Ted and (he, himself) are good friends now.

11. They (theirselves, themselves) are going to put on a show.

Lesson 28
Indefinite Pronouns

An indefinite pronoun may or may not have an antecedent. Some indefinite pronouns are singular, and others are plural.

The word *indefinite* means "vague, not sure or certain." A pronoun that may refer to a noun but does not indicate a definite person or thing is called an **indefinite pronoun**. Notice the pronouns in dark type in the sentences below.

Of the two hundred filmmakers, **few** have seen the new movie.
Years ago **someone** suggested making a movie about outer space.

In the first sentence, the indefinite pronoun *few* refers to its antecedent *filmmakers*, but it does not tell how many filmmakers have seen the new movie. In the second sentence, there is no antecedent for the indefinite pronoun *someone*.

Indefinite pronouns can be singular or plural. Some of the most commonly used indefinite pronouns are shown in the chart below.

Indefinite Pronouns			
Singular			Plural
another	either	one	both
anybody	everyone	somebody	few
anyone	neither	someone	many
each	no one	something	several
			others

Indefinite pronouns can be troublesome because people tend to think of most of them as plural forms. As the chart suggests, though, many of them are singular and take singular verbs. Some pronouns—*all, any, most, none,* and *some*—can be either singular or plural, depending on how they are used.

Exercise A
Underline the indefinite pronouns in each sentence below.

Example: I hope everyone will compete.
Answer: I hope <u>everyone</u> will compete.

1. Anyone can attend the event.

2. How could anybody miss it?

3. Someone might forget.

4. No one announced the place.

5. Many knew that.

6. Several asked about it.

7. Something should be done.

8. Neither knows about it.

9. Others have already heard.

10. Each will know soon.

Exercise B
Underline each indefinite pronoun once and its antecedent twice.

Example: These cameras are expensive, but others are cheap.
Answer: These <u>cameras</u> are expensive, but <u>others</u> are cheap.

1. Tourists were in town. Many visited the World Trade Center.

2. Tourists went to the top of the building. Several took photos.

3. The twins didn't take photos because both forgot the film.

4. My brothers wouldn't go. All are afraid of heights.

5. My sisters like the view, and each has seen it before.

Exercise C
Underline the indefinite pronoun in each sentence below, and write **S** if it is singular or **P** if it is plural.

Example: Everyone has responsibilities.
Answer: <u>Everyone</u> has responsibilities. <u>S</u>

1. Everyone knows about doing chores. _____

2. Each has agreed on a job. _____

3. Few would neglect carrying their own loads. _____

4. Several think their time is limited. _____

5. Others believe their schedules are not full. _____

6. Anybody forgets duties at times. _____

7. Either is able to do the tasks well. _____

8. Neither was pleased with the schedule. _____

9. Many are confident of their own abilities. _____

10. I hope someone will volunteer. _____

Lesson 29
Subject and Object Pronouns

Subject pronouns are used as subjects of sentences. Object pronouns can be used as direct objects, indirect objects, or objects of prepositions.

When a pronoun is used as the subject of a sentence, the pronoun is in the nominative case and is called a **subject pronoun**. Notice the pronouns in the chart and then read the sentences.

Subject Pronouns			
Singular	I	you	he, she, it
Plural	we	you	they

I borrowed Marta's bike.   Bill and **I** rode bikes.

    The sentence on the right has a compound subject. To check that you are using the correct pronoun in a compound subject, use the pronoun by itself with the verb. For the compound subject *Bill and I*, you would say *I rode*, which makes sense (Not: *me rode*).

    Personal pronouns can also be used as direct and indirect objects and objects of prepositions. Then the pronoun is in the objective case and is called an **object pronoun**. Study the object pronouns in the chart and then read the sentences.

Object Pronouns			
Singular	me	you	him, her, it
Plural	us	you	them

    When the sandwiches were ready, Kay ate **them**. (direct object)
    Mrs. Rosario gave **me** and **her** some orange juice too. (indirect objects)
    When Nolan arrived, we ate lunch with Mrs. Rosario and **him**. (object of preposition)

    To check that you are using the correct pronoun in a compound object, say the sentence with just one pronoun as the object.

Exercise A

Circle the correct pronoun.

> **Example:** Jill and (I, me) are in the same history class.
> **Answer:** (I)

1. Our teacher gave an assignment to (she, her) and (I, me)—a report on peasant life in the Middle Ages.

2. Toni and (they, them) are studying medieval home life.

3. (He, Him) and Manuel are researching knighthood.

4. Our teacher gave Jill and (I, me) a good grade.

5. She congratulated Toni and (they, them) on their report.

Exercise B

Write the pronoun that can be substituted for the underlined word or groups of words.

> **Example:** France was an important center for painters.
> **Answer:** It

1. Women were not accepted as artists until quite recently. _____

2. People ignored Mary Cassatt for years. _____

3. Mary's parents raised Mary and her brothers and sisters. _____

4. Eventually, Mary and her family settled in Pennsylvania. _____

5. Mary surprised her parents when she decided to become an artist. _____

6. The decision was unusual for a woman of her time. _____

7. Mary's decision was supported by Mr. Cassatt and her older brother. _____

8. In 1866 Mary went to France with her parents and her sister. _____

9. In Paris Mary studied art done by Impressionists. _____

10. These painters experimented with the effects of light and color. _____

11. Edgar Degas, an Impressionist, and Mary became friends. _____

12. Degas introduced Mary to other painters and sculptors. _____

13. Her paintings show the influence of the French Impressionists. _____

14. Today people from around the world know Mary Cassatt and her paintings. _____

Lesson 30

Pronouns as Subject Complements

A subject pronoun is used as a subject complement.

When a word follows a linking verb and refers to the subject, it is called a
subject complement. A pronoun that follows a linking verb such as *am*, *is*,
are, *was*, and *were* and identifies the subject is used as a subject complement. A
subject pronoun is always used as a subject complement in formal English.
Compare the following pairs of sentences. The subjects are underlined; the
subject complements are in dark type.

<u>She</u> is the **judge.**   The <u>judge</u> is **she.**
<u>They</u> are the **players.**   The <u>players</u> are **they.**
<u>Tim and I</u> are **alternates.**   The <u>alternates</u> are **Tim and I.**

In the sentences on the left, the subject complement *judge* refers to the
subject *she*, the subject complement *players* refers to the subject *they*, and the
complement *alternates* refers to the subject *Tim and I.* The subject and subject
complement in each sentence refer to the same people. Therefore, the
sentences can be turned around as they are on the right without changing the
meaning. Notice that the pronoun forms do not change when the sentences
are turned around. The same pronoun form —a subject pronoun— is used as
subject and as subject complement.

If someone asks you "Who is it?" you probably use an object pronoun and
say "It is me" or "It's me" rather than "It is I." When you are speaking to
family or friends, "It's me" is acceptable. However, in writing or in more
formal situations such as a job interview, use "It is I." Also use "It is she," "It is
we," and so on.

Exercise A

Circle the correct form of the pronoun in parentheses to use in formal
situations.

Example: It was (she, her) who had the idea.
Answer: (she)

1. It was (they, them) who made the posters.

2. It was Lucia and (I, me) who distributed them.

3. They thanked Lucia and (I, me).

4. It was (we, us) who helped.

5. The person who benefited most was (he, him).

Exercise B

Write **S** if the underlined pronoun in each sentence is used as a subject or **SC** if it is used as a subject complement.

Example: According to Scooter, <u>he</u> and I must prepare a report.
Answer: **S**

1. <u>We</u> were puzzled about being chosen to do a report. _____

2. The only two students that were selected were Scooter and <u>I</u>. _____

3. <u>He</u> and I both like the novelist Daniel Defoe. _____

4. It was <u>he</u> that we chose for our report. _____

5. <u>We</u> had both enjoyed reading *Robinson Crusoe*. _____

6. <u>It</u> is the novel based on the life of Alexander Selkirk. _____

7. It was <u>he</u> whom Defoe used to create Crusoe. _____

8. The main characters are Friday and <u>he</u>. _____

9. Scooter thought it was <u>he</u> who made the novel interesting. _____

10. <u>I</u> wrote about the lives of Selkirk and Defoe. _____

Exercise C

Circle the correct pronoun to complete each sentence. Write **SP** if it is a subject complement or **OP** if it is an object complement.

Example: Between Scooter and (I, me), we finished the report.
Answer: (me)—OP

1. Scooter and (I, me) practiced giving our report many times. _____

2. It was (I, me) who was nervous, not Scooter. _____

3. It was (he, him) who introduced the report. _____

4. The only two speakers today are Scooter and (I, me). _____

5. First, (he, him) will speak about the life of Daniel Defoe. _____

6. (I, Me) will also say something about Defoe. _____

7. About (he, him) we know very little. _____

8. (We, Us) know, however, that Defoe was a novelist, journalist, and secret agent. _____

9. It was (he, him) that Queen Anne threw in prison in 1702. _____

10. To Scooter and (I, me), *Robinson Crusoe* is his best novel. _____

11. To (we, us), Friday is one of the most important characters. _____

12. It is (he, him) who makes the story exciting. _____

13. The phrase "man Friday" comes from (he, him). _____

Lesson 31
Pronoun Agreement

A pronoun should agree with its antecedent.

As you know, an **antecedent** is the word to which a pronoun refers. When the antecedent is singular, the pronoun referring to it should be singular. When the antecedent is plural, the pronoun should be plural. Here are examples.

The **cowboy** went out riding on **his** horse.
The **cowgirl** attended to **her** horse at the stable.
The **horses** served **their** owners well.

The pronouns and antecedents above also agree in gender. That means the masculine pronoun *his* refers to the masculine noun *cowboy*. The feminine pronoun *her* agrees with the feminine noun *cowgirl*.

If a driver is careful, **he or she** can avoid many accidents.
If drivers are careful, **they** can avoid many accidents.
A careful driver can avoid many accidents.

Since the noun *driver* can refer to either a man or a woman, some writers use the phrase *he or she*. Another, less repetitious, solution is to reword the sentence, if possible.

Although in everyday conversation you sometimes hear *they* or *you* used with a singular antecedent, this use of a plural pronoun should be avoided in formal writing.

Do not write: If a driver is careful, **they** can avoid many accidents.
                  If a driver is careful, **you** can avoid many accidents.

Singular indefinite pronouns like *each*, *anybody*, *everyone*, *either*, *someone*, and *neither* should be referred to by singular pronouns. Although in conversation plural pronouns are sometimes used, this should be avoided in formal speech and in all writing. Plural indefinite pronouns like *both*, *few*, *many*, and *several* should be referred to by plural pronouns.

Each of the girls displayed **her** entry. (Not: their)
Both of the winners proudly held up **their** prizes. (Not: her)

Exercise A
Place a check before each sentence in which the underlined pronoun is used correctly.

_____   **1.** Has either of the women had <u>their</u> turn yet?

_____   **2.** Each of the boys offered <u>his</u> help.

_____   **3.** If a person is wrong, <u>they</u> should admit the fact.

_____   **4.** Many of the participants brought <u>their</u> radios.

Exercise B
Write a pronoun that correctly completes each sentence in formal English.

Example: A female member of the expedition unpacked _____ gear.
Answer: her

1. Each person had _____ own backpack.

2. Many of the women carried cameras around _____ necks.

3. Every explorer had _____ own goal.

4. Several of the hikers followed _____ guide along a river.

5. On the third day somebody lost _____ sleeping bag.

6. Neither of the guides ever lost _____ patience.

7. Both of the guides carried equipment on _____ heads at times.

8. Everyone knew that _____ should wear sunglasses.

9. At night no one was to leave _____ tent.

10. The explorers took time to write about _____ discoveries that day.

11. Each of the guides had _____ own tent.

12. Some of the party did voice _____ other complaints.

13. Most said _____ were covered with insect bites.

14. A few of the explorers said _____ would be glad to get home.

15. Everybody said _____ had a great time.

Exercise C
Circle the pronoun that agrees with each indefinite pronoun in formal English.

Example: If someone on the boys' team volunteers, (they, he) should be prepared to work.
Answer: (he)

1. Everyone on the boys' team did (their, his) work.

2. Each of the girls spent (their, her) time at the car wash.

3. Many of the girls brought (their, her) towels and sponges.

4. Neither of the twins brought (their, her) old clothes.

5. Neither of them had time for (her, their) lunch.

6. Many of the boys also gave (their, his) time at the retirement home.

7. Each of the boys was using (their, his) parents' lawnmower.

8. Many of them spent (their, his) time trimming hedges.

Exercise D

If the antecedent and pronoun in a sentence agree, write **Correct**. If they do not agree, rewrite the sentence, correcting the pronoun.

    Example: Each of the bakers has their own specialty.
    Answer: Each of the bakers has his own specialty.

1. If a repair person will be late, they should call.

_____

_____

2. Each of the mechanics bought their own tools.

_____

_____

3. If you are a plumber, you must take care of your tools.

_____

_____

4. Neither of the chefs owned their own restaurant.

_____

_____

5. Before a lawyer can practice, they must pass a bar exam.

_____

_____

6. If a farmer has a good crop, they feel lucky.

_____

_____

Lesson 32
Using *who* and *whom*

Who is generally used as a subject. *Whom* is used as a direct object or object of a preposition.

Who is usually used as a subject of a sentence or clause.

> **Who** knows anything about books?
> The man **who** brought the message left immediately.

In the first sentence, *who* is the subject of the verb *knows*. In the second sentence *who* is the subject of *brought* in the clause *who brought the message*.

The pronoun *whom* is used as the direct object of an action verb or with a preposition such as *for*, *from*, *to*, and *with*. Look at these two uses of *whom* in the sentences below.

> **Whom** do we call for information?
> Is this the man **whom** the bank president hired?
> From **whom** did you hear the news?

In the first sentence the pronoun *whom* is the direct object of the sentence (*we do call whom*). In the next sentence *whom* is the direct object of the verb *hired* in the clause *whom the bank president hired* (*the bank president hired whom*). In the third sentence the pronoun *whom* is the object of the preposition *from*.

Who is being used as a subject in the sentences on the left. *Whom* is being used as an object in the sentences on the right.

Who is the next appointment?	**Whom** do you see at 3:00?
Those **who** arrived can sign in.	To **whom** do I give this?

In everyday conversation *who* is often used in place of *whom*, especially at the beginning of questions. *Who did you write?* However, in writing and formal speech, use *whom* as a direct object or object of a preposition: *Whom did you write?*

Exercise A
Write **S** if the underlined word is a subject or **O** if it is an object.

1. <u>Whom</u> did you sell the ticket to? _____

2. The one <u>who</u> sold the most tickets was Patty. _____

3. That is the actor <u>whom</u> I admire. _____

Exercise B

Circle the word that correctly completes each sentence below.

> **Example:** (Who, Whom) called you yesterday?
> **Answer:** (Who)

1. (Who, Whom) wants a ride downtown?

2. From (who, whom) did you get a ride?

3. (Who, Whom) gave you an invitation?

4. This is the girl (who, whom) Jon invited.

5. (Who, Whom) do you usually invite?

6. Ramon was the one (who, whom) thought of the idea.

7. I don't know anyone (who, whom) wouldn't like it.

8. Ramon and Pia are the ones (who, whom) we should thank.

9. (Who, Whom) arranged the flowers on the tables?

10. (Who, Whom) cooked these delicious foods?

Exercise C

Complete each sentence with **who** or **whom**.

> **Example:** Do you know for _____ this hairstyle is named?
> **Answer:** Do you know for <u>whom</u> this hairstyle is named?

1. Rudolph Diesel was the German engineer _____ invented the diesel engine.

2. For _____ was the state of Virginia named?

3. Jean Martinet was a military leader _____ people hated.

4. Someone _____ is too strict is called a martinet.

5. The man _____ ran from Marathon to Athens in 490 B.C. became famous.

6. People for _____ running is a sport enter marathons.

7. _____ was the Earl of Sandwich?

8. He is the person after _____ the sandwich is named.

9. _____ was Napoleon Bonaparte?

10. From _____ did you receive that biography about Napoleon Bonaparte's life?

Lesson 33
Identifying Verbs

Some verbs express action. Other verbs link the subject with a word or words in the predicate.

The most important word in the predicate is the verb. A verb that expresses action, or tells what action is taking place, is called an **action verb**. Some action verbs show physical action. Other action verbs show mental action.

Sara **ran** in the marathon in Springfield last year.
She **believed** in herself and in her ability.

Both *ran* and *believed* are action verbs. The verb *ran* expresses physical action, and the verb *believed* expresses mental action.

Another kind of verb, called a **linking verb**, joins the subject with a word or words in the predicate that describe or name the subject. Linking verbs express no action. Some of the most common linking verbs are forms of *be*, including *is*, *am*, *are*, *was*, and *were*.

The runners in the race **were** competitive.
The first prize **was** a huge, gold-plated trophy.

In the first sentence, the linking verb *were* joins the subject with the word *competitive*. *Competitive* describes the subject *runners*. In the second sentence, the linking verb *was* joins the word *prize* to the word *trophy*.

The verbs *seem*, *appear*, *become*, *feel*, *look*, *taste*, *sound*, and *smell* can also be linking verbs. Read the examples below.

The joggers **seem** eager.   These socks **feel** wet.
That runner **appears** weary.   The snack **tastes** salty.

Exercise A
Complete each sentence with an action verb.

Example: Jason _____ quite rapidly.
Answer: Jason <u>runs</u> quite rapidly.

1. Runners _____ daily.

2. Exercise _____ your health.

3. The athletes _____ records.

4. Two contestants _____.

5. Fans _____ the track meet.

6. I _____ the water.

7. The water _____ everywhere.

8. Soon the meet _____.

9. Everyone _____ for home.

10. The athletes _____ well.

Exercise B
Complete each sentence with a linking verb. Use a variety of verbs.

Example: A new goal _____ ahead.
Answer: A new goal <u>was</u> ahead.

1. My performance _____ best.

2. Her time _____ the fastest.

3. My lunch _____ good.

4. The day _____ too short.

5. Everything _____ so easy.

6. The attendance _____ higher.

7. The crowd _____ noisy.

8. That _____ a good sign.

9. The runners _____ happy.

10. Track meets _____ wonderful.

Exercise C
Underline the verb in each sentence and write whether it is an action or a linking verb.

Example: Bill and I bicycled to the lakefront.
Answer: <u>bicycled</u>—action verb

1. The athletes all traveled to New Orleans. _____

2. New Orleans is the largest city in Louisiana. _____

3. The Mississippi River flows past New Orleans. _____

4. The trip was my first one ever outside Missouri. _____

5. The best restaurants seemed rather expensive. _____

6. Many of the buildings in New Orleans are old. _____

7. Tourists walk through the French Quarter every day. _____

8. Many of them buy *beignets* at the French Market. _____

9. These pastries taste warm and sweet. _____

10. Some tourists purchase antiques in fancy shops. _____

Lesson 34
Action or Linking Verb

Some verbs can be either action verbs or linking verbs.

Some verbs may be used as either action verbs or linking verbs. These verbs include *appear*, *become*, *feel*, *grow*, *look*, *remain*, *smell*, *sound*, and *taste*. How a verb is used in a sentence determines whether it is an action verb or a linking verb. Study these examples.

Ben **smelled** the soup.   Hope **felt** the confining walls.
The soup **smelled** delicious.   She **felt** panicky.

I **grow** dates on those trees.   Ann **looked** at the dresses.
I **grow** anxious to taste them.   None **looked** right for her.

In the first sentence in each pair, the subject is performing an action. In the second sentence, no action is performed. Instead, the verb links the subject to a word in the predicate.

The easiest way to tell whether a verb is used as an action verb or a linking verb is to try to replace it with a form of the verb *be*. Look at these sentences.

Ernie **looks** happy with his new library books.
Michael **looks** out the window in boredom.

In the first sentence, *looks* is a linking verb. It may be replaced with the verb *is* without changing the meaning of the sentence. In the second sentence, however, *looks* cannot be replaced with *is*. The meaning of the sentence would be completely different. In this sentence, *looks* is an action verb. Try this test on the sentence pairs above.

Exercise A
Write **A** if the sentence contains an action verb or **L** if it contains a linking verb.

Example: Something in the kitchen smelled wonderful.
Answer: L

_____ **1.** Suddenly Mother appeared with bread from the oven.

_____ **2.** The brown, crispy loaf looked delicious.

_____ **3.** Kim became very hungry.

_____ **4.** She eagerly tasted the bread.

_____ **5.** She remained in the kitchen for another slice.

Exercise B
Underline the verb in each sentence on the next page and write whether it is an action or linking verb.

Example: The mountain looked impossibly high.
Answer: The mountain <u>looked</u> impossibly high. —linking verb

1. The mountaineers looked at the peak from a distance.

   _____

2. They felt hopeful and courageous. _____

3. Few trees or shrubs grew in the rocky soil. _____

4. The air smelled clean and pure. _____

5. The water in a nearby stream looked clear and blue. _____

6. The climbers felt their way up slowly. _____

7. The click of their crampons sounded against the rocks.

   _____

8. They became more cautious. _____

9. The climbers remained calm during the first hour. _____

10. Suddenly dark clouds appeared in the sky above the mountain.

    _____

Exercise C

Follow the same directions as for Exercise B.

1. Some people look for adventure in their lives. _____

2. They appear at exciting places. _____

3. Edmund Hillary's desire for adventure grew stronger each year.

   _____

4. As a young man, he looked after bees in New Zealand. _____

5. Later, he became a famous mountain climber. _____

6. Mt. Everest, the world's tallest mountain, remained the ultimate challenge
   for him. _____

7. Hillary and his guide remained at the top for a short time.

   _____

8. The final victory at the summit, 29,028 feet above sea level, tasted sweet
   to him. _____

9. On May 29, 1953, he looked down at the world beneath him.

   _____

10. He remained only a short time but felt the thrill of his feat.

    _____

Lesson 35
Verb Phrases

A verb phrase consists of a main verb and one or more helping, or auxiliary, verbs.

The verb, or simple predicate, may sometimes be one word. Often, though, the verb consists of two or more words—a main verb and one or more helping verbs. This is called a **verb phrase**.

> Mr. Velazquez **is planting** beans and tomatoes in his garden.
> He **should have been finished** yesterday.

The **main verb** is always the final word in the verb phrase. It tells what action is happening. The **helping**, or **auxiliary**, **verbs** precede the main verb and help it express meaning and tense. Study the chart.

Helping Verbs
am, are, is, was, were, be, being, been
has, have, had
do, does, did
can, could, must, may, might, shall, should, will, would

Some verbs in the chart, if used alone, can be main verbs.

Main Verbs	**Helping Verbs**
He **had** the tools.	The beans **had sprouted** quickly.
The tools **were** good ones.	Onions **were growing** well.

The helping verb or verbs usually come right before the main verb. But sometimes an adverb will come in between. In questions, the helping verb and main verb are often separated by the subject.

He **will** not **plant** corn.	He **has** always **planted** squash.
Am I **planting** the peas?	**Have** you **pulled** the weeds?

Exercise A
Underline the verb phrase or phrases in the sentences.

Example: Diane has been studying electronics.
Answer: Diane <u>has been studying</u> electronics.

1. She may have been attending classes this afternoon.

2. Diane should have come home twenty minutes ago.

3. What is keeping her?

4. She probably will be arriving soon.

5. Mrs. Velazquez and Connie are teaching at Union School.

6. Did Juan run in the track meet yesterday?

7. Mr. Velazquez has been working in the garden again today.

8. Should we help him, or would we only get in the way?

9. The garden can be planted in no time at all.

10. Mr. Velazquez had already prepared the soil last week.

Exercise B

Underline each main verb once and each auxiliary verb twice.

> **Example:** Carlos has not yet finished his report on tennis.
> **Answer:** Carlos <u>has</u> not yet <u>finished</u> his report on tennis.

1. He had at one time studied the history of the game.

2. The game of tennis was first played in France.

3. Years ago, players would usually hit the ball with their hands.

4. Now, of course, they must always use a racket, or a foul would be called.

5. Tennis back then was also played on grass courts.

6. A variety of other surfaces are widely used now, but some famous tournaments are still played on grass.

7. Ancient tennis courts were often enclosed, and players could easily participate during any season.

8. Most people could not afford such a sport, so it was customarily enjoyed by nobles.

9. Tennis has in time become a more affordable sport.

10. Have you ever seriously played the game?

Lesson 36
Simple Tenses

Verbs have simple present, past, and future tenses.

The **tense** of a verb can help tell the time of the action. The present, the past, and the future tense are known as the **simple tenses**.

Both action and linking verbs change form to show tense. Study the tenses of the verbs in this chart.

Present Tense	Past Tense	Future Tense
I **walk** alone.	I **walked** alone.	I **will walk** alone.
She **names** it.	She **named** it.	She **will name** it.
He **tries**.	He **tried**.	He **will try**.
I **am** sad.	I **was** sad.	I **will be** sad.
They **begin** today.	They **began** yesterday.	They **will begin** tomorrow.

When you write about events or incidents and you begin writing in the past tense, do not carelessly change to the present tense. Keep writing in the tense you began in unless you have a good reason to change. Notice the unnecessary tense changes in the following paragraph.

Harold walked with uncertainty to the open field. Suddenly, he spots Heloise, his lost dog, rolling in some waist-high weeds. He called the dog to his side, and Heloise, after a few seconds of indecision, runs up to him. "I will never let you loose in a strange neighborhood again," Harold vows.

Exercise A
Underline the verb in each sentence and write whether it is present, past, or future.

Example: Tim will finish his assignment on the shuttle tomorrow.
Answer: Tim <u>will finish</u> his assignment on the shuttle tomorrow. —future

1. In 1969, American astronauts landed on the moon. _____

2. The idea of space travel started long ago. _____

3. In 1687, Sir Isaac Newton described the laws of motion.

_____

4. In 1865, Jules Verne wrote *From the Earth to the Moon*, the first science-fiction story about space travel. _____

5. In 1919, Robert Goddard explained the value of rockets.

_____

6. In 1957, the Soviet Union launched *Sputnik I* into orbit.

_____

7. The space shuttle makes interplanetary travel possible. _____

8. The shuttle crews will continue the launching of satellites and space telescopes.

_____

9. The space shuttle measures about 184 feet in length. _____

10. Perhaps someday shuttle crews will build a space station. _____

Exercise B

There are several unnecessary tense changes in the following paragraph. On your own paper, rewrite the following paragraph. Change verb tenses to make the paragraph smooth and consistent.

     We carried our canoe to the edge of the stream. The sky is clear blue, and the morning was still cool. Slowly, we lower the canoe into the water. I held it steady, and my partner climbs in. She knelt down in the stern and waits for me. I push the canoe into deeper water and jumped in. "This will be a great day!" I remark. We paddled into deep water. The overhanging trees formed a green tunnel over the stream. Suddenly, the channel widened, for the stream will enter a lake. The lake was absolutely empty. Not a soul is in sight! Occasionally an eagle or falcon circles overhead and will land in a tree. Wild rice even grew in the shallow areas. No houses cluttered the banks, and no motorboats disturb the peacefulness of these surroundings. Canoeing on that lake was truly a memorable experience.

Lesson 37
Principal Parts of Verbs

Verbs have four basic forms, which are called principal parts. They are used to form tenses.

The four main forms of a verb are called its **principal parts**. They are the **present**, the **present participle**, the **past**, and the **past participle**. Study the following chart. It shows how to form the principal parts of **regular verbs**, verbs spelled alike in their past and past participle forms.

Present	Present Participle	Past	Past Participle
open	(is) opening	opened	(has, have, had) opened
like	(is) liking	liked	(has, have, had) liked
try	(is) trying	tried	(has, have, had) tried
grin	(is) grinning	grinned	(has, have, had) grinned
omit	(is) omitting	omitted	(has, have, had) omitted

The first form is the present. Next is the present participle, which is formed by adding *-ing* to the present. It is used with a form of the helping verb *be*. (Verbs like these, which show action in progress, are sometimes said to be in the **progressive tense**.)

The past and past participles are formed by adding *-ed* to the present. The past participle uses a form of the helping verb.

Follow these rules for adding endings to regular verbs.

- For verbs ending in *e*, the *e* is dropped before *-ing* or *-ed* is added.
- For verbs ending in a consonant plus *y*, the *y* changes to *i* before *-ed* is added.
- For one-syllable verbs ending in a single vowel followed by a single consonant, the final consonant doubles before *-ing* or *-ed* is added.
- For two-syllable verbs ending in a single vowel followed by a single consonant, the final consonant doubles before *-ing* or *-ed* is added.
- For two-syllable verbs ending in one vowel and one consonant, and having the accent on the final syllable, the final consonant also doubles.

Some verbs form their past and past participles in other ways—like *ring, ringing, rang, rung*. These are called **irregular verbs**. A dictionary shows the principal parts of these verbs. You will learn more about them later in this book.

Exercise A
Underline the verbs in the sentences and write what principal part each was formed from.

Example: Mighty dinosaurs had once roamed North America.
Answer: Mighty dinosaurs <u>had</u> once <u>roamed</u> North America. —past participle

1. Dinosaurs lived in many parts of the world. _____

2. Some dinosaurs had measured over forty-five feet in length. _____

3. I have looked at many dinosaur skeletons in museums. _____

4. Every year, experts are discovering more and more about them. _____

5. Scientists consider a new discovery extremely important. _____

6. I am attending some lectures on dinosaurs this week. _____

7. They are helping me with my report for science. _____

8. Dinosaurs long ago disappeared from the face of the earth. _____

9. Even so, they still capture our imagination. _____

10. The lectures interest me a great deal. _____

Exercise B
Complete the chart.

Present	Present Participle	Past	Past Participle
climb	1.	climbed	climbed
2.	trying	tried	tried
ski	skiing	skied	3.
yell	yelling	yelled	4.
receive	5.	received	received
patrol	patrolling	6.	patrolled
permit	permitting	7.	8.
9.	10.	liked	liked

Lesson 38
Perfect Tenses

Verbs have present, past, and future perfect tenses.

The **perfect tenses** express actions that were completed or will be completed by a certain time. The perfect tenses are made by using certain forms of *have* with the past participle of the verb.

Perfect Tenses	Time	Sample Sentences
Present	Begun in the past, continuing, or completed now	I **have called** my best friends.
Past	Begun in the past, completed in the past	Earlier I **had compiled** a list of these friends.
Future	Begun in the past or present, completed in the future	By tonight, I **will have invited** everyone.

Notice in the chart that the words *called*, *compiled*, and *invited* are the past participle forms.

Exercise A
Read the following sentences and then answer the questions about the verbs.

She has listened to your every word.
We both had sympathized with your position until quite recently.
I will have stated my own point very soon now.

1. What helping verb is used with *listened* to form the present perfect tense?

_____

2. What kind of action does the present perfect tense show?

_____

3. What helping verb is used with *sympathized* to show the past perfect tense?

_____

4. What two helping verbs are used with *stated* to form the future perfect tense?

_____

Exercise B
Underline the perfect tense verbs and write what tense they are.

Example: I have enjoyed all kinds of sports.
Answer: I <u>have enjoyed</u> all kinds of sports. —present perfect

1. I have taken swimming lessons since October. _____
2. By June 20, I will have attended thirty lessons. _____
3. My teacher has complimented me on my Australian crawl. _____
4. My diving also has improved. _____
5. I have practiced even more lately. _____
6. By the end of August I will have raced in several events. _____
7. Neither of them had swum before. _____
8. In a week each of them will have taken three lessons. _____
9. By last May I had taken four tennis lessons. _____
10. Tennis has become my friend Rita's favorite sport. _____

Exercise C

Rewrite the sentences, adding the suggested form of the verb.

Example: I _____ a great experiment. (*complete*, present perfect)
Answer: I have completed a great experiment.

1. I _____ about a life without friends. (*wonder*, present perfect)

_____

2. Now I _____ it is no life at all. (*conclude*, present perfect)

_____

3. I _____ at this conclusion by a simple experiment. (*arrive*, present perfect)

_____

4. Until yesterday I _____ to no one for thirty days. (*talk*, past perfect)

_____

5. I _____ no phone calls. (*answer*, past perfect)

_____

6. I _____ no one. (*visit*, past perfect)

_____

7. For thirty days I _____ without friends. (*live*, past perfect)

_____

8. I finally _____ what friendship means. (*learn*, present perfect)

_____

Lesson 39
Transitive and Intransitive Verbs

Action verbs with direct objects are transitive. Action verbs without direct objects are intransitive, as are linking verbs.

Some verbs are followed by **direct objects**—nouns or pronouns that complete a verb's meaning. When an action verb is used with a direct object, the verb is said to be **transitive**. Look at the following examples.

         V   **DO**   **V**   **DO**
  Kiku **played** the piano for hours.   Gene **baked** a cake today.

Piano is the direct object of the verb *played*, and *cake* is the direct object of the verb *baked*. The objects receive the action expressed by the transitive verbs. To locate the object of the action, ask *what* or *who* receives the action expressed by the verb.

An action verb is called **intransitive** when it does not need an object to complete its meaning.

  Kiku **played** for hours.   Gene **baked** today.

The verb in the first sentence is *played*. Because there is no direct object, *played* is intransitive.

As you can see, action verbs like *play* and *bake* can be either transitive or intransitive. It depends on whether they have a direct object.

Linking verbs are always intransitive. They never have objects.

  Maynard **is** a good actor.   The play **seemed** a bit dull.

Exercise A
Write **T** if the verb is transitive or **I** if it is intransitive.

1. Dino plays first base for the Scooters. _____

2. He is a good hitter. _____

3. He also runs well. _____

4. His team won their last three games. _____

5. They play the Cyclones tomorrow. _____

Exercise B
Label each verb **V** and each direct object **DO**.

  Example: Jockeys ride thoroughbred horses.
               V   **DO**
  Answer: Jockeys ride thoroughbred horses.

1. Cortés first brought horses to America.

2. Native Americans had never seen animals like horses before.

3. Some of the horses escaped their owners.

4. They roamed the West in wild herds.

5. Native Americans later captured these horses.

6. In time, Native Americans tamed their horses.

7. Herds of horses represented wealth.

8. They rode horses on buffalo-hunting trips.

9. Besides food, the buffalo provided hides for clothing.

10. Horses gave a new way of life to Native Americans.

Exercise C

Underline the verbs in the sentences and write **T** if they are transitive or **I** if they are intransitive.

Example: Texas has a proud history.
Answer: Texas <u>has</u> a proud history. —**T**

1. Today four-lane highways cross old cattle trails. _____

2. The state seems both old-fashioned and modern. _____

3. Ranch hands still herd cattle on the range. _____

4. Skyscrapers form the skylines of Dallas and Houston. _____

5. Tourists find numerous attractions in Texas. _____

6. The state continually expands its many cultural attractions. _____

7. The Lyndon Johnson Library stores presidential papers. _____

8. Visitors flock to the Alamo in San Antonio. _____

9. Texas was an independent republic for almost ten years. _____

10. It eventually became a state in 1845. _____

Lesson 40
Principal Parts of Irregular Verbs

The past and past participle forms of irregular verbs do not end in *-ed*.

All verbs have four principle parts. They are the present, the present participle, the past, and the past participle. The past and past participle forms of regular verbs end in *-ed* —for example, *followed, have followed,* and *prepared, have prepared.*

The past and past participle of irregular verbs are not formed in the same way. The chart below shows principal parts of common irregular verbs.

Present	Present Participle	Past	Past Participle
run	(is) running	ran	(has, have, had) run
come	(is) coming	came	(has, have, had) come
become	(is) becoming	became	(has, have, had) become
go	(is) going	went	(has, have, had) gone
begin	(is) beginning	began	(has, have, had) begun
see	(is) seeing	saw	(has, have, had) seen

Two guidelines will help you use the past and past participle forms of irregular verbs correctly.

1. Don't use the participle form without an auxiliary verb such as *have, has,* or *had.*

   Ian **has become** an expert on whales. (Not: Ian become)
   We **have seen** the whales out at sea. (Not: We seen)

2. Don't use the past form with an auxiliary verb.

   Ian **began** a book about whales. (Not: Ian has began)
   He **went** to the science museum. (Not: He had went)

Some irregular verbs can be grouped according to the patterns by which they change. Try to learn these patterns. Note that the past participle is always used with a helping verb like *has, have, or had.* (Since the present participle presents no problem it is not included in the chart.)

Present	Past	Past Participle
grow	grew	(has, have, had) grown
know	knew	(has, have, had) known
throw	threw	(has, have, had) thrown
blow	blew	(has, have, had) blown
fly	flew	(has, have, had) flown
draw	drew	(has, have, had) drawn
wear	wore	(has, have, had) worn

Present	Past	Past Participle
tear	tore	(has, have, had) torn
swear	swore	(has, have, had) sworn
ring	rang	(has, have, had) rung
sing	sang, sung	(has, have, had) sung
sink	sank, sunk	(has, have, had) sunk
swim	swam	(has, have, had) swum
spring	sprang, sprung	(has, have, had) sprung
drink	drank	(has, have, had) drunk
shrink	shrank, shrunk	(has, have, had) shrunk

Exercise A

Complete each sentence with either the past or past participle form of the verb in parentheses.

1. Yesterday Ian _____ a blue whale for the first time. (see)

2. It had _____ near his boat. (swim)

3. I have _____ interested in studying whales. (grow)

4. I had _____ to the marine museum one day. (go)

5. There Ian and I _____ into each other. (run)

6. Ian _____ many facts about whales. (know)

7. He had _____ a wonderful picture of a whale. (draw)

Exercise B

Complete each sentence with the correct past or past participle form of the verb in parentheses.

   Example: Track has _____ a very popular sport. (become)
   Answer: Track has <u>become</u> a very popular sport.

1. Sharon had _____ to one track meet. (go)

2. A week later she _____ to another one. (go)

3. She _____ someone who was a runner. (know)

4. She had _____ this person in both races. (see)

5. Soon Sharon _____ a runner herself. (become)

6. She _____ herself into the activity. (throw)

7. She had _____ to get stronger and faster. (begin)

8. The day of the race _____ near. (draw)

9. Finally, the big day had _____. (come)

10. Before the race, everyone _____ the national anthem. (sing)

11. The starting bell had _____ loudly. (ring)

12. Sharon _____ forward ahead of the other runners. (spring)

13. The coach had never _____ her run so well. (see)

14. That day she _____ the 220-meter race and won. (run)

15. Her team _____ to the national meet in Idaho. (fly)

Exercise C

Circle the correct past or past participle form of the verb.

Example: The players (drank, drunk) water during the time-out.
Answer: drank

1. The referee had (blew, blown) the whistle.

2. The quarterback dropped back and (threw, thrown) a pass.

3. He had (threw, thrown) the ball to the receiver.

4. The receiver (ran, run) to catch the ball.

5. The receiver had (sprang, sprung) high in the air but still missed the ball.

6. The audience (began, begun) to shout and boo the players.

7. Clearly the crowd had (became, become) upset.

8. The team (drew, drawn) into a close huddle.

9. In the huddle the quarterback had (sank, sunk) to his knees.

10. At first he had not (knew, known) what play to call.

11. An idea (grew, grown) in his mind while he knelt there.

12. The players (went, gone) back to their positions.

13. The quarterback had (began, begun) to give signals.

14. He had (sang, sung) out the signals loudly and clearly.

15. A cry of disappointment (rang, rung) out from the crowd.

16. The quarterback had (threw, thrown) the ball to a running back.

17. The running back had not (saw, seen) a tackler behind him.

18. Both players had (went, gone) down.

19. The ball had (flew, flown) out of the running back's hands.

20. Everyone had (knew, known) it would be a close game.

Exercise D

Rewrite each sentence to make the verb correct.

    Example: The tire had sprang a leak.
    Answer: The tire had sprung a leak.

1. I had grow to love my old car.

_____

_____

2. I had swore never to get rid of it.

_____

_____

3. At one time it flown over the highways.

_____

_____

4. Now its engine has wore out somewhat.

_____

_____

5. It has blow many tires.

_____

_____

6. The muffler has sink closer to the ground.

_____

_____

7. The seat belt buzzer has rang its last warning.

_____

_____

8. Among my friends I have sang its praises.

_____

_____

Lesson 41

More Irregular Verbs

The irregular verbs *break*, *drive*, and *bring* represent three more patterns.

In each group of irregular verbs shown below, the changes from present to past to past participle are similar. Study the chart and look for the patterns.

Present	Past	Past Participle
break	broke	(has, have, had) broken
speak	spoke	(has, have, had) spoken
steal	stole	(has, have, had) stolen
freeze	froze	(has, have, had) frozen
choose	chose	(has, have, had) chosen
drive	drove	(has, have, had) driven
eat	ate	(has, have, had) eaten
fall	fell	(has, have, had) fallen
ride	rode	(has, have, had) ridden
write	wrote	(has, have, had) written
give	gave	(has, have, had) given
take	took	(has, have, had) taken
bring	brought	(has, have, had) brought
think	thought	(has, have, had) thought
buy	bought	(has, have, had) bought
teach	taught	(has, have, had) taught
lead	led	(has, have, had) led
lend	lent	(has, have, had) lent
leave	left	(has, have, had) left
find	found	(has, have, had) found
say	said	(has, have, had) said
sting	stung	(has, have, had) stung
swing	swung	(has, have, had) swung

Exercise A

Circle the correct past or past participle form of the verb in parentheses.

  Example: Zack and Zena had (ate, eaten) lunch at their grandmother's.
  Answer: (eaten)

1. Zack and Zena had (chose, chosen) to ignore each other.

2. They had (ate, eaten) lunch in angry silence.

3. Zack thought Zena had (took, taken) his book.

4. Zena believed Zack had (broke, broken) her bike.

5. Finally, Zena (spoke, spoken) angrily to Zack.

6. "Well, you (stole, stolen) my book," replied Zack.

7. The two (froze, frozen) in their tracks.

8. At least they had (broke, broken) their silence.

9. "I have not (stole, stolen) your book," Zena said.

10. "Remember, you (gave, given) it to me to read," she continued.

11. Zack forgot he had (gave, given) Zena the book.

12. Zack (spoke, spoken) next.

13. "I (rode, ridden) your bike to the store."

14. "On the way there, I (fell, fallen)."

15. "I (chose, chosen) not to tell you because I was embarrassed."

16. "I am sorry that I have (fell, fallen) with your bike."

17. Zena (gave, given) her brother a hug.

18. Then she said, "I have (wrote, written) for a new reflector."

19. "I (wrote, written) the letter two days ago."

20. Now Zack has (gave, given) Zena money for a new reflector.

Exercise B

Write the correct past or past participle form of the verbs in parentheses.

Example: We (speak) about Socrates in class today.
Answer: We spoke about Socrates in class today.

1. I have _____ (buy) a book about him.

2. This Greek philosopher and teacher has _____ (give) much to us.

3. His ideas have _____ (bring) us wisdom and knowledge.

4. Socrates had _____ (choose) to live a humble life.

5. Socrates believed that it was people's natures that _____ (lead) them to behave correctly.

6. He had _____ (think) that people acted wrongly because of ignorance.

7. He _____ (say) that the unexamined life is not worth living and that no person knowingly does evil.

8. He _____ (teach) many students by questioning them.

9. He had _____ (lead) his students to answer their own questions.

10. Socrates' students _____ (find) him to be a respectable teacher.

11. However, the general public _____ (think) he should not be trusted.

12. He had _____ (fell) from honor among influential Athenians.

13. The Athenians _____ (bring) Socrates to trial.

14. Socrates _____ (give) good arguments during the trial.

15. He had not _____ (freeze) on the witness stand.

16. The jury _____ (find) Socrates guilty of corrupting the young and being disrespectful to religion.

17. They _____ (give) him the death sentence.

18. Socrates never _____ (write) a book.

19. Others have _____ (write) about his beliefs.

20. He has _____ (leave) behind many lessons that are still studied.

Exercise C
Write a description of a misunderstanding between two friends. Include forms of at least four of the following verbs: *bring*, *speak*, *eat*, *give*, *lead*, *lend*, and *take*.

_____

_____

_____

_____

_____

_____

_____

_____

_____

_____

_____

_____

Lesson 42

Forms of *be*

Use the forms of the verb *be* correctly.

These forms of the verb *be*—*am*, *is*, *are*, *was*, *were*—can be used as linking verbs or as auxiliary verbs.

Nina **is** a student. Nina **is studying** American history.

Study the chart for forms of *be* to use with subject pronouns.

	Pronoun	Present	Past	Past Participle
Singular	I	am	was	(have, had) been
	you	are	were	(have, had) been
	he, she, it	is	was	(have, had) been
Plural	we	are	were	(have, had) been
	they	are	were	(have, had) been

I **am** the first. (Not: I is)
You **were** second. (Not: You was)
We **are** the prize winners. (Not: We is)

Use the present participle *being* with the auxiliary verbs *am*, *is*, *are*, *was*, and *were*. Use the past participle *been* with *has*, *have*, and *had*.

He **is being** silly. (Not: He being)
He **has been** that way all day. (Not: He been)

The form *be* should not be used in place of *am*, *is*, or *are*.

He **is** foolish. (Not: He be)

The word *ain't* is not a correct form and should not be used in place of *isn't* or *aren't*.

Jerry **isn't** going with us. (Not: Jerry ain't)
His friends **aren't** leaving yet. (Not: His friends ain't)

Exercise A
Circle the verb in parentheses that correctly completes each sentence.

1. Two women (was, were) the originators of it.

2. The name of its first teacher (was, were) Yim Wing Chun.

3. She (had been, been) the teacher of Ng Mui.

4. Ng Mui and others (is, are) the ones who popularized the art.

5. We (is, are) about to go to a karate tournament.

6. Concentration (is, be) the most important ability in karate.

7. Probably you (will be, being) most familiar with judo and karate.

8. They (have been, been) considered common arts of self-defense.

Exercise B
Rewrite each sentence, correcting the form of *be* where necessary.

1. The meaning of *judo* are "gentle way."

_____

2. Judo were for fighting, but now it's a sport.

_____

3. The idea of it ain't to overpower your opponent.

_____

4. The moves been designed to use the opponent's strength to your own advantage.

_____

5. Courtesy and confidence is gained from judo.

_____

6. New students being given a white belt to wear.

_____

7. Black belts ain't worn by anyone except masters of the art.

_____

8. Judo be an Olympic event for the first time in 1964.

_____

9. That year Tokyo been the site for the Olympics.

_____

10. Did you know some moves in karate was originally imitations of the movements of animals?

_____

Lesson 43

Forms of *have*

Use the forms of the verb *have* correctly.

Forms of the verb *have*—*have*, *has*, *had*—can be used by themselves as main verbs to form verb phrases.

Chiyoko **has** a question.
Chiyoko **has asked** a question.

Study the chart to learn what form of *have* to use with subject pronouns.

	Pronoun	Present	Past	Past Participle
Singular	I	have	had	(have, had) had
	you	have	had	(have, had) had
	he, she, it	has	had	(have, had) had
Plural	we	have	had	(have, had) had
	they	have	had	(have, had) had

Emma **has** the answer. (Not: Emma have)
We **have heard** it. (Not: We has heard)
I **had** another question. (Not: I has)

Do not write the word *of* in place of the word *have* in phrases like *would have, should have, could have,* and *must have.*

Joshua **must have** heard the answer. (Not: must of heard)

Exercise A
Circle the verb form in parentheses that correctly completes each sentence.

1. We (has, had) visitors last week.

2. They (have, had) visited us last year too.

3. You (could have, could of) met them.

4 The Burkes (has, have) gone home now.

5. Their visit (has, have) left our family excited.

6. I (has, had) the time of my life.

Exercise B
In the sentences on the next page, underline the verb that completes each sentence correctly.

Example: The students (has, have) their reports ready.
Answer: <u>have</u>

1. Flora (have, had) her report on H. G. Wells ready at least a week early.

2. She (hasn't, haven't) read much science fiction before this.

3. I (has, have) loaned her the novel *The Time Machine*.

4. The bookstores all (have, has) copies of that novel.

5. I (haven't, hasn't) read his novel *The Island of Dr. Moreau*.

6. Flora (have, has) promised to lend it to me.

7. Our library (have, has) copies of *The Invisible Man*.

8. Wells (have, has) written many books besides novels.

9. Those books (haven't, hasn't) been read as much as the novels.

10. Several of his novels (have, has) been made into movies.

Exercise C

Rewrite each sentence, using the correct form of *have*.

Example: H. G. Wells should of lifted weights as a child.
Answer: H. G. Wells should have lifted weights as a child.

1. Wells have poor health as a child.

_____

_____

2. Early in life he must of had an interest in science.

_____

_____

3. We know he have worked in a drapery factory and as a science teacher in a small school.

_____

_____

_____

4. Many of his books has scientific-sounding titles.

_____

_____

5. He have written one book called *The First Men on the Moon*.

_____

_____

Lesson 44
Forms of *do*

Use the forms of the verb *do* correctly.

Three forms of the verb *do* are *do*, *does*, and *did*. These forms can be used alone as main verbs or as auxiliary verbs.

> Janitors **do** the work.
> A janitor **does** things professionally.
> The janitor **did** fix the furnace.
> He **did** it quickly.

Study the forms of *do* in the chart below.

	Pronoun	Present	Past	Past Participle
Singular	I	do	did	(have, had) done
	you	do	did	(have, had) done
	he, she, it	does	did	(have, had) done
Plural	we	do	did	(have, had) done
	they	do	did	(have, had) done

Study the example sentences, which show correct uses of forms of the verb *do*.

> Our janitor **did** all the cleaning. (Not: Our janitor done)
> He had **done** a good job. (Not: He done)
> He has **done** it by himself. (Not: He done)

Exercise A
Circle the verb in parentheses that completes the sentence correctly.

> **Example:** (Do, Does) you know anything about Sir Ronald Ross?
> **Answer:** (Do)

1. Ross (had done, done) research on malaria.

2. (Do, Does) you think most people know he discovered the malaria parasite?

3. He (don't, doesn't) get talked about often.

4. Many scientists (do, does) know about Ross's discovery.

5. Scientists (don't, doesn't) forget about Giovanni Grassi either.

6. Grassi (did, done) research on malaria also.

7. (Does, Do) the name Charles Laveran mean anything to you?

8. He was another scientist who (had done, had did) research on malaria.

9. Laveran (did, do) important work on other diseases too.

10. Grassi did not receive a Nobel prize, but Laveran and Ross (did, do).

11. Malaria (don't, doesn't) worry people as much as it used to.

12. It (doesn't, don't) worry me.

13. I (does, do) not think you can catch malaria from another person.

14. I (do, does) know what the symptoms are.

15. (Does, Do) you know much about the disease?

Exercise B

Use **do**, **does**, **did**, or **done** to complete the sentences.

> **Example:** Giovanni Grassi has _____ important work on malaria.
> **Answer:** Giovanni Grassi has <u>done</u> important work on malaria.

1. Grassi had _____ work on eels and white ants.

2. He _____ recognize malaria as a problem in Italy around 1898.

3. Few scientists had _____ studies on mosquitoes.

4. _____ you know there are over thirty kinds of mosquitoes?

5. Grassi _____, and he tried to find the ones causing malaria.

6. He _____ his work in the nastiest swamps in Italy.

7. In time he had _____ over one hundred experiments.

8. _____ his work seem interesting to you?

9. We have _____ a science report on Grassi.

10. _____ you want to read it?

Lesson 45

Troublesome Verb Pairs

Some pairs of verbs are confusing because they have similar meanings or because they look alike.

Notice the difference in the principal parts of each pair of verbs below. These verb pairs are frequently confused. The examples and definitions will help you use the verbs correctly.

Present	Past	Past Participle
lay	laid	(has, have, had) laid
lie	lay	(has, have, had) lain

Lay your coat over there. ("put or place")
Lie down for a nap. ("rest or recline; be at rest")

set	set	(has, have, had) set
sit	sat	(has, have, had) sat

Set your books on that table. ("put something somewhere")
Sit here and rest awhile. ("sit down")

let	let	(has, have, had) let
leave	left	(has, have, had) left

Let me help you. ("allow")
I **leave** at six. ("go away")

lend	lent	(has, have, had) lent
borrow	borrowed	(has, have, had) borrowed

Lend me a pen. ("give")
I **will borrow** one from Pat. ("get")

teach	taught	(has, have, had) taught
learn	learned	(has, have, had) learned

Rob **taught** me to play chess. ("gave knowledge")
I **learned** to play chess from Bob. ("gained knowledge")

bring	brought	(has, have, had) brought
take	took	(has, have, had) taken

Bring the book here. ("carry something toward")
You can **take** the book home. ("carry something away")

rise	rose	(has, have, had) risen
raise	raised	(has, have, had) raised

Rise when the judge enters. ("get up")
Please **raise** the window. ("lift something up; make it higher")

Exercise A
Circle the verb in parentheses that correctly completes the sentence.

1. You have (laid, **lain**) in the sun long enough.
2. You should (set, **sit**) in the shade awhile.
3. Will you (**lend**, borrow) me some sunscreen?
4. (Bring, **Take**) the towel over here.
5. Is Juan (**teaching**, learning) you to swim?
6. He won't (**let**, leave) me swim by myself yet.
7. The water in the lake (**rises**, raises) higher every year.

Exercise B
Circle the verb in parentheses that correctly completes the sentence.

1. An experiment I did (**taught**, learned) me about plants.
2. Mr. Roberts, our science teacher, (**brought**, took) a white carnation from home.
3. He (**laid**, lay) the carnation on the table.
4. He (borrowed, **lent**) me his penknife to slit the carnation stem vertically.
5. I (**set**, sat) half the stem in a glass of plain water and the other half in a glass of water with blue ink in it.
6. I didn't (leave, **let**) any water touch the flower.
7. Then I (**let**, left) the carnation in water overnight.
8. That night as I (laid, **lay**) in bed, I wondered what would happen to the carnation.
9. After twenty-four hours, I (**took**, brought) the carnation out of the water and looked at the petals.
10. On the side where the stem (**lay**, laid) in blue water, the petals were blue.
11. I (taught, **learned**) that there are little tubes inside the carnation's stem.
12. The water (**rises**, raises) through these tubes into the petals and leaves.
13. The next day Mr. Roberts (**lent**, borrowed) me a book about plant experiments.
14. I (set, **sat**) at my desk for hours and read it.
15. I finally (lay, **laid**) the book down to try another experiment.

Exercise C

Circle the verb in parentheses that correctly completes each sentence.

1. My brothers, Sid and Ernie, (taught, learned) me the basics of softball.

2. They (borrowed, lent) a softball and a bat from our gym teacher.

3. He (let, left) us practice on the athletic field after school.

4. Some softball players (lay, laid) on the grass.

5. Sid told me to (rise, raise) the bat to shoulder height.

6. I (rose, raised) my bat even more before Sid pitched to me.

7. I swung and watched the ball (let, leave) my bat.

8. Ernie simply (set, sat) there and watched the ball.

9. I (laid, lay) the bat next to him.

10. Now I (borrow, lend) the softball and bat every day and work on my hitting.

Exercise D

Write the verb form needed to complete each sentence. Use the verbs given in parentheses.

Example: Ken has _____ the table. (past participle of *set*)
Answer: set

1. Sara has _____ the lasagna out of the oven. (past participle of *take*)

2. Mom has _____ down the napkins. (past participle of *lay*)

3. Please ask Uncle Leo to _____ here. (present of *sit*)

4. I _____ next to my grandmother at the table. (past of *sit*)

5. My brothers each had _____ second helping of lasagna. (past participle of *take*)

Lesson 46

Active and Passive Verbs

Active verbs are used most often because they express action directly and naturally. Passive verbs are used less often.

A verb is called **active** when the subject of a sentence is the doer of the action. A verb is called **passive** when the subject receives the action.

Diego **hit** the ball.

Diego, the subject of the sentence, performed the action. *Hit* is the active verb. *Ball* is the direct object of the sentence. It receives the action.
Now look at the sentence below.

The ball **was hit** by Diego.

Ball still receives the action, but in this sentence it is the subject. The verb *was hit* is passive. Passive verbs consist of some form of *be*, such as *was*, plus a past participle.
Writers generally use active verbs because they express action in a direct, natural way. There are two cases, however, when writers prefer to use passive verbs.

A passive verb is used to emphasize the receiver of the action rather than the doer of the action.

The winning run **was scored** by the Trenton catcher.

A passive verb is used when the doer of the action is unknown or unimportant.

Some equipment **had been taken** from the locker room.

Exercise A

Write **P** if the sentence is passive; write **A** if it is active.

1. Sandi broke the record a second time. _____

2. Toby played the game well. _____

3. The record was broken by Sandi. _____

4. A speech was given by the coach. _____

5. Mr. Baker handed Sandi her trophy. _____

6. The play was directed by Rudy. _____

7. Rita played the lead. _____

8. The costumes were made by Elena and Louise. _____

9. Sam sold tickets to all his friends. _____

10. Sam's parents also bought tickets from him. _____

Exercise B

Rewrite the sentences below, changing the passive verbs to active verbs.

1. Shells were collected by Bonnie.

_____

2. The shells were displayed by her on a velvet cloth.

_____

3. Two large albums of foreign stamps were brought by Willis.

_____

4. The stamp collection had been started by his father.

_____

5. Hand-carved marionettes were exhibited by Maya.

_____

6. The marionettes had been carved by her father.

_____

7. The marionettes were worked for us by Maya.

_____

8. A prize was awarded by the judges to the best exhibit.

_____

9. The prize was won by Barry Handelman.

_____

10. A miniature theater was built by him.

_____

Lesson 47

Subject-Verb Agreement

A singular subject agrees with a singular verb. A plural subject agrees with a plural verb.

When the subject and verb of a sentence are both singular or both plural, they agree in number. This is called **subject-verb agreement**. Read the sentences below.

The <u>road</u> **is** icy. (singular subject; singular verb)
The <u>roads</u> **are** icy. (plural subject; plural verb)

Pronouns generally follow this rule. However, *I* and *you* always take plural verbs.

<u>I</u> **iron**. <u>She</u> **scrubs**. <u>You</u> **watch**. <u>We</u> **complain**.

Use the following two rules to help you make compound subjects and their verbs agree.

Rule 1.   Most compound subjects joined by *and* or *both . . . and* are plural and are followed by plural verbs.

<u>Sarah and Helga</u> **drive** to the mountains on weekends.
<u>Both Sarah and Helga</u> **like** the area very much.

Rule 2.   A compound subject joined by *or, either . . . or*, or *neither . . . nor* is followed by a verb that agrees in number with the closer subject.

<u>Either Sarah or Helga</u> **drives** to the mountains on weekends.
<u>The twins or the girls</u> **drive** to the mountains on weekends.
<u>Neither the twins nor Brian</u> **goes** with the girls.

In the first sentence both subjects are singular, so the verb is singular. In the second sentence both nouns are plural, so the verb is plural. In the third sentence, the noun closest to the verb is singular, so the verb is singular.

Exercise A
Circle the correct singular or plural form of the verb in parentheses.

1. Two dogs and a cat (lives, live) in that house.

2. They (is, are) always playing together.

3. Neither the dogs not the cat (likes, like) strangers.

4. Mr. Terry and one dog (takes, take) long walks.

5. Either Mr. Terry or his housekeeper (feeds, feed) the animals.

6. Neither the cat nor the dogs (strays, stray) far from home.

7. Either the dogs or the cat (sleeps, sleep) with Mr. Terry.

8. Both my mother and father (disapproves, disapprove) of my dog sleeping with me.

9. Both cats and dogs (is, are) easy to care for.

10. Neither the cat nor the dogs (is, are) any trouble.

Exercise B
Follow the directions for Exercise A.

1. Juan and his sisters (wants, want) to put on a pet show.

2. Neither his parents nor the neighbors (objects, object).

3. Both Cindy and Maria (has, have) agreed to help.

4. They (has, have) put on a show before.

5. Two boxers and a cat (is, are) entered already.

6. Either the twins or Jamie (has, have) entered a snake.

7. Jamie or the twins (is, are) also entering a myna bird.

8. Either a blue ribbon or some treats (is, are) to be first prize.

9. Both Ron and the twins (expects, expect) to win a prize.

10. I (know, knows) that it will be a good pet show.

11. You (remember, remembers) what fun it was last year.

12. The twins and Juan (hopes, hope) to win a prize again this year.

Exercise C
Use the compound subjects below to make sentences of your own. Be sure your subjects and verbs agree.

1. some artists and writers

   _____

2. either Karen or the boys

   _____

3. both the boys and Karen

   _____

4. neither the girls nor Cal

   _____

5. either the cyclist or the runners

   _____

Lesson 48
Subjects Separated from Verbs

Agreement between subject and verb is not affected by words or phrases that come between the subject and the verb.

Subjects and verbs must agree in number. A common agreement problem occurs when the subject of a sentence is separated from the verb by a prepositional phrase. Notice that the subject and verb in the sentence below agree.

> <u>Reports</u> of a gigantic earthquake **were** greatly exaggerated.

The verb *were* is plural to agree with the plural subject *reports*. The prepositional phrase *of a gigantic earthquake* comes between the subject and the verb. Although the noun *earthquake* appears just before the verb, it does not affect the number of the verb. The verb agrees in number with the subject.

Here are some other examples of subjects separated from verbs.

> The <u>report</u> about many injured people **was disproved**.
> The <u>objection</u> of the city manager and the two commissioners **has received** much publicity.
> The newspaper <u>column</u> of questions and answers **gives** all the necessary information.
> The <u>cars</u> in the driveway next to the house **belong** to our visiting relatives.

Exercise A

Circle the form of the verb in parentheses that correctly completes the sentence.

> **Example:** Tracks of a large animal (has, have) been found.
> **Answer:** (have)

1. Scientists from a nearby university (has, have) examined them.

2. The spokesperson for the scientists (says, say) that the tracks resemble those of a dinosaur.

3. A reporter for two magazines (wants, want) an interview.

4. The citizens of the town (welcomes, welcome) the excitement.

5. A group of parents (has, have) formed a dinosaur watch.

6. One parent of six-year-old twins (states, state) that his children will stay home from school until the animal is found.

7. A parent of two boys (describes, describe) the news as scary.

8. Rumors of a prank (is, are) beginning to spread.

9. The opinion of my friends (is, are) that someone is fooling us.

10. An animal with such big feet (has, have) not been seen yet.

Exercise B

Rewrite the sentences. Correct the agreement mistakes.

> **Example:** The stories of great pranks is found in this book.
> **Answer:** The stories of great pranks are found in this book.

1. The history of pranks are a fascinating one.

   _____

   _____

2. Victims of a prank quite often does not know they're being fooled.

   _____

   _____

3. Once, scientists from a British university was fooled by the skull of an animal.

   _____

   _____

4. A 1938 radio drama about Martian invaders have been broadcast every Halloween to fool listeners.

   _____

   _____

5. Reports of a UFO invasion still scares many people.

   _____

   _____

6. People in an Illinois town has believed in "Big Foot."

   _____

   _____

7. Descriptions of "Big Foot" has varied greatly.

   _____

   _____

8. The footprints of the creature is found in the snow.

   _____

   _____

Lesson 49
Sentences in Inverted Order

The position of a subject in a sentence does not affect subject-verb agreement.

In most sentences the subject comes before the verb. In some sentences, though, especially in questions, the verb or part of the verb usually comes first and the subject follows. When the subject follows the verb, the sentence is said to be in **inverted order**. To make sure that such sentences have subject-verb agreement, reverse the order.

> Down the street **walks** <u>Jean</u>.
> <u>Jean</u> **walks** down the street.
> **Does** <u>Jean</u> **practice** today?
> <u>Jean</u> **does practice** today.
> Where **are** her <u>instruments</u>?
> Her <u>instruments</u> **are** where?

In the first sentence pair the verb *walks* agrees with the singular subject *Jean*. The verb phrase *does practice* in the second pair agrees with the singular subject *Jean*. In the third pair the plural verb *are* agrees with the plural subject *instruments*.

In sentences that begin with *here* or *there*, the words *here* and *there* are not subjects. To find the subject, reverse the order of the sentence.

> There **are** no <u>seats</u>.
> No <u>seats</u> **are** there.
> Here **is** a <u>book</u> of songs.
> A <u>book</u> of songs **is** here.

The plural verb *are* agrees with the plural subject *seats*. The singular subject *song* agrees with the singular verb *is*.

Remember that *here's* and *there's* are contractions of *here is* and *there is*.

Incorrect:	Here**'s** the <u>programs</u>. There**'s** our <u>seats</u>.
Correct:	Here **are** the <u>programs</u>. There **are** our <u>seats</u>.

Exercise A
Write **S** over the subject and **V** over the verb.

1. When does Natusa go to science class?

2. Here's a copy of her schedule.

3. There are your books on the table.

4. Does Ollie know about the meeting?

5. Where have Sandy and Duncan gone?

Exercise C

Put one line under the prepositional phrase in each sentence and two lines under the word the phrase describes. Write what kind of prepositional phrase you underlined.

Example: Many areas of the world require more energy.
Answer: Many <u>areas</u> of the world require more energy.—Adjective phrase

1. Windmills offer hope for a larger energy supply. _____

2. A windmill of great size could serve several homes. _____

3. In many places, steady winds blow. _____

4. The high cost of wind machinery is a problem. _____

5. Remote areas with steady winds produce electricity now. _____

6. Another source of power is the sun. _____

7. The rays of the sun can heat water. _____

8. Water heats at a low cost if this method is used. _____

9. Heat collectors operate in sunny climates. _____

10. The sun's heat collects in panels. _____

Exercise D

Complete each sentence with the kind of prepositional phrase indicated in parentheses. You may want to begin your phrases with some of these prepositions: *in, on, by, near, around, above, about,* or *from.*

Example: The scouts camped _____. (adverb phrase)
Answer: The scouts camped by the river.

1. Their fire was built _____. (adverb phrase)

2. The scouts fished _____. (adverb phrase)

3. They bathed and swam _____. (adverb phrase)

4. The beach _____ was wide. (adjective phrase)

5. Even when it rained the scouts hiked near the camp _____. (adverb phrase)

6. The birds _____ chirped for their young. (adjective phrase)

7. Animals _____ were hidden from view. (adjective phrase)

8. At night the scouts studied the stars _____. (adjective phrase)

9. During the day they learned _____. (adverb phrase)

10. Next year the troop will travel _____. (adverb phrase)

Lesson 65
Identifying Conjunctions

A conjunction joins words or groups of words. The terms *coordinating conjunction* **and** *correlative conjunction* **describe how certain conjunctions are used in sentences.**

A **conjunction** is a word that links one part of a sentence to another. It can join words, phrases, or entire sentences.

A **coordinating conjunction** is used to join words or groups of words of equal value in a sentence. The most common coordinating conjunctions are *and*, *but*, and *or*.

The coordinating conjunction *and* shows the addition of one thing to another. The conjunction *but* shows contrast between one thing and another. The conjunction *or* shows choice between things. Study these examples.

I am wearing red socks **and** a red shirt today.
My brother is in the crowd, **but** I can't see him.
We didn't know whether the actor was laughing **or** crying.

In the first sentence, *and* joins the words *red shirt* and *red socks*. *But* shows a contrast in the second sentence between what the speaker knows and what he or she can see. In the third sentence, *or* shows a choice between the verbs *laughing* and *crying*.

Other coordinating conjunctions include *so*, *yet*, *for*, and *nor*.

I have read that book, **so** I know the plot.
She liked the painting, **yet** she didn't buy it.
We should win the game, **for** we have more talented players.
He didn't thank Lisa **nor** anyone else.

Conjunctions that are used in pairs are called **correlative conjunctions**. Some correlative conjunctions are *both . . . and*, *either . . . or*, and *neither . . . nor*. A pair of correlative conjunctions is always separated by a word or group of words.

Both the inventor **and** her assistant were surprised.
They went to see **either** a play **or** a musical in the city.
Neither the drummer **nor** the guitarist knew "Stardust."

Exercise A
Use coordinating or correlative conjunctions to complete the sentences.

1. On our trip we will travel first to Memphis _____ then on to New Orleans.

2. Sam wants to drive, _____ I don't think it's a good idea.

3. I'm sure we can get there just as easily _____ by train _____ by plane.

4. _____ Mom _____ Dad want to go to Preservation Hall.

5. Sam and I can go with them, _____ we can do something else that evening.

6. I like television, _____ I don't like everything on it.

7. I watched an entire day _____ night of television once.

8. On a quiz show, the contestants kept clapping _____ jumping.

9. On a soap opera, everyone was _____ in trouble _____ dying.

10. _____ the quiz show _____ the soap opera devoted almost as much time to commercials as they did to the programs.

Exercise B

Underline the coordinating conjunctions in the sentences below.

Example: The girl and boy knew the song but didn't sing it.
Answer: <u>and</u>, <u>but</u>

1. I have three brothers, four sisters, and two parents.

2. We get along well, but we do disagree about money.

3. Two of my brothers and three of my sisters have jobs.

4. I don't care much about money, nor am I careless with it.

5. I occasionally borrow money from a brother or sister.

6. I try to pay them back promptly, for I know they need money.

7. A barter system would end all our disagreeing, yet I cannot convince the family of this.

8. No one except me finds my idea interesting or acceptable.

9. My brothers and sisters laughed when I explained it, so I talked to them one at a time.

10. I convinced one parent, one brother, and two sisters, but no one else in the family will budge.

Exercise C

Underline the ten pairs of correlative conjunctions in the sentences below.

Example: Neither Jennifer nor Lenore had anything to trade.
Answer: <u>Neither</u> . . . <u>nor</u>

1. Both my parents and the rest of my family have given in to me.

2. The bartering will be either a success or a disaster.

3. Neither my brother Fozzie nor my sisters like bartering very much.

4. Fozzie wanted both my favorite pen and my pet duck for his oldest, most worn-out hiking boots.

5. I told him the trade would be fair neither to me nor to my duck, who dislikes Fozzie intensely.

6. "Either leave out the duck or it's no deal," I said.

7. Both he and I made new offers for other trades.

8. I wanted either his backpack or his new T-shirt for my pen.

9. Neither Fozzie nor I could come to any agreement.

10. Both my family and I have decided to forget bartering.

Exercise D

Add to the thoughts begun below. Use a conjunction to join your ending to each statement. Vary your conjunctions. If you can, make a few of your endings humorous, like the example in parentheses.

>   **Example:** They say that the best things in life are free . . . (and I would pay a lot to learn what they are!)

1. What you don't know won't hurt you _____

   _____

2. Everything comes to those who wait _____

   _____

3. A penny saved is a penny earned _____

   _____

4. An apple a day keeps the doctor away _____

   _____

5. They who laugh last, laugh best _____

   _____

6. Birds of a feather flock together _____

   _____

7. Every cloud has a silver lining _____

   _____

8. Let a smile be your umbrella _____

   _____

Lesson 66
Identifying Interjections

An interjection is a word or phrase used to express strong emotion.

An **interjection** is an exclamation of feeling. It usually stands alone or at the beginning of a sentence. It may consist of one word, a few words, or the spelling of a certain sound. Here are some of the feelings expressed by interjections.

Joy:	**Yahoo!** I made the basketball team!
Surprise:	**Wow,** that is an amazing Halloween costume!
Pain:	**Ow!** That's my sore toe you just squashed!
Fear:	**Oh no,** a train is coming down the tracks!

Use a comma after an interjection that expresses mild emotion. Use an exclamation mark after one that expresses stronger feelings. Remember not to overuse interjections in your writing or they will lose their effectiveness.

Exercise.
Make up sentences, using these interjections to express the feelings described in parentheses. Use either commas or exclamation marks with your interjections.

1. goodness (surprise)

_____

2. okay (approval)

_____

3. ouch (pain)

_____

4. aha (triumph)

_____

5. well (mild surprise)

_____

6. all right (joy)

_____

7. ah (pain)

_____

8. my (surprise)

_____

Lesson 67

Punctuating the Ends of Sentences

The punctuation mark used at the end of a sentence depends on the kind of sentence.

A sentence may end with a period, a question mark, or an exclamation mark. Study the sentences below.

Declarative:	Eve visited the White House last summer.
Interrogative:	Have you ever been there?
Exclamatory:	What a beautiful mansion it is!
Imperative:	Notice the lovely rooms and rare paintings.
	You really must take the tour next year!

A question mark is used to signal an interrogative sentence. A period is used to signal a declarative sentence. An exclamation mark is used to signal an exclamatory sentence.

Notice the end punctuation for the last two example sentences. An imperative sentence usually ends with a period. If the sentence expresses strong feeling, an exclamation mark is used.

End punctuation helps make the meaning of a sentence clear. Notice how your voice changes if you read the three sentences below aloud. Pay close attention to the end punctuation in each.

The TV isn't working.
The TV isn't working?
The TV isn't working!

Exercise A
Add the appropriate punctuation mark for each kind of sentence.

1. Melinda, this is Beth _____ (declarative)

2. What are you doing this afternoon _____ (interrogative)

3. I'm cleaning my room and vacuuming the rug _____ (declarative)

4. How long will it take you _____ (interrogative)

5. It's really a mess this time _____ (declarative)

6. Well, hurry up _____ (imperative)

7. It may take me all afternoon _____ (exclamatory)

8. I wanted you to go to the movies with me _____ (declarative)

9. I'd like to, but I can't finish in time _____ (declarative)

10. Let me come over and help you _____ (imperative)

11. I couldn't ask you to do that _____ (declarative)

12. I'll come right over on my bike _____ (declarative)

13. Do you mean it _____ (interrogative)

14. Of course I do _____ (exclamatory)

15. I'll see you soon _____ (declarative)

Exercise B

Read each sentence and decide what kind of sentence it is. In the space before the sentence, write **D** for declarative, **I** for interrogative, **E** for exclamatory, or **Im** for imperative. Then add a punctuation mark to the end of each sentence.

1. _____ Is that a bear over there in the park _____

2. _____ That's a black bear beyond the evergreens _____

3. _____ Oh, how friendly he looks _____

4. _____ Don't go near him or you may be sorry _____

5. _____ He may not be so friendly up close _____

6. _____ Please take a picture of him for our album _____

7. _____ How does the homing pigeon find its way home _____

8. _____ I read an interesting magazine article about pigeons _____

9. _____ Read this article if you want to learn about them _____

10. _____ Did you know that pigeons can see special light rays _____

11. _____ These light rays are invisible to humans _____

12. _____ Pigeons use their vision to find the sun's position _____

13. _____ How remarkable that pigeons can do this _____

14. _____ Imagine the world from a pigeon's-eye view _____

15. _____ How different it must look _____

Lesson 68

Commas in Sentences

Use a comma to show a pause or separation between words or word groups in a sentence.

Commas are used to indicate pauses between words and word groups in sentences. Commas are also used to make the meaning clear. Read the sentence below.

Oh, we're having a party, and Harvey, Lee, and Glen are coming.

Without the commas, you might not know that Harvey and Lee are two different people.

Listed below and on the next page are six rules for using commas. Follow these rules as you work through the practices.

Rule 1. Use commas to separate items in a series.

Jan, Dot, Steve, and Cory are coming to the party.
I've called the guests, bought the food, and warned the neighbors.
I think this will be a loud, enjoyable, and exciting party.

Use two commas when there are three items in a series. Use three commas when there are four items in a series.

Rule 2. Use a comma after introductory words and phrases.

By the way, can you bring plates?
Oh, I'm sure we have paper plates in the kitchen.

Rule 3. Use commas to set off nouns in direct address.

Mike, will you come? I'd love to, Marsha.
Remember, friends, to bring some olives.

Use one comma if a noun is the first or last word in the sentence. Use two commas if the noun is in the middle of the sentence.

Rule 4. Use commas to set off interrupting words and appositives.

We've borrowed chairs from Mr. Wilson, our next-door neighbor.
Rosa, of course, will bring her folding table.

If the interrupting words or appositive is at the end of a sentence, use one comma. If it is in the middle, use two.

Rule 5. Use a comma after a dependent clause that begins a sentence. Do not use a comma before a dependent clause that follows the independent clause.

If Mr. Wilson complains, we'll invite him in for a snack.
When he arrives, we'll ask him about his vacation.
We'll invite Mr. Wilson in for a snack if he complains.

Rule 6. Use a comma before the conjunction in a compound sentence. Omit the comma, however, in a short compound sentence.

> Herman wanted to play charades, but no one else would play.
> The party ended and we went home.

Exercise A
Add commas where needed in each sentence.

1. Will you remember Wanda to call the twins Pat and Michelle?

2. I've bought green gold white and brown crepe paper.

3. Luis Dan will decorate two of the rooms and you can help him.

4. Henry of course will help too Luis.

5. If you finish early you can start choosing the music.

Exercise B
Add commas where necessary and underline each. You will add eighteen commas.

(1) "Jerry I want to ask you something. (2) The Encounter a new rock group is performing this afternoon. (3) Unfortunately I can't use my ticket. (4) I need to replace a filling and it just can't wait. (5) If you are interested I'll sell you my ticket."

(6) "I wish I could buy it Samantha. (7) My problem as usual is that I am broke. (8) Of course I could borrow the money from Ivan my brother's friend. (9) He's not here now but he should be back soon. (10) Since I can't promise to get the money you might want to ask someone else."

(11) "If you don't mind Jerry I will. (12) Barry Mike and June are all crazy about The Encounter. (13) They tried to buy tickets but the concert was all sold out."

Exercise C
Rewrite each sentence, inserting commas where they are needed.

1. If you are horror-film fans ladies and gentlemen we have some news for you.

_____

_____

2. Do remember Count Dracula the stranger from Transylvania?

_____

_____

3. The count is the father of a terrifying daughter Draculana.

_____

_____

4. These terrible creatures are appearing together in *Daughter Of Dracula* a new movie.

_____

_____

5. Every scene needless to say is packed with action suspense chills and thrills.

_____

_____

6. You won't know whether to laugh cry gasp or shiver.

_____

_____

7. We won't give the story away but you'll definitely be scared.

_____

_____

8. If you go take a friend.

_____

_____

9. People in Texas Ohio and Maine really enjoyed the movie.

_____

_____

10. Another film *Daughter of Dracula: Part Two* is being made.

_____

_____

11. As usual people will wait in long lines to see it.

_____

_____

Lesson 69
Other Uses of Commas

Use commas to separate items in addresses and dates. Also use commas in figures and in friendly letters.

Remember that commas are used in sentences to indicate natural pauses and to make the meaning clear. The following rules explain some other uses of commas.

Rule 1. Use commas to separate items in a date. If a date is within a sentence, put a comma after the year.

> The art show opened on Sunday, February 2.
> The artist was born on April 5, 1960, in a small Pennsylvania farmhouse.

Rule 2. Use a comma to separate items in an address. The number and street are considered one item. The state and Zip Code are also considered one item. Use a comma after the Zip Code if it is within a sentence.

> Jeremy Taylor   Ms. Julie Cohan
> 512 E. Washtenaw Avenue   1956 Beeker Street
> Joliet, IL 60411   Tulsa, OK 74129

> The letter is addressed to Sara Smith, 5019 Topanga Avenue, Los Angeles, California 98421, but was delivered to me by mistake.

Rule 3. Use a comma to separate numerals greater than three digits.

> There are 86,400 seconds in a day.
> The attendance on Monday was 15,825.
> One painting sold for $4,900.
> The new house cost $94,750.

Rule 4. Use a comma when a person's last name appears before the first name.

> Appleton, Maria   Chen, Lin
> Arden, John   Jones, Lela
> Cardozo, Victor   Torres, Isabel

Rule 5. Use a comma after the greeting in a friendly letter and after the closing in all letters.

> Dear Jonah,   Yours truly,
> Dear Uncle Stan,   Sincerely,

Exercise A
Write the number of the rule that explains the punctuation in each sentence.

1. Please send a card to Cindy Perez, 3318 Plainfield Avenue, Chicago, Illinois 60634. _____

2. My little sister was born on January 8, 1979, in New York. _____

3. That building was just sold for $2,765,300. _____

Exercise B
Add commas to the letter below where they are necessary. You will add fourteen commas.

> 65 River Road
> Potomac MD 20853
> March 20 1988

Dear Martha

    I just got back from a family reunion in Woodstock Virginia. We celebrated my grandparents' anniversary on Saturday March 12. They were married on March 12 1930. My aunt and uncle flew in from Bangor Maine for the weekend. My cousin drove in from San Francisco California. Then he drove to see his sister in El Paso Texas. He must have driven over 10000 miles in his car during his trip!

    Woodstock is a friendly town but Potomac Maryland has one big advantage. It's my home!

> Your pal
> Carrie

Exercise C
Listed below and on the next page is information about the Grand Prize Winners in the Bubble-up Soap Contest. Read each listing and add commas where necessary.

Example:	Answer:
$1000000 Winner	$1,000,000 Winner
Barker John	Barker, John
248 Lerner Street	248 Lerner Street
Niles MI 49120	Niles, MI 49120

1. $500000 Winner

2. Anderson Rodney

3. 132 Valley Terrace

4. Santa Fe CA 90670

5. Birthday: October 7 1966

6. $250000 Winner

7. Muhs Neil

8. 6 Jasper Way

9. Boston MA 01432

10. Birthday: April 26 1955

11. $100000 Winner

12. Smith Janice

13. 863-B Roper Road

14. Gaithersburg MD 20760

15. Birthday: July 17 1972

16. $50000 Winner

17. Zim Roland

18. 101 Foundry Road

19. Pecos TX 79772

20. Birthday: March 30 1958

Exercise D

The following letter will be sent to all the parents of seventh graders at Leroy Junior High School. Add commas to the letter where they are needed. You will add twelve commas.

November 25 1996

Dear Parents

Come and join the fun on Saturday December 3. We're holding a bazaar at Leroy Junior High School 201 Washington Street San Diego. Books clothing and baked goods will be on sale. Help us raise the $4000 we need for new library books. Our target date for purchasing the books is January 2 1998. If you can't come in person please contact Ms. Melissa Raymond. Her address is 136 Mooney Road San Diego California 92117.

Gratefully yours

The 7th Grade Class

Lesson 70
Other Punctuation Marks

Other marks of punctuation can help make the meaning of your writing clearer.

Punctuation marks can have different uses. Study the following explanations and examples.

Colon   The colon is used after the greeting in a business letter, and it has these additional uses.

1. A colon is used after expressions that introduce a list.

    You need the following: a notebook, pencil, pen, and eraser.

2. A colon is used between the hour and minutes when you write time in numbers.

    The meetings are at 6:15, 8:30, and 10:45 A.M.

Hyphen   The hyphen is used to divide a word that breaks at the end of a line. It has two other common uses.

1. Hyphens are used to join compound words that are thought of as one.

    My older brother is a well-known favorite of the vice-president.

2. Hyphens are used in writing numbers from twenty-one to ninety-nine as words.

    The quarterback yelled, "Thirty-four, sixty-eight, hike."

Dash   The dash is used to show a sudden change in thought or to set off words that interrupt the main thought of a sentence.

    We will finish the reading—if we can—by Tuesday.
    The clumsy outfielder—he was my brother's friend—lost the final game of the season.

Parentheses   Parentheses have these two uses.

1. Parentheses are used to enclose words that interrupt the thought of the sentence. The words in the parentheses usually explain or add to the sentence.

    The best answer (and the easiest answer) is no answer.

2. Parentheses are used to enclose references to dates, numbers, or chapters.

    Mozart (1756–1791) composed music as a child (see chapter 4).

Period   The period is an end mark. It also is used after titles, initials, and other abbreviations.

    Maj. Jay B. Bennington, M.D., arrived at 9:00 A.M.

Apostrophe   An apostrophe is used in possessive words and in contractions. It is also used to form the plurals of letters and numbers if the plurals would be confusing without it.

> Dot your *i*'s and cross your *t*'s.

Semicolon   A semicolon is used to separate the two parts of a compound sentence when they are not joined by a comma and a coordinating conjunction.

> Mary played the villain; Jack played the hero.
>
> **Compare:**   Mary played the villain, and Jack played the hero.

Exercise A

Rewrite each sentence, adding necessary punctuation.

Example: Did you read that article pages 12–19 about Dr. Di?
Answer: Did you read that article (pages 12–19) about Dr. Di?

1. The spelling bee starts at 830 AM

_____

2. I signed up that was my first mistake last month.

_____

3. Here are the names of the judges Vito Cardello, Lisa Wong, and Margaret Fenton.

_____

4. Cara Chen always wins I'm glad she's not going to enter this year.

_____

5. Can you I mean anyone study for a spelling bee?

_____

6. I'd pay special attention to the medical words pages 31–42.

_____

7. There are fifty two words on a page.

_____

8. Your know it all attitude sometimes annoys me.

_____

9. Are there two *m*s, *t*s, and *e*s in the word *committee?*

_____

10. My dentist, Dr Mildred N Mann, won a contest.

_____

Exercise B

Write a sentence for each item below.

    Example: a colon after an expression introducing a list
    Answer: Mr. Jay had the following: a dog, a cat, and a pen.

1. a colon between the hour and minutes in time

_____

2. the number *67* written out

_____

3. two hyphens in a compound word

_____

4. a dash showing a sudden change of thought

_____

5. a period in an abbreviation

_____

6. an apostrophe with the plural of a letter or number

_____

7. parentheses enclosing dates

_____

8. a semicolon in a compound sentence

_____

9. a colon that introduces a list

_____

10. a period in an initial

_____

Lesson 71

Quotation Marks

Quotation marks enclose a speaker's exact words. Quotation marks are also used to enclose some titles.

When you use someone's exact words in your writing, signal your reader with **quotation marks**. Follow these rules.

Rule 1. Enclose all quoted words within quotation marks.

Rule 2. The first word of a direct quotation begins with a capital letter. When a quotation is broken into two parts, use two sets of quotation marks. Use one capital letter if the quote is one sentence. Use two capital letters if it is two sentences.

> **"Let's go home," Kate suggested, "and get some lemonade."**
> **"Can we leave right away?" Marta asked. "I'm really thirsty."**

Rule 3. Use a comma between the words that introduce the speaker and the words that are quoted. Place the end punctuation or the comma that ends the quotation inside the quotation marks. Begin a new paragraph each time the speaker changes.

> Kate said, "There's my mom at the front door."
> "Hello," Kate's mom said. "Would you like some lemonade?"

Rule 4. Do not use quotation marks with an indirect quotation—that is, a quotation that does not give the speaker's exact words.

> **Indirect:** Mom told Kate that she had been waiting for her.
> **Direct:** Mom told Kate, "I've been waiting for you."

Rule 5. Quotation marks are also used to enclose the titles of songs, stories, poems, articles in newspapers and magazines, and chapters in books. They are not used to indicate book titles.

"The Raven"   Chapter 1, "Nouns"   "Over the Rainbow"

<u>War and Peace</u>

Exercise A

Rewrite these sentences. Add quotation marks to the direct quotations. If a sentence is correct, write *Correct*.

1. Let's go to the beach, Ky said.

_____

2. Would you like a picnic lunch? Pedro asked. I'm starved!

_____

3. Why don't we invite Harriet? Ky suggested.

_____

4. Pedro said that he didn't think she was feeling well.

_____

5. She was out of school Thursday and Friday, he commented.

_____

6. Ky said, Why don't you call her?

_____

7. OK, I will, said Pedro.

_____

8. When Harriet answered the phone, she said, What a shame!

_____

9. I'd like to come, she explained, but I have a terrible cold.

_____

10. She said she had been sitting around feeling sorry for herself.

_____

Exercise B

Add quotation marks to the direct quotations and titles in the following sentences.

    Example: I just read The Tell-Tale Heart, a spooky story.
    Answer: I just read "The Tell-Tale Heart," a spooky story.

1. Many students were reading May Swenson's poem The Centaur.

2. Others were writing down the lyrics to America, the Beautiful.

3. Attention, class! Mrs. Gordon said. Listen carefully.

4. I'm going to put a list of stories and articles for recommended reading on the board, she said.

5. The list included the following titles: Thank You, by Alex Haley; A Haircut, by I. S. Nakata; and Drouth, by Ben Logan.

6. Should we write answers to the discussion questions? Lu asked.

Lesson 72
Capitalizing First Words

Capitalize the first words in sentences, in direct quotations, and in the greetings and closings in letters.

When you write a sentence or a direct quotation, begin the first word with a capital letter. Read the sentences that follow.

> **M**y sister is interested in a radio career.
> **M**y dad said, "**Y**ou could be a sports announcer."
> "**M**aybe I'd like that," she replied. "**H**ow do I find out about sports announcing?"
> "**T**here are colleges you could write to," said Dad, "or why not try calling a local radio station for information?"

In the first example, the first word of the sentence is capitalized. In the second, the first word of the direct quotation is also capitalized. Notice that both *Maybe* and *How* are capitalized in the third example because each word begins a new sentence in the quote. In the fourth example, only *There* is capitalized. *Or* continues the quotation, but it does not start a new sentence.

When you write the greeting and closing of a letter, always begin the first word with a capital letter.

> **D**ear Bill,   **Y**our friend,
> **D**ear Dr. Wade: **S**incerely,
> **D**ear Uncle Ted,   **V**ery truly yours,

Dear is capitalized in the greeting because it is the first word. *Your*, *Sincerely*, and *Very* are capitalized because they are the first words of the closings.

Exercise A
Underline the words that should be capitalized in each of the following.

1. dear aunt nell,

2. thank you for the birthday present.

3. when she saw it, my mom said, "what a beautiful bracelet!"

4. "aren't you lucky," Dad kidded me, "to have a rich relative?"

5. are you coming for a visit soon?

6. gratefully yours,

Exercise B
Decide whether the items on the next page are capitalized correctly or incorrectly. Write *Correct* or *Incorrect* for each. If an item is incorrect, rewrite it correctly.

Example: dear fred,
Answer: Incorrect   Dear Fred,

1. Dear bonnie, _____

2. it is snowing hard here. _____

3. school is closed today _____

4. Please write soon. _____

5. Sincerely, _____

6. Dear Barbara, _____

7. here is a surprise. _____

8. I know you like cats._____

9. have a happy birthday! _____

10. Yours truly, _____

Exercise C

Rewrite the following, inserting capital letters where necessary.

Example: the case was solved with the help of a letter.
Answer: The case was solved with the help of a letter.

1. we waited for the inspector. the atmosphere was tense. soon the inspector arrived.

   _____

2. he said, "the case is over. we have found the thief."

   _____

3. "it's not me," Harry said.

   _____

4. "relax, Harry," the inspector said, "because you're innocent."

   _____

5. the inspector had a note. everyone listened eagerly.

   _____

6. "dear Sir," he read. "max stole the jewels. he buried them in the yard. sincerely yours, Pat the Rat."

   _____

7. "impossible!" Kay cried. "my dog is a good dog and is not a thief. the thief wrote that!"

   _____

Lesson 73

Capitalizing Proper Nouns and Adjectives

Capitalize all proper nouns and all adjectives formed from proper nouns.

A **proper noun** names a particular person, place, or thing. Proper nouns fall into many categories. They may name geographical areas, historic events, companies, organizations, and other persons, places, or things.

The list that follows shows the kinds of proper nouns to capitalize.

people: Jackie Robinson
initials: L. J. Bell
streets, roads: Linden Road
cities: Chicago, Madison
states: Texas, Vermont
countries: Japan, India
continents: Australia, Asia
counties: Lake County
areas, regions: South Pole, the Far East, Midwest
months, days: June, Monday
holidays: Memorial Day
schools: Sullivan High School
organizations: Board of Trade
documents: Bill of Rights

companies: Barbury Company
buildings: World Trade Center
government bodies: State Department, Congress
institutions: Booth Hospital
monuments: Lincoln Memorial
relatives: Uncle Steve
languages: English, Polish
planets: Saturn, Venus
geographical features: Gulf of Mexico, Mt. McKinley
events: World Series
periods of time: Ice Age
product names: Lemon Fizz
brand names: Washton soap

Proper nouns may consist of one word or several words. All important words in a proper noun are capitalized.

Notice the difference between product names and brand names, the last two items on the list. *Lemon Fizz* is a specific name made up and given to a product, so all the words in it are capitalized. In *Washton soap*, however, only *Washton* is the brand name, so only *Washton* is capitalized.

Here are some nouns that are not capitalized:

- the names of the seasons—*fall*, *winter*, *spring*, *summer*
- the words *north*, *south*, *east*, *west* when they refer to compass directions rather than regions of a country

A **proper adjective** is an adjective formed from a proper noun. Like a proper noun, a proper adjective begins with a capital letter. Some proper adjectives consist of more than one word. Study the following chart.

Proper Noun	Proper Adjective + Noun
Italy	**Italian** pastry
Congress	**Congressional** committee
Puerto Rico	**Puerto Rican** sunset
Midwest	**Midwestern** steak
Canada	**Canadian** mountains
Spain	**Spanish** music

You will notice that proper adjectives may have endings that differ from the noun endings. Use a dictionary to be sure that you correctly spell a proper adjective.

Exercise A

Rewrite the sentences. Capitalize all proper nouns and initials.

Example: Settlers followed the oregon trail almost to the pacific.
Answer: Settlers followed the Oregon Trail almost to the Pacific.

1. Before lewis and clark, no one knew much about the west.

_____

2. Many thought there was a great desert west of missouri.

_____

3. oregon was still british, but yankees yearned to settle it.

_____

4. st. joseph and independence were popular start-off cities.

_____

5. hiram sloane joined a wagon train in early spring.

_____

6. The plan was to cross the cascade mountains before winter.

_____

7. The party skirted the missouri river and headed northwest.

_____

8. It followed the valley of the platte river to the rockies.

_____

9. It passed through areas that are now nebraska and colorado.

_____

10. In early october, the party finally got through south pass.

_____

Exercise B

Rewrite the sentences, capitalizing all proper nouns, initials, and proper adjectives.

1. chris johnson and I went with jason.

_____

2. We stayed at the drake hotel near pennsylvania avenue.

_____

3. We toured the white house on wednesday.

_____

4. A white house guard told us to visit the jefferson memorial.

_____

5. We met roger j. collins from the house of representatives.

_____

6. We visited both the british and french embassies.

_____

7. In the evening we took a boat ride on the potomac river and went through the georgetown channel.

_____

8. There was a group of swedish tourists on our bus trip to mount vernon, george washington's home.

_____

9. chris got acquainted with them because he knows some swedish.

_____

10. We also went to gettysburg, pennsylvania.

_____

11. That's where abraham lincoln made his famous address during the civil war.

_____

12. In jamestown, virginia, we saw a replica of fort james.

_____

13. jamestown was settled by englishmen led by john smith.

_____

14. Before going home, we visited aunt dora in richmond.

_____

15. aunt dora teaches at jefferson high school there.

_____

Lesson 74
Capitalizing Titles

Capitalize the first, last, and every important word in a title.

When you write a title, capitalize the first word, the last word, and every word that is important. Study the following examples.

book: *The Adventures of Sherlock Holmes*   **song:** "Home on the Range"
story: "A Day in May"   **play:** *The Miracle Worker*
poem: "To a Skylark"   **film:** *Jurassic Park*
magazine: *Science World*   **TV Series:** *Sesame Street*
newspaper: *The Taos Post*   **work of art:** *Mona Lisa*
          article: "Rhythmic Gymnastics"

Note the book title *The Adventures of Sherlock Holmes*. *The* is capitalized because it is the first word of the title, but *of* is not capitalized because it is not an important word. Do not capitalize *a, an, and, of, in, on, to,* and *the* unless they are the first or last word in a title.

Notice that the titles of whole words, such as books, magazines, newspapers, plays, films, TV series, or works of art, are printed in italics. When you write one of these titles, underline it. Use quotation marks when writing the title of a story, poem, song, or article.

Begin a title with a capital letter when it is used with a person's name. Study these examples.

Ms. Ellen Murphy   **O**fficer Blake   **P**rince Rainer
Dr. Maria Rivera   **R**everend Thomas   **C**aptain Cook
Mr. Henry C. Fein   **G**overnor Meyers   **G**eneral Washington

When a title is used in place of a full name, capitalize the title.

Good morning, **M**ayor.   How are you, **D**octor?

Exercise A

Capitalize the following titles. Remember to underline italicized titles.

> **Example:** *giants in the earth*
> **Answer:** <u>Giants in the Earth</u>

1. "a dinner at poplar walk"

   _____

2. *julie of the wolves*

   _____

3. *oliver twist*

   _____

4. *the old curiosity shop*

   _____

5. "the three sailors"

   _____

6. *a christmas carol*

   _____

7. "a day in the sun"

   _____

8. *great expectations*

   _____

9. *a tale of two cities*

_____

10. "the lady, or the tiger?"

_____

Exercise B

Capitalize the titles of plays and the names of people. Underline italicized titles.

Example: *death of a salesman*   **Answer:** <u>Death of a Salesman</u>

1. *the queen of hearts*

_____

4. mrs. mary todd lincoln

_____

2. king leopold

_____

5. general robert e. lee

_____

3. sir isaac newton

_____

6. commodore oliver h. perry

_____

Exercise C

Rewrite the sentences. Capitalize the necessary words.

Example: peggy mann wrote *the street of the flower boxes*.
Answer: Peggy Mann wrote *The Street of the Flower Boxes*.

1. mayor bailey met with governor frey to discuss the bus strike.

_____

2. officer patricia cabot was awarded a medal for bravery.

_____

3. dr. robert conklin proved that chimpanzees can communicate.

_____

4. *never a dull moment* is hailed as the year's best film.

_____

5. The TV play *children of tomorrow* will be shown next week.

_____

6. The poem "my father is a simple man" is one of my favorites.

_____

7. Millions of people watched the weddings of prince charles and prince andrew.

_____

VOCABULARY ANSWER KEY

Lesson 1

The Value of Context

EXERCISE A

1. smaller
2. lives
3. dollars
4. disasters
5. law
6. spills
7. life
8. winter
9. navigate; guide
10. storms

EXERCISE B

1. k.
2. p.
3. f.
4. n.
5. l.
6. j.
7. m.
8. q.
9. e.
10. d.
11. c.
12. a.
13. i.
14. o.
15. h.

Lesson 2

Context and Multiple Meanings

EXERCISE A

1. d.
2. a.
3. b.
4. f.
5. e.

EXERCISE B

1. l.
2. h.
3. g.
4. i.
5. a.
6. b.
7. k.
8. c.
9. d.
10. n.
11. o.
12. j.
13. e.
14. f.
15. m.

EXERCISE C

1. hue, tint
2. total
3. solid, sturdy
4. client
5. consistent

Lesson 3

Context and Unfamiliar Words

EXERCISE A

1. small boat
2. huddled
3. They would need food and shelter from the weather; personality conflicts.

EXERCISE B

1. a.
2. a.
3. c.
4. b.
5. b.

Lesson 4

Direct and Indirect Context Clues

EXERCISE

1. direct; animals with backbones
2. direct; creatures living both in water and on land
3. direct; thriving in many parts of the world
4. indirect; a large fish net
5. indirect; dwellers, inhabitants
6. indirect; good to eat, eatable
7. indirect; hunters, killers

Lesson 5

More Indirect Context Clues

EXERCISE

1. c.
2. b.
3. c.
4. b.
5. a.
6. c.
7. b.

Lesson 6

Common Sense and Context

EXERCISE

1. D
2. A
3. C
4. B
5. C

Lesson 7

Recognizing Word Structure

EXERCICE

1. y
2. er
3. ite
4. tri
5. extra
6. every
7. inter; al
8. fire; er
9. out; ing
10. Answers will vary.

Lesson 8

Compound Words

EXERCICE A

1. Time-honored, bright-eyed
2. Ringmaster, loudspeaker, bandleader, spotlights, gentlemen
3. Big Top, brigadier general

EXERCICE B

1. sunlight—light from the sun
2. Bareback—without a saddle
3. breakneck—very fast
4. handstands—to balance upside down on hands
5. high-stepping—raise legs up; prance
6. overhead—up above one's head; high
7. earrings—rings worn in ears
8. cannonball—ball from a cannon

EXERCICE C

Answers will vary. Accept compound words that are written as one word, written as two words, or connected by a hyphen.

Lesson 9

Recognizing Root Words

EXERCICE A

1. unfriendly
2. befriend
3. friendless
4. friendship
5. friendly

EXERCICE B

cream
pride
muscle
age
turn

EXERCICE C

1. prewash
2. statement
3. darkness
4. greatly
5. tasteful
6. sheepish
7. airless
8. deface
9. nonsense
10. reread
11. singable
12. semicircle
13. subway
14. management
15. basically

EXERCICE D

1. development
   redevelop
   overdevelop
   developmental
   underdevelop
   developable
2. discolor
   colorless
   bicolor
   colorfully
   discoloration
   colorful
3. actor
   reaction
   interact
   activist
   transaction
   inactive
4. payable
   payment
   prepay
   nonpayment
   payless
   repay

Lesson 10

Root Words with Spelling Changes

EXERCICE A

1. memory
2. happy
3. activity
4. hurry
5. busy
6. whistle
7. dive
8. swim
9. fog
10. leaf
11. paddle
12. grab
13. pierce
14. scramble
15. grin
16. fury
17. fun
18. crazy

EXERCICE B

1. baggy — final consonant doubled
2. merriest — y changed to i
3. worrier — y changed to i
4. calves — f changed to v

5.	having	final e dropped
6.	leaving	final e dropped
7.	funniest	y changed to i
8.	imaginable	final e dropped
9.	shelves	f changed to v
10.	leggy	final consonant doubled

Lesson 11
Using Prefixes
EXERCISE A

<u>re</u>cover   <u>mis</u>behave   <u>ad</u>verb

<u>sub</u>soil   <u>super</u>market   <u>anti</u>freeze

<u>un</u>happy   <u>in</u>correct   <u>pre</u>heat

<u>ab</u>normal   <u>inter</u>city   <u>post</u>war

<u>de</u>bug   <u>under</u>ground   <u>re</u>make

EXERCISE B
1. reappear
2. pregame
3. overpaid
4. inflated
5. vice-president

EXERCISE C
1. superpower; super-
2. outgrow; out-
3. redecorate; re-
4. imprint; im-
5. misfire; mis-

Lesson 12
Negative Prefixes
EXERCISE A
1. un-, mis-, non-
2. not   *unpleasant*
    without   *nonstop*
    badly   *mismatched*

EXERCISE B
1. ir-; not, without
2. non-; not
3. il-; not, without
4. im-; not, lack of
5. dis-; not, opposite of

EXERCISE C
1. impossible
2. incorrect
3. illegal
4. irregular
5. dislike

Lesson 13
Prefixes with Several Meanings
EXERCISE A
1. A, C
2. B, D
3. F
4. E, G

EXERCISE B
1. upon
2. not
3. not
4. not
5. opposite of
6. not
7. into
8. in
9. not
10. reverse

Lesson 14
Using Suffixes
EXERCISE A
1. fish<u>ing</u> equip<u>ment</u>; wood<u>en</u>; not<u>ed</u>; differ<u>ent</u>; bright<u>ness</u>; thank<u>ful</u>; sun<u>ny</u>; clear<u>ly</u> predict<u>able</u>
2. end

EXERCISE B
1. excite; -ment
2. previous; -ly
3. construct; -ion
4. pink; -ish
5. luck; -y

EXERCISE C
1. barely breathing, pulled; -ly, -ing, -ed
2. unfriendly, tired; -ly, -ed
3. teacher, diver; -er, -er
4. going, hiking; -ing, -ing
5. finalist, performances; -ist, -es
6. assignment, finally; -ment, -ly
7. Going, passed, working; -ing, -ed, -ing
8. joyful, celebration; -ful, -tion
9. approaching, retirement; -ing, -ment
10. driver, working; -er, -ing

READING ANSWER KEY

Lesson 1
Reading for Different Purposes
EXERCISE A
1. just the headlines; yes
2. What are the five parts of a cell? How are cells and tissues related?

EXERCISE B
1. Everyone seems to be saying how lonely the city is.
2. talking, laughing, staring
3. She is not afraid.
4. gentleness
5. carefully

Lesson 2
Helps for Setting Purpose
EXERCISE
1. Answers will vary.
2. Answers will vary.
3. Answers will vary.

Lesson 3
Adjusting to Structure
EXERCISE A
Students should check paragraph B.
1. A
2. B
3. A

EXERCISE B
1. c.
2. a.
3. b.
4. freedom
5. to read
6. There were none for black people.
7. founded a school for black girls; advisor to Roosevelt, etc.

EXERCISE C
8. Answers will vary; Victoria Woodhull
9. Victoria Woodhull
10. Victoria Woodhull

Lesson 4
Using Patterns to Help You Read
EXERCISE A
1. cause-effect
2. time order
3. listing
4. comparison-contrast
5. comparison-contrast
6. cause-effect
7. time order

EXERCISE B
1. listing
2. comparison-contrast
3. time order
4. cause-effect
5. cause-effect
6. comparison-contrast

Lesson 5
More About Patterns
EXERCISE A
1. By giving the date 5500 B.C.
2. listing
3. Flooding assured a rich harvest; cause-effect.
4. Rainwater from the monsoons flowed into tributaries of the Nile; cause-effect.
5. listing
6. other lands; comparison-contrast

EXERCISE B
1. however
2. listing
3. time order
4. listing
5. Hunters killed too many of them.

Lesson 6
Surveys to Guide Your Study
EXERCISE
1. Maria Tallchief
2. Answers will vary.
3. slow or normal
4. listing; time order
5. the leading female dancer of a ballet company
6. dancing in the Chopin Concerto

Lesson 7
Putting Your Reading Skills to Work
EXERCISE
1. in an ancient Mayan city
2. life-size
3. The Mitchell-Hedges skull with other Mayan skulls made of clay, wood, bone, and crystal.
4. Unusual noises; things scattered all over; causes deaths; changes its appearance; strange odor; observers experience tightness of muscles and rise in pulse and blood pressure.
5. The people who made it had a sophisticated understanding of physics.

Lesson 8
What Is Imagery?
EXERCISE
1. wild horses running free; sleek-bodied horses stampeded
2. untamed
3. stampeded
4. siren
5. stallions traveling in bands with their mares and colts
6. the words "modern ranching methods"
7. a corral disguised by sagebrush
8. Answers will vary.

Lesson 9
Recognizing Imagery
EXERCISE A
1. sound, sight, feeling
2. smell, sight
3. sight
4. taste, sound
5. feeling

EXERCISE B
1. a.
2. b.
3. b.
4. a.
5. a.

EXERCISE C
huddled closer to what was left of the fire
the dying light of the campfire
black bean soup
gulped it down in thick spoonfuls without water
smeared with insect repellent
crackle of a fire
Some large creature was rustling through the bushes.
a beaver slapped its tail
screeching
soft murmurs, sighs, scufflings, squeaks
flying squirrels

Lesson 10
Responding to Imagery
EXERCISE A
1. growling, throbbing
2. slim blonde
3. thick with fumes
4. heat, hair, grease mark
5. The starter's flag drops.

EXERCISE B
1. c.
2. c.
3. a.
4. b.
5. b.
6. no; the word "blast"
7. excited, happy
8. Answers will vary. Sample answers may include: grease-smeared clothing; mechanics talking; smell of gasoline, exhaust, rubber tires, heat, nervousness, sweat.

Lesson 11
Visualizing What Happens
EXERCISE A
1. c.
2. d.
3. c.
4. The heat waves rippling above the beach
5.

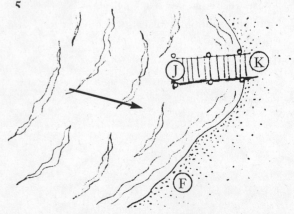

Grade Seven SkillBook, Reading Answer Key

EXERCISE B

1. a.
2. a. T
  b. F
  c. T
  d. T
  e. F
  f. CT
  g. F
  h. T
  i. F
3. Floundering and grasping for help; bobbing
4. Her fear of deep water
5. afraid, frantic, desperate
6. d.

Lesson 12
Reviewing the Use of Imagery
EXERCISE

1. Answers will vary. Sample answers include:
  a. a cap of worn coonskin
  b. door creaked
  c. fire; cooking rabbit
  d. his face and ears burned
2. b.
3. b.
4. c.
5. a. Y
  b. N
  c. Y
  d. Y
  e. Y
  f. Y

Lesson 13
What Is Figurative Language?
EXERCISE A

1. gulps; b.
2. sandpaper; c.
3. nervous as a racehorse; b.
4. she pulls herself into her shell; a.

EXERCISE B

1. a.
2. b.
3. b.
4. a.
5. b.

Lesson 14
Making Sense of Figurative Language
EXERCISE A

1. A toaster and a dragon
2. the coils of the toaster glowing red
3. They pop up
4. Answers will vary.

EXERCISE B

1. b.
2. a.
3. a.
4. c.
5. b.

EXERCISE C

1. white
2. No; very soft
3. That it could jump with a lot of strength; its legs are very strong.
4. The cat has physical qualities of royalty—it looks and moves like a king, a god.
5. Long and graceful, part of it straight, but the end curved in an arc

EXERCISE D

The <u>gold,</u> the <u>iron,</u> the <u>waterfall,</u>
The <u>nut,</u> the <u>peach, apple, granite</u>

Lesson 15
Figurative Language in Literature
EXERCISE

1. Answers will vary.
2. b.
3. A diatom is so small that a pan of water is as large as an ocean in comparison.
4. Literal: An idea suddenly occurred to her.
  Figurative: (accept expression that conveys same meaning.)
5. Answers will vary. Accept any that include idea they're impossible to see except under special conditions.

Lesson 16
Reviewing Figurative Language
EXERCISE

1. He tires her out until she's ready to collapse. He "kills" her.

2. figurative. He thinks Jacky's use of the golf ball is funny, that the little boy's actions are "cute."

3. He's a real killer.

4. No; his golf ball. Both torpedo and gold ball are hurled at a target and meant as weapons.

5. No. The hot-pink might refer to her swimsuit or tanned burned skin. She looks part-girl, part-fish as she rises up.

Lesson 17
Making Inferences
EXERCISE A

1. no

2. Afraid, nervous, concerned, troubled

3. frowning deeply; jumped slightly; grabbed the back of a chair; But still she stood

4. leave by the kitchen door

5. walked quickly across the room toward the door to the kitchen and to the back stairs; glanced toward the kitchen door

EXERCISE B

1. She did not do well.

2. The tire is bad. The friend doesn't know much about tires.

3. The tryout went well.

4. The movie was sad.

5. She is a substitute teacher.

Lesson 18
Identifying Clues
EXERCISE A

1. Whoever murdered him was looking for something.

2. No. The body was lying face down.

3. The carnation or the canister

4. in the flour canister because he was holding it— an innocent person wouldn't know Hugh wore a flower.

5. That Mimms was involved in the murder

EXERCISE B

1. yes

2. rapidly; dashed across the street; skipped; ran up

3. A letter she received

4. happy

5. Grinning broadly; jumped up and down

Lesson 19
Inferences About People
EXERCISE A

1. folded her arms

2. no expression at all

3. suddenly sat up straight

4. looked directly at her father

5. her actions

EXERCISE B

1. b.

2. c.

3. a.

4. No; her statement "I bet it wouldn't," and her belief that Brady will hear "harsh words later."

5. What the characters say

Lesson 20
Inferring Time and Place
EXERCISE A

1. July 10, 1875. In the middle of the afternoon

2. Main Street in Santa Fe

3. Another planet

4. planetary government; Boskavel, the capital slight excess of orange; softly on six heavily clawed feet; big overlapping plates covering its body made it look like a reptile; an ambassador from Earth learns to expect surprises on any new world

5. The future

6. The existence of a planetary government; an ambassador from Earth to another planet; the laser gun

EXERCISE B

1. b.

2. d.

3. a ship, the Atlantic Ocean

4. leaving Ireland; take Maureen and the boys to America; the *Star* pitched forward and Maureen gripped the sides of the bunk; on the deck overhead; into the hold; topside

5. Before the 1950s

6. On a mountain

7. high above them; He tied one end around Joby's waist and wrapped the other end around his own hand; they were still tied together; high on the slope above; "Avalanche!"

Lesson 21

Reviewing Inferences

EXERCISE

1. b.   6. c.
2. b.   7. c.
3. a.   8. b.
4. a.   9. b.
5. a.   10. a.

Lesson 22

Finding the Main Idea

EXERCISE A

1. c.
2. a.

EXERCISE B

1. c.
2. a.
3. b. and c.

Lesson 23

Direct Statement of Main Idea

EXERCISE A

1. d.
2. a.

EXERCISE B

1. c.
2. The M.G. TC is the car that started the sports-car revolution in the United States.

EXERCISE C

Not only does it seem that everybody is juggling these days, they seem to be tossing around just about anything you can imagine.

Lesson 24

Implied Main Idea

EXERCISE A

1. c.
2. d.

EXERCISE B

1. c.
2. b.

EXERCISE C

a.

Lesson 25

Reviewing Main Idea

EXERCISE

1. "Detective" or secret cameras
2. If a male spy set out on a mission armed with every type of sneaky camera that has come out in the last one hundred years, he'd be clicking from head to toe.
3. c.
4. The detective cameras—designed with tiny plates and often circular images—were indeed popular.
5. But many of these detective cameras were not quite as sneaky as they might appear.
6. a.

Lesson 26

What Are Judgments?

EXERCISE A

1. The Grapplers will win the football game.
2. He looked at the strengths and weaknesses of both teams and decided which was stronger.
3. experienced quarterback, leading runner, better defense, home fields
4. a better kicker
5. yes

EXERCISE B

1. good
2. bad
3. good
4. bad
5. bad

Lesson 27

Fact and Opinion

EXERCISE

1. F   6. O
2. F   7. F
3. O   8. F
4. F   9. O
5. F   10. O

Lesson 28

Mixed Statements

EXERCISE

1. F
2. M *Pinocchio* cost 2.8 million dollars to make,

which was a great deal of money to spend on
a motion picture in those days.

3. F
4. O
5. F
6. F
7. M For the *Fox and the Hound*, which is one of the
best Disney films, the artist used his own pet
fox for a model.
8. M Disney artists also act out the movements of
animals, even though they look foolish to
studio visitors.
9. F
10. O

Lesson 29

Valid Opinions

EXERCISE A
A.
1. O
2. F
3. F
4. F
5. valid
B.
1. F
2. O
3. O
4. F
5. valid

EXERCISE B
1. d.
2. b.
3. a.
4. c.
5. e.

EXERCISE C
1. no authority
2. X   authority
3. personal interest
4. X   authority
5. X   authority
6. no authority, no facts
7. X   authority, fact
8. no authority, no facts
9. X   authority
10. personal interest
11. X   authority

12. personal interest
13. no authority, no facts
14. X   authority
15. no authority
16. personal interest
17. X   authority
18. no authority

Lesson 30

Emotional Effect of Words

EXERCISE A
1. b.
2. a.
3. b.
4. b.
5. a.
6. b.
7. a.
8. a.
9. b.
10. b.

EXERCISE B

Negative effect: terrible, frightening; Screaming,
cursing; invaded; spoiled brats
sneaked; stuffed their bellies; shout
me down; nerve; tyrant; tyrants; deny
me

Positive effect: lovely; dear family; loyal friends;
honor; fair-minded; freedom of
speech

WRITING ANSWER KEY

Lesson 1

Main Idea in a Paragraph

EXERCISE A

1. at the end, as a conclusion
2. He is bold in leaping on the table and seems to enjoy the fracas. A broom is needed to drive him out.

EXERCISE B

   Jody clung to the fence. He was numb. He could neither feel nor think. Flag scented him, lifted his head, and came bounding to him. Jody climbed down into the yard. He did not want to see him. As he stood, Flag cleared, as lightly as a mockingbird in flight, the high fence on which he had labored. Jody turned his back on him and went into the house. He went to his room and threw himself on his bed and buried his face in his pillow.

1. **b.** Jody was shocked and upset by Flag's behavior.
2. **c.** Answers may include details underlined in paragraph.

EXERCISE C

The main idea is underlined once; supporting details twice.

1. Melissa wanted to prove that she could do her share on the camping trip with her dad. She rushed to unpack the tent and camping gear while her dad removed stones from their site. She helped put up the tent and set out the necessary items for dinner. Melissa then insisted that she do all the cooking as well as build the fire. After sunset she even contributed a number of scary stories as they sat by the dying fire.
2. Beth and Luisa first met in kindergarten. During fourth grade they joined Girl Scouts and did projects together. In the fifth grade, they both started guitar lessons. Last year they had fun in the park-district softball program. Now, in seventh grade, they are taking swimming lessons together.
   Main Idea: Beth and Luisa have shared activities for many years.

Lesson 2

Topic Sentences

EXERCISE A

1. first
2. third
3. second

EXERCISE B

1. In spring, the marsh echoed with the cries of wild birds.
2. On that misty morning, the lake was quiet.
3. The pond seemed empty of life until we looked closely.

EXERCISE C

1. middle
2. Sight: lightning, lamplight flickering: smell: dank odor; sound: rain lashing down, great weather raging.

Lesson 3

Writing a Narrative Paragraph

EXERCISE A

1. At first, then
2. Papa, Roberto, and the narrator are packing up the car.

EXERCISE B

Answers may include the words and phrases shown.

1. Next
2. then
3. after
4. At first
5. then
6. Meanwhile
7. Finally

EXERCISE C

Paragraphs will vary slightly, but should follow the correct sequence.

4. After a while, Noni neared home, dragging the sled.
6. Even before he arrived, he could hear the sled dogs barking.
2. Then, as Noni came close to the cabin he panicked.
5. Smoke was coming from a side window near the stove.
1. Immediately he rushed past the dogs and stormed into the cabin.
7. Then he ripped flaming curtains from the wall.
3. At last, he rushed out the front door with them, flinging them into the snow.

Lesson 4

Conflict in Story Plots

EXERCISE A

1. See first sentence of summary.
2. Answers will vary.

3. conflict between character and outside force
4. See last sentence of summary.
5. See last sentence of summary.
6. They are going to move.

EXERCISE B
Summaries will vary but should identify the plot's conflict, climax, and resolution.

EXERCISE C
The conclusions of the plot summaries will vary, but students should address the questions suggested in the text.

Lesson 5
Characters and Dialogue
EXERCISE A
Suggested responses are given.
1. Thoughtful; he is a serious boy.
2. He lets the older boy think and talk for them both.
3. He introduces himself, sometimes sneaks into movies, and chooses a trip to the zoo over a day in a movie theater.

EXERCISE B
Descriptions will vary.

Lesson 6
Classifying
EXERCISE A
1. sight
2. sound, taste, sight
3. Answers will vary.
4. touch, smell
   Details will vary.

EXERCISE B
1. broccoli
2. Utah
3. poverty
4. tulip
5. glasses
6. cat
7. calm
8. walk
9. teeth
10. break

EXERCISE C
1. emotions
2. languages
3. sounds
4. hand parts
5. games you play with a ball
6. bodies of water
7. tastes
8. literature, written words
9. objects in sky
10. "ent" rhyming words

Lesson 7
Arranging Details in Spatial Order
EXERCISE A
1. As far along the coast as the eye could see
2. toward the shore, up and down the edge, in the distance
3. far to near

EXERCISE B
1. into, closer, below, farther down, submerged, straight ahead
2. top to bottom
3. into, closer, below, farther down, straight ahead

EXERCISE C
Paragraphs will vary but should include spatial-order words.

Lesson 8
Writing a Descriptive Paragraph
EXERCISE A
1. sight
2. Answers will vary.
3. top to bottom

EXERCISE B
Details will vary.

EXERCISE C
Details will vary but should follow the guidelines provided.

EXERCISE D
Paragraphs will vary but should include the points in the checklist.

Lesson 9
Comparing and Contrasting
EXERCISE A
1. long, round
2. wings
3. contrast

EXERCISE B
Suggested answers are provided.

	Shape		Stage of Life Cycle
Caterpillar	long, round, many legs		
Butterfly	long, skinny, wings		adult

EXERCISE C

Sentences will vary but should use words and phrases that compare and contrast.

Lesson 10

Writing a Comparison/Contrast Description

EXERCISE A

1. ballet dancers and football players
2. Comparison: see 2nd-6th sentences; contrasts: other sentences.
3. Comparison: both, likewise, same, as
   Contrast: differ, however, differently, in contrast
4. point-by-point comparison; then contrast

EXERCISE B

- has porch roof to block sun **P**
- lets you see front sidewalk **P**
- private place in backyard **D**
- family gathering place **D, P**
- place to sit and talk **D, P**
- no porch roof to block sun **D**
- lets you see backyard **D**
- attached to or near house **D, P**

EXERCISE C

Answers will vary but students should write at least six similarities and/or differences.

EXERCISE D

Paragraphs will vary but should include the elements of comparison and contrast.

Lesson 11

Transitions in Paragraphs

EXERCISE A

1. then, First, Next, Finally
2. Because of; next to
3. More than; For example

EXERCISE B

1. The doctor looked at the X-ray and still felt uncertain about Tony's injuries. <u>Because of</u> his uncertainty, Tony's doctor ordered more tests and X-rays. <u>As a result,</u> severe injuries were found. <u>It was evident</u> that Tony needed an operation.
2. Planning your route for a long trip is a good investment of time. <u>First,</u> buy a good, up-to-date map. <u>Then,</u> mark your starting point and your end point. <u>Finally,</u> with a brightly colored marker, trace the route you prefer. Whether you choose the scenic drive or the most direct route, your preparation will result in a more pleasant trip.

3. The road sign was a real surprise. <u>Above</u> the cornfield it loomed, bright blue and tall. <u>On</u> the metal rectangular face were printed the words: Enter at your own risk. <u>Under</u> the sign we saw rows of corn that extended to the horizon. Perhaps, we thought, the sign was meant to be a joke.

Lesson 12

Writing an Explanatory Paragraph

EXERCISE A

1. ravens' intelligence
2. drops shellfish from air to break them open; work in pairs to take food from cat
3. Answers are underlined.

   Ravens are known for their intelligence <u>as well as</u> for their playfulness. <u>While</u> most other birds act mainly by instinct, ravens show curiosity, learn quickly from experience, and even use this experience to solve problems in new situations. <u>For example</u>, after watching its parents, a young raven puts nearly everything new into its mouth to find out if it's edible. <u>But later</u> it learns many different food-gathering skills. <u>Like</u> gulls, it drops shellfish from high in the air to break them open. A scientist observed one pair of ravens working together to take food from a cat. <u>While</u> one bird swooped low to make the cat drop the mouse it had caught, the second bird grabbed the dinner. This was not habit or instinct on the ravens' part— the birds had figured out how to solve a problem.
   —*from* **"One Smart Bird"** by Katherine Hauth

EXERCISE B

Words and phrases are underlined.

To most people, bees seem to fly aimlessly from place to place. <u>However,</u> to other bees, the pattern and speed of their flight communicate very important information. <u>For example,</u> to tell other bees that food is within a hundred yards of the hive, a scout bee will fly in a circle. <u>On the other hand,</u> if the food is farther away, the bee will move in a figure-eight formation. <u>In addition</u> to telling the distance to the food, the scout will cross from one loop of the figure eight to the other to indicate the direction of the food. The speed with which the bee flies also tells the distance to the food. <u>As a result,</u> if a bee sees another bee flying very fast in a circle, it knows that food is very close.

EXERCISE C

Completion of activities will vary.

EXERCISE D

Paragraphs will vary but should follow the guidelines in the checklist.

Lesson 13

Cause and Effect

A; Overeating and the flu

B; headache, sunburn

EXERCISE A

Causes are underlined once; effects, twice.

1. Jake broke his leg; therefore, he couldn't play in the game and had to use crutches to walk.
2. As a result of last night's power shortage, we ate a cold dinner by candlelight.
3. Jane forgot to put the top on the grasshopper's box; consequently, the insect escaped.
4. Since it has not rained in several days and because it has been cold, the new seedlings have died.
5. Joe's dad left his car's headlights on last night; hence, the car won't start.
6. The farmland meant everything to the Hutchisons because it had been in the family for generations.
7. Rosemary overslept this morning, and as a result, she didn't have time to eat breakfast and was late for work.

EXERCISE B

1. the Mongol conquest
2. See last three sentences in paragraph.

Lesson 14

Writing a Cause-Effect Paragraph

EXERCISE A

Presenting information in a graph is an effective way to help people understand information. When, for example, you put data you have collected as part of a science project into graph form, people notice and remember what you did. A colorful, clear graph makes people pay attention and, as a result, helps them understand your research.

EXERCISE B

Answers are underlined.

Our school needs more plants. First, plants are beautiful to look at; consequently, the school would be a more visually pleasing place. Their presence would encourage student attendance. Finally, all plants could be labeled and presented with descriptions and care instructions. As a result, they would have educational value. Plants would be appreciated by our eyes, noses, and brains.

EXERCISE C

Answers will vary.

EXERCISE D

Paragraphs will vary but include the points given in the checklist.

Lesson 15

Writing a Persuasive Paragraph

EXERCISE A

Topic sentences will vary.

EXERCISE B

Reasons will vary.

EXERCISE C

Paragraphs will vary.

Lesson 16

Writing a Summary Paragraph

EXERCISE A

1. Patience and virtue are rewarded.
2. No, although some individual words and phrases can be questioned.

EXERCISE B

(A) Tom's father tries to persuade his son to go to the farm so that he and Tom's mother can take a trip to Europe. One thing Tom's father mentions is that Tom will be able to go swimming each day. Tom resists his father's reasoning. Finally, Tom's father recalls a time that Tom's mother sacrificed a trip because Tom got sick. If Tom doesn't go to the farm, he could ruin this trip for his mother because she would worry about him.

(B) First, Tom's father tells his son there's a pond at the farm. He says that Tom can go swimming every day. Tom reminds his father that he isn't much of a swimmer. Then Tom's father says that Tom can learn. He also says that two months on a farm could make a mental and physical difference in Tom. Tom responds that he likes the way he is and continues working on his model. Tom's father asks him to put the model down. Finally, Tom's father says that this trip means a lot to his mother. He reminds Toms that she didn't go to the Smokies, stayed home, nursed Tom when he got the measles, and never complained. Tom's father wants her to go to Europe and see everything she's wanted to see her whole life. If Tom does not go to the farm, she will worry.

1. A, first sentence
2. second sentence
3. sentences are underlined; A
4. B; Answers will vary

EXERCISE C

Paragraphs will vary.

Lesson 17

Research: Choosing a Topic

EXERCISE A

Narrowed topics will vary.

EXERCISE B

Research questions will vary.

EXERCISE C

Inventories will vary.

Lesson 18

Research: Using Reference Sources

EXERCISE A

1. almanac
2. encyclopedia
3. atlas
4. *Readers' Guide*

EXERCISE B

1. atlas
2. encyclopedia
3. *Readers' Guide*
4. nonprint media
5. book of quotations
6. almanac

Lesson 19

Research: Taking Notes

1. p., +, =
2. Answers will vary.

EXERCISE A

Summaries will vary. Check for correct format.

EXERCISE B

Information will vary.

Lesson 20

Research: Organizing Information

EXERCISE A

The order is problem and solution. Numbers 2–5 can have varying order.

2 **1.** Ban cars entirely from certain areas of the inner city

1 **2.** The problem of noise pollution in large cities

3 **3.** Make laws on auto mufflers stricter

5 **4.** Pass laws against playing portable radios on buses

4 **5.** Move airplane flight paths farther from populated areas

EXERCISE B

Students may be able to justify additional methods.

1. Problem and solution
2. Time order
3. Cause and Effect
4. Order of importance
5. Order of importance
6. Time order
7. Cause and effect
8. Order of importance
9. Cause and effect
10. Order of importance

EXERCISE C

Information will vary. You may want to review students' note cards.

Lesson 21

Research: Outlining

EXERCISE A

Walt Disney

I. Introduction
II. Early life
   A. Born in Chicago
   B. Moved to Missouri when a child
   C. At 16 studied art
   D. Made first cartoons at 19
III. Motion Pictures
   A. Cartoon Characters
      1. Mickey Mouse
      2. Minnie Mouse
      3. Donald Duck
   B. Nature Films
      1. Showed animals in nature
      2. Rare scenes of animal life
IV. Amusement Parks
   A. Disneyland in California
   B. Disney World in Florida
V. Conclusion

EXERCISE B

Outlines will vary. Check for proper format.

GRAMMAR, USAGE, AND MECHANICS ANSWER KEY

Lesson 1
Kinds of Sentences
EXERCISE A

1. imperative	11. declarative
2. exclamatory	12. interrogative
3. declarative	13. exclamatory
4. declarative	14. declarative
5. declarative	15. declarative
6. declarative	16. declarative
7. interrogative	17. declarative
8. exclamatory	18. interrogative
9. declarative	19. declarative
10. declarative	20. imperative

EXERCISE B

1. Soon the town asked for help from outside.
2. Please send some helicopters right away!
3. Do you suppose that worked?
4. The birds scattered at first but returned again, later.
5. Whew, were the townspeople disappointed!
6. The whole town was awakened at sunrise by the birds.
7. What did the people try next?
8. Experts arrived with special loudspeakers.
9. They aimed loud, high-pitched sounds at the birds.
10. How frustrated the people were by yet another failure!
11. Guess what happened next? or!
12. Someone tried playing loud music on very large speakers.
13. It took a while, but it actually worked! *or* .
14. What a happy day it was when the birds left!

Lesson 2

Subjects and Predicates
EXERCISE A

1. It | was made of wood and traveled at only twelve miles per hour.
2. The first double-decker buses | appeared in London in the 1850s.
3. Horses of great size | pulled them on tracks.
4. The first true submarine | was used in 1776.
5. No American President | rode in one until Harry Truman.
6. Alexander Graham Bell | invented the telephone in 1876 yet had originally intended a hearing aid for the deaf.
7. Telephone service from coast to coast | began in 1914.
8. The invention of the radio by Marconi in 1895 | revolutionized communications almost overnight.
9. Boats at sea | could send messages and distress signals.

EXERCISE B

1. Both <u>Greece</u> and <u>Egypt</u> <u>claim</u> credit for its invention.
2. A <u>man</u> from Greece <u>became</u> the first organist.
3. Egyptian <u>inventors</u> further <u>developed</u> the instrument.
4. Their <u>instrument</u> <u>had</u> a keyboard and <u>ran</u> on water power.
5. <u>Historians</u> and <u>researchers</u> <u>have studied</u> the origins of the first pipe organ and <u>have discovered</u> these ancient models.
6. <u>Someone</u> <u>built</u> and <u>played</u> a wind-powered organ in the tenth century.
7. <u>Innovators</u> and <u>musicians</u> <u>produced</u> later improvements.
8. <u>Handel</u> and <u>Bach</u> <u>were</u> great organ composers.
9. <u>Gottfried Silbermann</u> <u>improved</u> the organ's sound and <u>added</u> more voices.

Lesson 3

Sentences with Modifiers
EXERCISE A

1. Two nervous, for the baseball field.
2. wooden, quickly with noisy fans.
3. into pieces from the impact of the bat.
4. in the bleachers, loudly

EXERCISE B

1. A <u>small wooden</u> <u>house</u> <u>on our street</u> was on fire.
2. The <u>electric</u> <u>heater</u> <u>in the living room</u> had exploded.
3. <u>Some flimsy lace</u> <u>curtains</u> had caught fire.
4. An <u>alert</u> <u>neighbor</u> called the police.
5. <u>Ten</u> <u>firefighters</u> <u>from various stations</u> answered the alarm.
6. <u>Deep, blowing</u> <u>snow</u> hindered their job.
7. A <u>large</u> <u>family</u> <u>trapped in the house</u> was saved.
8. <u>Many</u> <u>residents</u> <u>in adjoining houses</u> fled to safety.
9. The <u>terrible</u> <u>fire</u> could have cost many lives.
10. The <u>brave</u> <u>firefighters</u> should receive medals.

EXERCISE C

1. The dirty wet snow <u>melted</u> <u>slowly</u>.
2. Birds <u>chirped</u> <u>noisily in the budding trees</u>.
3. The sun <u>rose</u> <u>earlier on each new morning</u>.
4. People <u>often</u> <u>smiled</u> <u>now</u>.
5. The grass <u>grew</u> <u>quickly</u> <u>in people's yards</u>.
6. Storms <u>sometimes</u> <u>blew</u> <u>in from the west</u>.
7. Trees <u>bent</u> and <u>swayed</u> <u>in the heavy rains</u>.
8. Telephone lines <u>sometimes</u> <u>broke</u>.
9. Schools <u>closed</u> <u>occasionally</u>.
10. On sunny days, children <u>ran</u> <u>outside</u> <u>into the</u> <u>warmth</u> and <u>played</u> <u>excitedly</u>.

Lesson 4
Inverted Order in Sentences
EXERCISE A

1. Near the stream in our pasture stands a huge <u>tree</u>.
2. Have <u>you</u> noticed its golden branches in the springtime?
3. There was <u>mud</u> all around it after the recent heavy rains.
4. Was <u>Tom</u> in the basement during that last storm?

EXERCISE B

1. <u>Is</u> your <u>homework</u> on the desk?
2. <u>Did</u> <u>you</u> <u>get</u> the assignment from Dan?
3. <u>Is</u> <u>it</u> difficult work?
4. <u>Will</u> <u>you</u> <u>help</u> me?
5. <u>Do</u> <u>you</u> <u>want</u> a snack?
6. <u>Are</u> the <u>apples</u> sweet and juicy?
7. <u>Are</u> <u>they</u> <u>studying</u> hard?
8. <u>Can</u> <u>you</u> <u>discuss</u> the assignment?
9. <u>Have</u> <u>you</u> <u>finished</u> already?
10. <u>Have</u> the <u>others</u> <u>left</u>?

EXERCISE C

Subjects are underlined once; verbs, twice.

1. Here <u>is</u> <u>Uncle Chet</u> in his sports car.
2. Here <u>is</u> a birthday <u>present</u>.
3. There <u>are</u> many other great <u>gifts</u> as well.
4. Here <u>is</u> my favorite <u>one</u>.
5. There <u>is</u> my second <u>choice</u>.
6. Here <u>is</u> my new baseball <u>glove</u> from Mom and Dad.
7. There <u>is</u> the <u>baseball</u>.
8. Here <u>is</u> the <u>camera</u>.
9. There <u>are</u> several <u>pictures</u> of the guests.
10. Here <u>is</u> the best <u>one</u>.

EXERCISE D

1. Into the hall <u>went</u> my two <u>cousins</u> with their dog.
2. Under the shade trees <u>sat</u> my <u>aunts</u> and <u>uncles</u>.

3. Above them <u>floated</u> fat, puffy <u>clouds</u>.
4. Beyond the tree <u>flowed</u> the <u>river</u>.
5. Over the rocks <u>gushed</u> cool, clear <u>water</u>.

Lesson 5
Sentence Fragments
EXERCISE A

Answers will vary. Sample answers are provided.

1. Attach the fragment to the sentence it belongs with.
2. Attach the fragment to the sentence it belongs with.
3. Attach the fragment to the sentence it belongs with.
4. Add words.

EXERCISE B

1. They are often feared because they attack people.
2. Most tigers are really shy and avoid contact with people if possible.
3. Tigers sometimes attack people after being cornered.
4. Tigers can live almost anywhere, needing only food and water to survive.
5. They do not run well for long distances.
6. Nowadays tigers are no longer captured for zoos since enough are born in captivity.
7. Some zoos have special areas that are magnificent.

EXERCISE C

Answers for items 2. and 4.-7. will vary. Sample answers are provided.

1. Correct
2. My sister, who knows carpentry, builds her own furniture.
3. Correct
4. For her next project for her class at school, she will build a table.
5. Building a table requires precise measuring and cutting.
6. The table will be a secret surprise for Mom and Dad!
7. The family will be surprised by the creation.

Lesson 6
Run-On Sentences
EXERCISE A

1. Jean is an artist. She paints children's portraits.
2. Jean is an artist, and she paints children's portraits.
3. Jean is an artist; she paints children's portraits.

EXERCISE B

1. Wolfgang Amadeus Mozart was born in Austria. His father was a musician.
2. Mozart never attended school; his father taught him about music.
3. Correct
4. He wrote several operas and forty-one symphonies, and almost all of his works are still performed today.
5. Mozart had severe hardships and disappointments, but his music is cheerful and vigorous.
6. Correct
7. Correct

EXERCISE C

Answers will vary. A sample paragraph is provided.

Rock and roll is a form of contemporary music. It is especially popular among young people. This music grew out of the blues, and it also has its roots in gospel music. Chuck Berry is often considered a founder of rock music; he is a composer and performer. Rock songs often speak about current problems. Some people consider rock to be a way people communicate with each other. There are many rock 'n' roll performers, but Elvis Presley is regarded by some people as the most popular artist ever.

Lesson 7

Appositives

EXERCISE A

(1) My best friend, <u>Linda</u>, always gets lost. (2) Once I was supposed to meet her at Pages, <u>a bookstore in our neighborhood</u>. (3) She was thirty minutes late because she turned onto Grover, <u>the wrong street</u>.

EXERCISE B

1. Chinatown, a part of San Francisco, has about 35,000 people.
2. Some shoppers look for porcelain, a fine china.
3. Grant Avenue, the main street, is filled with Chinese shops.
4. Chinatown is near Union Square, the city's main shopping area.
5. Shoppers can ride a special trolley, the cable car.
6. Some people like squid, a common Chinese seafood.
7. I often eat with chopsticks, a pair of small, slender sticks.
8. Much of the cooking is done in a wok, a special kind of pot.
9. Visitors especially enjoy one holiday, the Chinese New Year.

EXERCISE C

1. Many ties are made of silk, a cloth that originated in China.
2. Lee practices Kung Fu, a form of self-defense.
3. Our friend, Ling, taught us how to make chow mein, a tasty dish made with fried noodles.
4. She stirred in cloud ears, a kind of mushroom, and soy sauce.

Lesson 8

Combining Subjects and Predicates

EXERCISE A

1. The teachers and their students want to organize a band.
2. Cara, Mitch, and Bo write music.
3. Allison and Monty study the clarinet.
4. Lisa and Barbara are late for practice.
5. Robert and Luis set up the chairs and instruments.
6. The oboe and the piano sound lovely.

EXERCISE B

1. These apes eat fruits and also like vegetables.
2. Gorillas eat in the morning and sleep in the afternoon.
3. Gorillas travel in groups and never stay in the same place for more than one night.
4. Group leaders signal the time to awaken and decide the time to rest.
5. Young adults like to wrestle with each other and enjoy playing games.
6. Gorillas live in zoos and perform in circuses.

Lesson 9

Direct Objects and Subject Complements

EXERCISE A

              SC
1. She is a good <u>actress</u>.

                DO
2. The audience applauded <u>her</u>.

              SC
3. She appeared quite <u>young</u>.

EXERCISE B

Subjects and verbs are underlined once; direct objects, twice.

1. Early baseball <u>cards</u> <u>included</u> <u>pictures</u> and <u>names</u> of players.
2. Young <u>hobbyists</u> <u>trade</u> the <u>cards</u> among themselves.

3. Some <u>people</u> <u>file</u> their <u>collections</u> by teams.
4. One <u>collector</u> <u>owned</u> twenty thousand <u>cards</u>.
5. Old <u>cards</u> <u>bring</u> the most <u>money</u>.
6. <u>Mistakes</u> on the cards <u>increase</u> their <u>value</u> tremendously.
7. <u>Collectors</u> <u>love</u> any <u>errors</u> in printing.

EXERCISE C
Subjects and verbs are underlined once; complements, twice.

1. My <u>friend</u> <u>became</u> an <u>expert</u> on monster costumes. PN
2. My friend's <u>talent</u> <u>is</u> <u>rare</u>. PA
3. His <u>creatures</u> <u>grow</u> <u>scarier</u> all the time. PA
4. His elaborate <u>costumes</u> <u>look</u> <u>unearthly</u>. PA
5. Rubber <u>masks</u> <u>are</u> the <u>heads</u>. PN
6. My friend's <u>work</u> <u>appears</u> <u>real</u>. PA
7. <u>He</u> <u>is</u> <u>helpful</u> to people giving parties. PA
8. His dreadful <u>outfits</u> <u>are</u> <u>works</u> of art. PN
9. <u>It</u> <u>is</u> <u>he</u> underneath those fake scars and bandages. PP
10. <u>I</u> <u>feel</u> <u>sure</u> about his future success. PA

Lesson 10
Indirect Objects
EXERCISE A
1. Sam sang a song for us.
√ 2. He sang us a new song.
3. Sam entered his song in a contest.
√ 4. The judge quickly gave Sam an entry.

EXERCISE B
1. The guitarist showed Sam the music.
2. The guitarist hummed the pianist some notes.
3. Ushers found people seats.
4. The ushers could not offer some spectators seats.
5. Other workers gave people programs.
6. Sam gave the leader of the band a nod.
7. Then Sam sang the audience his song.
8. Everyone gave the performance their full attention.
9. The audience gave Sam a big hand.
10. Sam sang the crowd two more songs.

EXERCISE C
Sentence parts are underlined.
1. The <u>whistlers</u>(S) <u>gave</u>(V) the <u>listeners</u>(IO) some <u>surprises</u>(DO).
2. The <u>contest</u>(S) <u>gave</u>(V) <u>everyone</u> (IO) a <u>chance</u>(DO).

3. Different <u>categories</u>(S) <u>offered</u> (V) <u>contestants</u>(IO) many <u>opportunities</u>(DO).
4. Senior <u>citizens</u>(S) <u>taught</u>(V) the <u>youngsters</u>(IO) old <u>tunes</u>(DO).
5. This unusual <u>event</u>(S) <u>brought</u>(V) Carson City(IO) <u>recognition</u>(DO).
6. The <u>judges</u>(S) <u>promised</u>(V) each <u>entrant</u>(IO) an <u>award</u>(DO).

Lesson 11
Simple and Compound Sentences
EXERCISE A
1. C
2. S
3. C

EXERCISE B
Subjects are underlined once; verbs, twice.
1. The <u>ducks</u> and <u>geese</u> <u>flew</u> south. CS
2. Some <u>birds</u> <u>swam</u> or <u>hunted</u> for grain. CV
3. Many <u>flocks</u> <u>landed</u> and <u>ate</u> in a bird refuge. CV
4. Loud <u>honks</u> and <u>quacks</u> <u>filled</u> the air. CS
5. The <u>hunters</u> and bird <u>watchers</u> <u>followed</u> the birds' flight. CS
6. Occasional <u>fog</u> and heavy <u>snow</u> <u>slowed</u> their flying speed. CS
7. The <u>birds</u> <u>glided</u> and <u>drifted</u> on the air currents. CV
8. The <u>weather</u> <u>warmed</u> and <u>mellowed</u> in the south. CV
9. Quiet <u>lakes</u> and active <u>rivers</u> <u>awaited</u> them. CS
10. Familiar <u>sights</u> and <u>sounds</u> <u>welcomed</u> their arrival. CS

EXERCISE C
1. C	6. S	11. C
2. S	7. S	12. S
3. C	8. C	13. S
4. C	9. S	14. C
5. C	10. S	15. S

Lesson 12
Independent Clauses
EXERCISE A
Subjects are underlined once, verbs twice.
1. My <u>book</u> <u>has</u> many pictures, but only the <u>photos</u> <u>are</u> in color.
2. That <u>cat</u> <u>is</u> a Siamese; <u>mine</u> <u>is</u> an Abyssinian.
3. <u>Cats</u> <u>see</u> well in daylight, but their <u>eyes</u> also <u>adjust</u>.

4. Wild <u>cats</u> often <u>hunt</u> at night, but <u>some</u> <u>prefer</u> dusk or dawn.

5. Angora <u>cats</u> <u>have</u> long hair; Siamese <u>cats</u> <u>have</u> short hair.

EXERCISE B

1. <u>Wild cats often hunt at night, but</u> some prefer dusk or dawn.

2. <u>Cats may meow softly, or</u> they may shrill loudly.

3. <u>Grassland leopards are tan with black spots; forest leopards are much darker.</u>

4. <u>Lions live in Africa, but</u> most of them are in national parks.

5. <u>Tigers are good swimmers, and</u> they may cross rivers for food.

6. <u>Most cats can extend their claws, but</u> the cheetah cannot.

7. <u>Domesticated cats do well as house pets, and</u> wild cats fare best in their natural habitats or in zoos.

8. <u>A cat's rough tongue is suited to eating, but</u> it is equally useful for grooming the cat's fur.

9. <u>Most cats have tails, but</u> a Manx cat does not.

10. <u>Angora cats have long hair; Siamese cats have short hair.</u>

11. <u>Tabbies may have stripes, or</u> they may be just black and white.

12. <u>Most cats like catnip, but</u> some do not.

13. <u>Cats purr when happy, but</u> they spit and hiss when angry.

14. <u>A cat's hearing is good, and</u> its sense of smell is excellent.

15. <u>Cats hate baths, but</u> they keep themselves clean.

EXERCISE C

Subjects are underlined once; verbs, twice.

1. Dan's <u>father</u> <u>works</u> at Benton's, and <u>Dan</u> <u>buys</u> his clothes there.

2. His <u>father</u> <u>sells</u> shoes, but <u>he</u> <u>prefers</u> the suit department.

3. <u>Dan</u> <u>may become</u> a salesman, but <u>he</u> <u>likes</u> recreational sports.

4. <u>He</u> <u>admires</u> professional athletes, and <u>he</u> <u>likes</u> most coaches.

5. <u>Dan</u> <u>skis</u> well, and <u>he</u> <u>plays</u> basketball with equal skill.

Lesson 13

Dependent Clauses

EXERCISE A

1. <u>Although she was in charge,</u> she was not bossy.

2. <u>We found the stack of firewood</u> that the ranger had mentioned.

3. <u>My cousin Jan was the one camper</u> who recognized the poison ivy.

EXERCISE B

1. DC	11. SS
2. SS	12. DC
3. SS	13. DC
4. DC	14. SS
5. DC	15. DC
6. SS	16. SS
7. SS	17. DC
8. DC	18. SS
9. SS	19. DC
10. DC	20. SS

EXERCISE C

1. IC
2. DC
3. IC
4. DC
5. IC

Lesson 14

Complex Sentences

EXERCISE A

1. that Ted found in the desk; Before he could examine it; which had been flickering

2. which had been flickering

3. While he searched for his matches

4. after he made several tries

5. Although he searched carefully *or* which had been on the desk

EXERCISE B

Answers will vary.

EXERCISE C

1. <u>Although the tree squirrel is a wonderful acrobat,</u> it sometimes misses its mark.

2. <u>If a squirrel should fall,</u> its tail will fan out and function as a parachute.

3. Some squirrels have a permanent home and a temporary one.

4. A temporary nest, <u>which is a loose pile of twigs and leaves,</u> is cool enough for hot weather.

5. <u>Because temporary nests fall apart easily,</u> squirrels build several during the summer.

6. Squirrels prefer nests in tree holes, but sometimes there aren't enough around for all of them.

7. An outside nest is called a "dray."

8. <u>Although tree squirrels do not hibernate in the winter</u>, they may stay in their nests for several days at a time.
9. Tree squirrels, <u>who are omnivorous</u>, can eat almost anything.
10. The seeds and nuts <u>that squirrels bury in the fall</u> are used for food all winter.
11. Squirrels are great foresters <u>because many of these seeds and nuts grow into new trees</u>.

Lesson 15
Adjective and Adverb Clauses
EXERCISE A
1. because he heard a cat crying. Adv.
2. which was shoulder-deep in snow Adj.
3. Before Pete could blink Adv.
4. when Pete offered it some leftovers   Adv.
5. which was the local newspaper. Adj.

EXERCISE B
Answers will vary.

Lesson 16
Combining Sentences
EXERCISE A
Answers will vary.
1. but
2. and
3. can't combine
4. or
5. can't combine
6. can't combine

EXERCISE B
1. The Senate has one hundred members, and the House of Representatives has more than four hundred.
2. Congress has a great deal of power, but the power is balanced by other branches of government.
3. Congress makes laws, and the President carries them out.
4. Congress can cooperate with the President, but sometimes it does not.
5. Cooperation is usually best, but this is not always true.
6. The President can sign a bill, or he can veto it.

Lesson 17
Combining Sentences with Modifiers
EXERCISE A
1. He leaped high over the fence and onto the trampoline.
2. He jumped vigorously, expertly, and intensely.

EXERCISE B
Answers will vary.

EXERCISE C
Answers will vary.

Lesson 18
Improving Sentences
EXERCISE A
Answers may vary.
1. We drove there in my uncle's new car.
2. We arrived at exactly 10:30 A.M.
3. The day was sunny, warm, and windy.
4. One zoo visitor with binoculars was studying the monkeys.
5. One monkey entertained its audience with its antics.
6. We thought the large birds at the lagoon were beautiful.
7. Just as we passed, a gorilla screamed loudly and menacingly.
8. The polar bears were sunning by their pool.
9. The giraffes moved slowly and gracefully.
10. All the animals in the zoo fascinate me.

EXERCISE B
Answers will vary.

Lesson 19
Identifying Nouns
EXERCISE A
Answers will vary.

EXERCISE B
1. tale, pirate, base
2. Searchers, coins, bars, silver
3. boy, group, path, beach
4. excitement, end, pier
5. weight, end, line
6. treasure, crab, mood

EXERCISE C
1. strangeness
2. wisdom

3. falsehood
4. observance

Lesson 20

Kinds of Nouns

EXERCISE A

1. common, abstract
2. common, concrete
3. common, abstract
4. proper, concrete
5. common, concrete

EXERCISE B

1. <u>Mr. Ferencik</u>, my <u>neighbor</u>, came to <u>America</u> from <u>Europe</u>.
2. This brave <u>man</u> wanted <u>freedom</u> from <u>persecution</u>.
3. He arrived in <u>New York City</u> on a <u>freighter</u>.
4. The <u>Statue of Liberty</u> appeared in the <u>distance</u>.
5. <u>Tears</u> of <u>joy</u> and <u>anticipation</u> welled up in his <u>eyes</u>.
6. His <u>loneliness</u> for his <u>country</u> turned to <u>happiness</u>.
7. <u>Mr. Ferencik</u> wanted the <u>advantages</u> of a <u>democracy</u>.
8. <u>America</u> had a <u>tradition</u> of <u>liberty</u> and <u>justice</u>.
9. The new <u>immigrant</u> would be free from unjust <u>treatment</u> here.
10. The <u>Constitution</u> guaranteed <u>Mr. Ferencik</u> equality.

EXERCISE C

Concrete nouns are underlined once; abstract nouns, twice.

1. He drew his <u>sketches</u> from his <u>thoughts</u>.
2. Using his <u>creativity</u>, he imagined two <u>characters</u>.
3. He painted them with dark <u>colors</u> for a <u>mood</u> of <u>sadness</u>.
4. The <u>faces</u> of these <u>people</u> were partly in <u>shadows</u> and <u>darkness</u>.
5. Their shabby <u>clothes</u> and <u>bundles</u> showed great <u>poverty</u>.

Lesson 21

Plural Nouns

EXERCISE A

1. potatoes
2. chiefs
3. branches
4. valleys
5. boxes

EXERCISE B

1. books
2. bunches
3. feet
4. allergies
5. thieves
6. aluminum
7. halves
8. spaghetti
9. lunchboxes
10. heroes

EXERCISE C

1. Zoos, cities, animals
2. Foxes, monkeys, ropes
3. Sea lions, seals, pools
4. Rhinos, hippos, enclosures
5. Children, adults, farms

Lesson 22

Personal Pronouns

EXERCISE A

1. <u>I</u> asked <u>my</u> friends, "Have <u>you</u> found the calculator today?"
2. "Oh, so the strange object <u>we</u> found is <u>yours</u>?" Ben kidded <u>me</u>.
3. "Why isn't <u>your</u> name on the back?" <u>his</u> brother Jack said.
4. <u>I</u> said <u>it</u> was not <u>mine</u>; <u>my</u> brother Julio owned the calculator.
5. "<u>You</u> should feel lucky <u>it</u> was found by <u>us</u>," Mara said.
6. "<u>Its</u> case is ripped, but <u>I</u> bet <u>your</u> father could repair <u>it</u>."
7. Later, <u>she</u> and <u>we</u> boys discussed <u>our</u> summer plans.
8. "Are <u>you</u> going to try out for <u>our</u> community play?" Ben asked.
9. "Yes, <u>I</u> would like the hero's role. Are <u>you</u> two trying out?" <u>I</u> asked <u>him</u> and <u>his</u> brother.
10. <u>They</u> said <u>they</u> would rather try <u>their</u> luck as villains.
11. Mara complained, "Jana told <u>me</u> the part of the heroine was already <u>hers</u> and <u>I</u> shouldn't waste <u>my</u> time trying for <u>it</u>."
12. "<u>We</u> will all be lucky if <u>they</u> choose <u>us</u>," <u>I</u> commented.

EXERCISE B

Pronouns are underlined. Antecedents are listed in order.

1. <u>They</u> saw Denise do <u>her</u> first magic trick. friends, Denise
2. <u>She</u> started <u>it</u> by borrowing Carmen's straw hat. Denise, trick
3. "What are <u>you</u> going to do with <u>my</u> hat?" <u>she</u> asked. Denise, Carmen, Carmen
4. Denise took off the ribbon and cut <u>it</u> into several pieces. ribbon
5. <u>She</u> told Carmen to put <u>them</u> into the hat and shake <u>it</u>. Denise, pieces, hat
6. Then <u>she</u> told Carmen to jump up and down with <u>her</u>. Denise, Denise
7. The crowd was amazed when Denise pulled the ribbon out of <u>her</u> hat and <u>it</u> was whole again. Carmen, ribbon
8. <u>They</u> applauded <u>her</u> magic, and Carmen waved <u>her</u> hat. crowd, Denise, Carmen

Lesson 23
Interrogative and Relative Pronouns
EXERCISE A

1. <u>Who</u> owned the horse?
2. <u>What</u> is the horse's name?
3. <u>Which</u> is the best saddle?
4. <u>Whom</u> did you ask?
5. <u>What</u> is the price of the harness?
6. <u>Whose</u> are these boots?
7. <u>Whom</u> did you pay?
8. <u>Which</u> of the trails is best?
9. <u>What</u> is calf roping?
10. <u>Which</u> is Gail's farm?

EXERCISE B

1. One photographer <u>whom</u> she congratulated won first prize.
2. Each photo <u>that</u> was selected pictured a person or landscape.
3. One man <u>who</u> was photographed wore overalls.
4. The man <u>whom</u> Harvey photographed was a veteran.
5. The photographer <u>who</u> won second prize is a good friend of mine.
6. She lives in Golden Gate Park, <u>which</u> is nearby.
7. The photograph <u>that</u> won third prize was taken on a boat.
8. The best photo, <u>which</u> took fourth prize, was of a farm.
9. A barn <u>that</u> is very old can be quite lovely.

10. One photographer, <u>whom</u> I didn't know, is on the school paper.

EXERCISE C

1. Relative
2. Interrogative
3. Interrogative
4. Relative
5. Relative

Lesson 24
Possessive Nouns
EXERCISE A

1. father's
2. thieves'
3. jockey's
4. men's

EXERCISE B

1. Washington's courage
2. Cornwallis's army
3. soldiers' hopes
4. army's bravery

EXERCISE C

1. teacher's; teachers'
2. fisherman's; fishermen's
3. plumber's; plumbers'
4. artist's; artists'
5. dancer's; dancers'
6. glass's; glasses'
7. doctor's; doctors'
8. woman's; women's
9. country's; countries'
10. baby's; babies'

Lesson 25
Plural or Possessive
EXERCISE A

1. years, Alaska's
2. mines'; miners
3. miners; inhabitants; territory's
4. states

EXERCISE B

1. ocean's
2. waves
3. chairs
4. passengers'
5. ship's
6. cabins
7. Jones's
8. engines
9. navigators
10. sun's

EXERCISE C
1. Edison's
2. voters'
3. world's
4. country's
5. lab's
6. world's
7. public's
8. Edison's

EXERCISE B

1. himself	7. himself
2. ourselves	8. themselves
3. themselves	9. me
4. I	10. he
5. ourselves	11. themselves
6. themselves	

Lesson 26

Pronoun Homophones

EXERCISE A
1. its
2. Who's
3. You're
4. their
5. Whose
6. It's

EXERCISE B

1. your	9. who's
2. It's	10. they're
3. whose	11. It's
4. there	12. there
5. Their	13. It's
6. Its	14. whose
7. they're	15. it's
8. its	16. their

Lesson 27

Reflexive and Intensive Pronouns

EXERCISE A
1. ourselves; reflexive
2. herself; intensive
3. themselves; reflexive
4. themselves; reflexive
5. himself; reflexive
6. himself; reflexive
7. himself; intensive
8. ourselves; reflexive
9. themselves; reflexive
10. themselves; intensive
11. myself; intensive
12. ourselves; reflexive
13. yourself; reflexive

Lesson 28

Indefinite Pronouns

EXERCISE A
1. Anyone
2. anybody
3. Someone
4. No one
5. Many
6. Several
7. Something
8. Neither
9. Others
10. Each

EXERCISE B
1. Tourists were in town. Many visited the World Trade Center.
2. Tourists went to the top of the building. Several took photos.
3. The twins didn't take photos because both forgot the film.
4. My brothers wouldn't go. All are afraid of heights.
5. My sisters like the view, and each has seen it before.

EXERCISE C
1. Everyone knows about doing chores. S
2. Each has agreed on a job. S
3. Few would neglect carrying their own loads. P
4. Several think their time is limited. P
5. Others believe their schedules are not full. P
6. Anybody forgets duties at times. S
7. Either is able to do the tasks well. S
8. Neither was pleased with the schedule. S
9. Many are confident of their own abilities. P
10. I hope someone will volunteer. S

Lesson 29

Subject and Object Pronouns

EXERCISE A

1. her, me
2. they
3. He
4. me
5. them

EXERCISE B

1. They	8. them
2. her	9. it
3. them	10. they
4. they	11. she
5. them	12. them
6. It	13. They
7. him	14. her

Lesson 30

Pronouns as Subject Complements

EXERCISE A

1. they
2. I
3. me
4. we
5. he

EXERCISE B

1. S	6. S
2. SC	7. SC
3. S	8. SC
4. SC	9. SC
5. S	10. S

EXERCISE C

1. I; SP	8. We; SP
2. I; SP	9. he; SP
3. he; SP	10. me; OP
4. I; SP	11. us; OP
5. he; SP	12. he; SP
6. I; SP	13. him; OP
7. him; OP	

Lesson 31

Pronoun Agreement

EXERCISE A

1. Has either of the women had <u>their</u> turn yet?
√ 2. Each of the boys offered <u>his</u> help.

3. If a person is wrong, <u>they</u> should admit the fact.
√ 4. Many of the participants brought <u>their</u> radios.

EXERCISE B

Possible answers are shown.

1. his, her, his or her
2. their
3. his, her, his or her
4. their
5. his, her, his or her
6. his, her, his or her
7. their
8. he, she, he or she
9. his, her, his or her
10. their
11. his, her, his or her
12. their
13. they
14. they
15. he, she, he or she

EXERCISE C

1. his	5. her
2. her	6. their
3. their	7. his
4. her	8. their

EXERCISE D

Answers may vary.

1. If a repair person will be late, he or she should call.
2. Each of the mechanics bought his own tools.
3. Correct
4. Neither of the chefs owned her own restaurant.
5. Before a lawyer can practice, she must pass a bar exam.
6. If a farmer has a good crop, he feels lucky.

Lesson 32

Using *who* and *whom*

EXERCISE A

1. O
2. S
3. O

EXERCISE B

1. Who	6. who
2. whom	7. who
3. Who	8. whom
4. whom	9. Who
5. Whom	10. Who

1. who
2. whom
3. whom
4. who
5. who
6. whom
7. Who
8. whom
9. Who
10. whom

Lesson 33
Identifying Verbs
EXERCISE A
Answers will vary.
EXERCISE B
Answers will vary.
EXERCISE C
1. traveled; action verb
2. is; linking verb
3. flows; action verb
4. was; linking verb
5. seemed; linking verb
6. are; linking verb
7. walk; action verb
8. buy; action verb
9. taste; linking verb
10. purchase; action verb

Lesson 34
Action or Linking Verb
EXERCISE A
1. A
2. L
3. L
4. A
5. A
EXERCISE B
1. looked; action verb
2. felt; linking verb
3. grew; action verb
4. smelled; linking verb
5. looked; linking verb
6. felt; action verb
7. sounded; action verb
8. became; linking verb
9. remained; linking verb
10. appeared; action verb
EXERCISE C
1. look; action verb
2. appear; action verb

3. grew; linking verb
4. looked; action verb
5. became; linking verb
6. remained; linking verb
7. remained; action
8. tasted; linking verb
9. looked; action verb
10. remained; action; felt; action

Lesson 35
Verb Phrases
EXERCISE A
1. She may <u>have been attending</u> classes this afternoon.
2. Diane <u>should have come</u> home twenty minutes ago.
3. What <u>is keeping</u> her?
4. She probably <u>will be arriving</u> soon.
5. Mrs. Velasquez and Connie <u>are teaching</u> at Union School.
6. <u>Did</u> Juan <u>run</u> in the track meet yesterday?
7. Mr. Velasquez <u>has been working</u> in the garden again today.
8. <u>Should</u> we <u>help</u> him, or <u>would</u> we only <u>get</u> in the way?
9. The garden <u>can be planted</u> in no time at all.
10. Mr. Velasquez <u>had</u> already <u>prepared</u> the soil last week.

EXERCISE B
Helping verbs are underlined once; main verbs twice.
1. He <u>had</u> at one time <u>studied</u> the history of the game.
2. The game of tennis <u>was</u> first <u>played</u> in France.
3. Years ago, players <u>would</u> usually <u>hit</u> the ball with their hands.
4. Now, of course, they <u>must</u> always <u>use</u> a racket, or a foul <u>would be</u> <u>called</u>.
5. Tennis back then <u>was</u> also <u>played</u> on grass courts.
6. A variety of other surfaces <u>are</u> widely <u>used</u> now, but some famous tournaments <u>are</u> still <u>played</u> on grass.
7. Ancient tennis courts <u>were</u> often <u>enclosed</u>, and players <u>could</u> easily <u>participate</u> during any season.
8. Most people <u>could</u> not <u>afford</u> such a sport, so it <u>was</u> customarily <u>enjoyed</u> by nobles.
9. Tennis <u>has</u> in time become a more affordable sport.
10. <u>Have</u> you ever seriously <u>played</u> the game?

Lesson 36

Simple Tenses

EXERCISE A

1. In 1969, American astronauts <u>landed</u> on the moon. Past
2. The idea of space travel <u>started</u> long ago. Past
3. In 1687, Sir Isaac Newton <u>described</u> the laws of motion. Past
4. In 1865, Jules Verne <u>wrote</u> *From the Earth to the Moon*, the first science-fiction story about space travel. Past
5. In 1919, Robert Goddard <u>explained</u> the value of rockets. Past
6. In 1957, the Soviet Union <u>launched</u> *Sputnik I* into orbit. Past
7. The space shuttle <u>makes</u> interplanetary travel possible. Present.
8. The shuttle crews <u>will continue</u> the launching of satellites and space telescopes. Future
9. The space shuttle <u>measures</u> about 184 feet in length. Present
10. Perhaps some day shuttle crews <u>will build</u> a space station. Future

EXERCISE B

Underlined verbs should be changed to past tense.

We carried our canoe to the edge of the stream. The sky <u>is</u> clear blue, and the morning was still cool. Slowly we <u>lower</u> the canoe into the water. I held it steady, and my partner <u>climbs</u> in. She knelt down in the stern and <u>waits</u> for me. I <u>push</u> the canoe into deeper water and jumped in. "This will be a great day!" I <u>remark</u>. We paddled into deep water. The overhanging trees formed a green tunnel over the stream. Suddenly, the channel widened, for the stream <u>will enter</u> a lake. The lake was absolutely empty. Not a soul <u>is</u> in sight! Occasionally an eagle or falcon <u>circles</u> overhead and <u>will land</u> in a tree. Wild rice even grew in the shallow areas. No houses cluttered the banks, and no motorboats <u>disturb</u> the peacefulness of these surroundings. Canoeing on that lake was truly a memorable experience.

Lesson 37

Principal Parts of Verbs

EXERCISE A

1. Dinosaurs <u>lived</u> in many parts of the world. Past
2. Some dinosaurs <u>had measured</u> over forty-five feet in length. Past part.
3. I <u>have looked</u> at many dinosaur skeletons in museums. Past part.

4. Every year, experts <u>are discovering</u> more and more about them. Present part.
5. Scientists <u>consider</u> a new discovery extremely important. Present
6. I <u>am attending</u> some lectures on dinosaurs this week. Present part.
7. They <u>are helping</u> me with my report for science. Present part.
8. Dinosaurs long ago <u>disappeared</u> from the face of the earth. Past
9. Even so, they still <u>capture</u> our imagination. Present
10. The lectures <u>interest</u> me a great deal. Present

EXERCISE B

1. climbed
2. try
3. skied
4. yelled
5. receiving
6. patrolled
7. permitted
8. permitted
9. like
10. liking

Lesson 38

Perfect Tenses

EXERCISE A

1. has
2. begun in the past and continuing or completed now
3. had
4. will have

EXERCISE B

1. I <u>have taken</u> swimming lessons since October. Pres. perf.
2. By June 20, I <u>will have attended</u> thirty lessons. Fut. perf.
3. My teacher <u>has complimented</u> me on my Australian crawl. Pres. perf.
4. My diving also <u>has improved</u>. Pres. perf.
5. I <u>have practiced</u> even more lately. Pres. perf.
6. By the end of August I <u>will have raced</u> in several events. Fut. perf.
7. Neither of them <u>had swum</u> before. Past perf.
8. In a week each of them <u>will have taken</u> three lessons. Fut. perf.
9. By last May I <u>had taken</u> four tennis lessons. Past perf.

10. Tennis <u>has become</u> my friend Rita's favorite sport. Pres. perf.

EXERCISE C
1. have wondered
2. have concluded
3. have arrived
4. had talked
5. had answered
6. had visited
7. had lived
8. have learned

Lesson 39

Transitive and Intransitive Verbs
EXERCISE A
1. T
2. I
3. I
4. T
5. T

EXERCISE B
Verbs are underlined once; direct objects twice.
1. Cortés first <u>brought</u> <u>horses</u> to America.
2. Native Americans <u>had</u> never <u>seen</u> <u>animals</u> like horses before.
3. Some of the horses <u>escaped</u> their <u>owners</u>.
4. They <u>roamed</u> the <u>West</u> in wild herds.
5. Native Americans later <u>captured</u> these <u>horses</u>.
6. In time, Native Americans <u>tamed</u> their <u>horses</u>.
7. Herds of horses <u>represented</u> <u>wealth</u>.
8. They <u>rode</u> <u>horses</u> on buffalo-hunting trips.
9. Besides food, the buffalo <u>provided</u> <u>hides</u> for clothing.
10. Horses <u>gave</u> a new <u>way</u> of life to Native Americans.

EXERCISE C
Verbs are underlined.
1. Today four-lane highways <u>cross</u> old cattle trails. T
2. The state <u>seems</u> both old-fashioned and modern. I
3. Ranch hands still <u>herd</u> cattle on the range. T
4. Skyscrapers <u>form</u> the skylines of Dallas and Houston. T
5. Tourists <u>find</u> numerous attractions in Texas. T
6. The state continually <u>expands</u> its many cultural attractions. T
7. The Lyndon Johnson Library <u>stores</u> presidential papers. T

8. Visitors <u>flock</u> to the Alamo in San Antonio. I
9. Texas <u>was</u> an independent republic for almost ten years. I
10. It eventually <u>became</u> a state in 1845. I

Lesson 40

Principal Parts of Irregular Verbs
EXERCISE A
1. saw
2. swum
3. grown
4. gone
5. ran
6. knew
7. drawn

EXERCISE B
1. gone
2. went
3. went
4. seen
5. became
6. threw
7. begun
8. drew
9. come
10. sang *or* sung
11. rung
12. sprang *or* sprung
13. seen
14. ran
15. flew

EXERCISE C
1. blown
2. threw
3. thrown
4. ran
5. sprung
6. began
7. become
8. drew
9. sunk
10. known
11. grew
12. went
13. begun
14. sung
15. rang
16. thrown
17. seen
18. gone
19. flown
20. known

EXERCISE D
1. I had **grown** to love my old car.
2. I had **sworn** never to get rid of it.
3. At one time it **flew** over the highways.
4. Now its engine **has worn** out somewhat.

5. It **has blown** many tires.
6. The muffler **has sunk** closer to the ground.
7. The seat belt buzzer **has rung** its last warning.
8. Among my friends I **have sung** its praises.

Lesson 41
More Irregular Verbs
EXERCISE A

1. chosen	11. given
2. eaten	12. spoke
3. taken	13. rode
4. broken	14. fell
5. spoke	15. chose
6. stole	16. fallen
7. froze	17. gave
8. broken	18. written
9. stolen	19. wrote
10. gave	20. given

EXERCISE B

1. bought	11. thought
2. given	12. fallen
3. brought	13. brought
4. chosen	14. gave
5. led	15. frozen
6. thought	16. found
7. said	17. gave
8. taught	18. wrote
9. led	19. written
10. found	20. left

EXERCISE C
Answers will vary.

Lesson 42
Forms of *be*
EXERCISE A
1. were
2. was
3. had been
4. are
5. are
6. is
7. will be
8. have been

EXERCISE B
1. The meaning of *judo* **is** "gentle way."
2. Judo **was** for fighting, but now it's a sport.
3. The idea of it **isn't** to overpower your opponent.

4. The moves **have been** designed to use the opponent's strength to your own advantage.
5. Courtesy and confidence **are** gained from judo.
6. New students **are** given a white belt to wear.
7. Black belts **aren't** worn by anyone except masters of the art.
8. Judo **was** an Olympic event for the first time in 1964.
9. That year Tokyo **had been** *or* **was** the site for the Olympics.
10. Did you know some moves in karate **were** . . .

Lesson 43
Forms of *have*
EXERCISE A
1. had
2. had
3. could have
4. have
5. has
6. had

EXERCISE B
1. had
2. hasn't
3. have
4. have
5. haven't
6. has
7. has
8. has
9. haven't
10. have

EXERCISE C
1. had
2. have had
3. had
4. have
5. had *or* has

Lesson 44
Forms of *do*
EXERCISE A
1. had done
2. Do
3. doesn't
4. do
5. don't
6. did
7. Does
8. had done
9. did
10. did
11. doesn't
12. doesn't
13. do
14. do
15. Do

EXERCISE B
1. done
2. did
3. done
4. Do *or* Did
5. did
6. did
7. done
8. Does
9. done
10. Do

Lesson 45
Troublesome Verb Pairs
EXERCISE A
1. lain
2. sit
3. lend
4. Bring
5. teaching
6. let
7. rises

EXERCISE B
1. taught
2. brought
3. laid
4. lent
5. set
6. let
7. left
8. lay
9. took
10. lay
11. learned
12. rises
13. lent
14. sat
15. laid

EXERCISE C
1. taught
2. borrowed
3. let
4. lay
5. raise
6. raised
7. leave
8. sat
9. laid
10. borrow

EXERCISE D
1. taken
2. laid
3. sit
4. sat
5. taken

Lesson 46
Active and Passive Verbs
EXERCISE A
1. A
2. A
3. P
4. P
5. A
6. P
7. A
8. P
9. A
10. A

EXERCISE B
1. Bonnie collected shells.
2. She displayed the shells on a velvet cloth.
3. Willis brought two large albums of foreign stamps.
4. His father had started the stamp collection.
5. Maya exhibited hand-carved marionettes.
6. Her father had carved the marionettes.
7. Maya worked the marionettes for us.
8. The judges awarded a prize to the best exhibit.
9. Barry Handelman won the prize.
10. He built a miniature theater.

Lesson 47
Subject-Verb Agreement
EXERCISE A
1. live
2. are
3. likes
4. take
5. feeds
6. stray
7. sleeps
8. disapprove
9. are
10. are

EXERCISE B
1. want
2. object
3. have
4. have
5. are
6. has
7. are
8. are
9. expect
10. know
11. remember
12. hope

EXERCISE C
Answers will vary, but subjects and verbs should agree.

Lesson 48
Subjects Separated from Verbs
EXERCISE A

1. have
2. says
3. wants
4. welcome
5. has
6. states
7. describes
8. are
9. is
10. has

EXERCISE B

1. The history of pranks is a fascinating one.
2. Victims of a prank quite often do not know they're being fooled.
3. Once, scientists from a British university were fooled by the skull of an animal.
4. A 1938 radio drama about Martian invaders has been broadcast every Halloween to fool listeners.
5. Reports of a UFO invasion still scare many people.
6. People in an Illinois town have believed in "Big Foot."
7. Descriptions of "Big Foot" have varied greatly.
8. The footprints of the creature are found in the snow.

Lesson 49
Sentences in Inverted Order
EXERCISE A

Subjects are underlined once; verbs, twice.
1. When <u>does</u> <u>Natusa</u> <u>go</u> to science class?
2. <u>Here's</u> a <u>copy</u> of her schedule.
3. There <u>are</u> your <u>books</u> on the table.
4. <u>Does</u> <u>Ollie</u> <u>know</u> about the meeting?
5. Where <u>have</u> <u>Sandy and Duncan</u> <u>gone</u>?

EXERCISE B

1. Do
2. Was
3. were
4. Do
5. have
6. dig
7. Are
8. have
9. has
10. do
11. are
12. are

EXERCISE C

Answers will vary. Possible answers follow.
1. Here in Hawaii is the famous volcano Kilauea.
2. Have there been many eruptions of this volcano over the years?
3. There are tourists who come just to see the eruptions.
4. Here are the footprints of some soldiers who were caught in an eruption.
5. Where is the viewing center for visitors to watch the volcanoes safely?

Lesson 50
Agreement with Collective Nouns
EXERCISE A

Subjects are underlined once; verbs, twice.
1. A <u>crew</u> of workers <u>is cleaning</u> up.
2. That <u>group</u> <u>disagree</u> about almost everything.
3. The <u>crowd</u> <u>has made</u> a path for the heroes.
4. The Rockville <u>team</u> <u>plays</u> a very fast game.
5. The <u>audience</u> <u>take</u> their seats.

EXERCISE B

1. is
2. is
3. are
4. was
5. is
6. are
7. is
8. is
9. has
10. has

EXERCISE C

Answers will vary. The noun should be labeled singular or plural.

Lesson 51
Agreement with Indefinite Pronouns
EXERCISE A

1. takes
2. look
3. is
4. trains
5. try

EXERCISE B

1. recognizes
2. was
3. understands
4. was
5. has
6. are
7. were
8. were

EXERCISE C

1. needs
2. have
3. is
4. turn
5. serves
6. is
7. show
8. knows
9. is
10. has
11. Has
12. say

Lesson 52

Identifying Adjectives

EXERCISE A

Answers will vary.

EXERCISE B

Adjectives and proper adjectives are underlined once; words modified, twice.

1. He flew in a supersonic jet to the Amsterdam airport.
2. Then he took a small plane to an Egyptian city.
3. These photographs are beautiful, and he took them with that old camera.
4. He has several photos of this ancient temple.
5. He also visited many European museums.
6. These three recipes are from famous French restaurants.
7. Uncle amused us with several legends about a German castle.
8. He took lengthy tours of a few gardens in the English countryside.
9. The trip also included a brief stop in the Austrian mountains.
10. Aunt Chloe joined him for eight days on the sunny island of Sardinia.

Lesson 53

Identifying Adverbs

EXERCISE A

Adverbs are underlined.

1. Yesterday Rita excitedly chose material for her prom dress.
2. First she pinned the pattern carefully to the material.
3. Then she quickly cut the various pieces.
4. She will soon start the skirt of the dress.

5. Now she is putting everything away.

EXERCISE B

Answers may vary.

1. late	9. completely
2. down	10. loudly
3. patiently	11. up
4. Finally	12. close
5. smoothly	13. carefully
6. Suddenly	14. certainly
7. strongly	15. also
8. gracefully	16. never

EXERCISE C

Adverbs are underlined once; words modified, twice.

1. Today we watched an exciting sailboat race on the lake.
2. Many crews enthusiastically competed for first prize.
3. The clear blue water glistened brightly in the sun.
4. Colorful pennants flapped loudly in the strong wind.
5. The crews scurried around to their captains' sharp commands.

Lesson 54

Functions of Adverbs

EXERCISE A

Answers will vary, but adverbs should be appropriate.

EXERCISE B

Adverbs are underlined.

1. very—intensifier
2. really, especially—intensifier, intensifier
3. quite, often—intensifier, time
4. constantly, extremely—manner, intensifier
5. Later, exceedingly, outside—time, intensifier, place
6. very, quickly—intensifier, time
7. rather, speedily—intensifier, manner

Lesson 55

Comparative Forms

EXERCISE A

1. quickly, more quickly, most quickly
2. cold, colder, coldest
3. tall, taller, tallest
4. bright, brighter, brightest
5. grumpily, more grumpily, most grumpily
6. steadily, more steadily, most steadily
7. tan, tanner, tannest

8. gracefully, more gracefully, most gracefully
9. young, younger, youngest
10. carefully, more carefully, most carefully
11. spicy, spicier, spiciest
12. pretty, prettier, prettiest
13. happy, happier, happiest
14. coolly, more coolly, most coolly
15. funny, funnier, funniest
16. near, nearer, nearest
17. likely, more likely, most likely
18. sad, sadder, saddest
19. practical, more practical, most practical
20. reasonably, more reasonably, most reasonably

EXERCISE B
1. The oldest Greek legend celebrated chariot racing.
2. A King loved one of his daughters most of all.
3. Each young suitor was worthier than the last.
4. Still he forbade even the noblest man her hand.
5. The best one must prove himself in a race.

Lesson 56

Using Comparative Forms
EXERCISE A
1. faster
2. less
3. fastest
4. best

EXERCISE B
1. best
2. more
3. less
4. least
5. worse
6. louder
7. longer
8. brightest
9. most
10. more

EXERCISE C
1. The largest of all snakes is the anaconda.
2. Some people think snakes are the creepiest of animals.
3. In some species, female snakes are larger than males.
4. A snake sheds its skin more quickly in warm weather.
5. Some desert snakes are hardier than other snakes.

Lesson 57

Good, well, bad, and *badly*
EXERCISE A
1. Does Ivan play water polo well?
2. He says he doesn't play it too badly.
3. I think Ivan can do well at almost any water sport.
4. One of his sisters is a good swimmer too.

EXERCISE B
1. well
2. well
3. badly
4. well
5. badly
6. well
7. well
8. badly
9. badly
10. badly

EXERCISE C
1. badly
2. well
3. badly
4. well
5. badly
6. well
7. badly
8. well
9. good
10. well
11. good
12. well

Lesson 58

Expanding Sentences with Modifiers
EXERCISE A
Answers will vary.

EXERCISE B
Answers will vary.

Lesson 59

Adjective or Adverb
EXERCISE A
1. I
2. I

3. C
4. I
5. I
6. I

EXERCISE B

1. This engine usually starts (regular, <u>regularly</u>). Adverb
2. We should have worked more (care, <u>carefully</u>). Adverb
3. Now the engine is running (smooth, <u>smoothly</u>). Adverb
4. Does it sound (<u>smooth</u>, smoothly) to you? Adjective
5. It started as (sudden, <u>suddenly</u>) as it stopped. Adverb
6. Don't you feel (<u>happy</u>, happily) to have it fixed? Adjective
7. Well, don't look so (<u>smug</u>, smugly). Adjective
8. We can repair any engine (easy, <u>easily</u>). Adverb
9. Jim worked (steady, <u>steadily</u>) on the repairs. Adverb
10. The engine now sounds (<u>different</u>, differently). Adjective
11. It seems to accelerate more (quick, <u>quickly</u>) than it did. Adverb
12. I hope the car is (<u>reliable</u>, reliably) now. Adjective

EXERCISE C

1. surely *or* really
2. surely *or* really
3. sure
4. really
5. real
6. surely *or* really
7. real

Lesson 60

This, that, these, and *those*

EXERCISE A

1. I don't like this kind of shorts.
2. Do you like those scissors?
3. Don thought that book was yours.
4. That magazine over there is mine.

EXERCISE B

"Do you want some of (1) <u>this</u> fruit I'm serving?" Dad asked.

"No, thanks," I said, "but (2) <u>that</u> cheese over there looks great!"

"I think you should have some of (3) <u>these</u> peaches," Dad said. "They are delicious."

" (4) <u>These/those</u> three pieces of cheese are enough for me," I answered. "Later, I'll eat (5) <u>those</u> pears in the refrigerator."

EXERCISE C

Adjectives and nouns are underlined.

1. Did you find <u>this</u> <u>book</u> on the sale table?
2. I found <u>these</u> <u>magazines</u> over near the door.
3. <u>These</u> <u>kinds</u> of magazines are hard to find.
4. I would like to read <u>that</u> <u>article</u>.
5. <u>That</u> <u>kind</u> of article is of interest to me.
6. I will buy <u>those</u> two <u>magazines</u>.
7. Julio bought <u>this</u> <u>book</u>.
8. <u>Those</u> <u>volumes</u> show cave paintings.
9. Cave dwellers drew <u>this</u> <u>kind</u> of scene.
10. <u>Those</u> <u>scenes</u> helped them in their hunting trips.
11. They thought that <u>these</u> <u>pictures</u> attracted animals.
12. <u>These</u> <u>animals</u> died long ago.
13. Yet they live forever in <u>these</u> cave <u>paintings</u>.
14. <u>Those</u> <u>artists</u> of long ago drew interesting pictures.
15. Many people have seen <u>this</u> <u>sort</u> of painting in books.
16. People are often amazed by <u>these</u> <u>sorts</u> of sketches.

Lesson 61

Using Negative Words

EXERCISE A

Answers will vary, but dropping *n't* will be most common.

EXERCISE B

1. anything
2. ever
3. any
4. anywhere
5. any

EXERCISE C

Answers will vary, but dropping *n't* works often.

Lesson 62

Prepositions and Prepositional Phrases

EXERCISE A

1. The actress <u>with red hair</u> held a book <u>in her hand</u>.
2. She stood <u>in the very center</u> <u>of the huge stage</u>.

3. She was auditioning <u>for the director and the producer</u>.
4. The stage manager sat <u>inside the wings</u> <u>to the right</u>.
5. <u>Behind him</u> stood various members <u>of the cast</u>.

EXERCISE B

Answers will vary.

EXERCISE C

1. I learned <u>about</u> the development <u>of</u> the modern theater.
2. Several texts <u>on</u> the theater were <u>in</u> our library.
3. First I looked <u>for</u> a recent book <u>with</u> information <u>about</u> theater history.
4. <u>Along</u> the shelf were books <u>by</u> many authors.
5. <u>During</u> my search, I examined the contents <u>of</u> many books.
6. Finally I reached <u>above</u> my head <u>for</u> two more books.
7. I tugged <u>at</u> one <u>between</u> two larger books.
8. It tumbled <u>off</u> the shelf and crashed <u>onto</u> my head.
9. <u>With</u> my hand <u>on</u> my head, I moaned and staggered <u>across</u> the room.
10. A friend <u>from</u> my English class thought I was practicing <u>for</u> the play.

Lesson 63

Preposition or Adverb

EXERCISE A

1. I looked <u>up</u> when I heard the shout from the water. A
2. I noticed a sailboat that had been sailing <u>around</u>. A
3. <u>Inside</u> the cockpit sat a woman with the tiller <u>in</u> her hand. P, P
4. She shouted <u>across</u> the water, telling me to come <u>along</u>. P, A
5. She told me to jump <u>into</u> the boat as she came <u>by</u>. P, A
6. I nervously looked <u>down</u> at the black water <u>below</u> me. A, P
7. <u>From</u> experience, I knew the water was cold <u>under</u> the surface. P, P
8. I waited until the boat came <u>near</u> before I jumped <u>in</u>. A, A
9. She guided the boat <u>by</u> the pier and slowed it <u>near</u> me. P, P
10. I leaped <u>over</u> the water to the deck as the boat went <u>past</u>. P, A

EXERCISE B

1. Una walked <u>to</u> the pier yesterday afternoon. P
2. The wind was whipping the waves <u>up</u>. A
3. She would have liked <u>to</u> sail across the lake. V
4. The wind was coming <u>on</u> too strong though. A
5. Una decided <u>on</u> a walk instead. P
6. She was soon walking <u>up</u> the beach. P
7. It was a good day <u>to</u> walk. V

EXERCISE C

Verbs are underlined once; prepositional phrases, twice.

1. <u>After my leap</u> <u>into the boat</u>, I had <u>to catch</u> my breath.
2. I was surprised <u>to find</u> that we were no longer <u>near the pier</u>.
3. The boat, <u>under full sail</u>, tilted <u>to the side</u>.
4. "Do you want <u>to steer</u> awhile?" the woman said <u>to me</u>.
5. It was all I could do <u>to keep</u> <u>on my feet</u>, going <u>to the helm</u>.
6. "You need <u>to keep</u> the sails filled <u>with wind</u>," she said.
7. I sat <u>by the tiller</u>, and the wind seemed <u>to decrease</u>.
8. The boat seemed <u>to want</u> <u>to go</u> <u>across the water</u> <u>to the north</u>.
9. <u>To my surprise,</u> the tiller seemed <u>to know</u> I was inexperienced.
10. All I needed <u>to do</u> <u>to turn</u> the boat was <u>to nudge</u> the tiller, first <u>to one side</u>, then <u>to the other</u>.

EXERCISE D

Answers will vary.

Lesson 64

Adjective and Adverb Prepositional Phrases

EXERCISE A

1. will be held-Adv.; Sunday-Adj.
2. Clothing-Adj.; has been collected-Adv.
3. will be run-Adv.; friend-Adj.
4. Put-Adv.; box-Adj.

EXERCISE B

1. The <u>skiers</u> on the lift <u>went</u> up the mountain. N, V
2. On each <u>side</u> of every chair <u>sat</u> a skier. N, V
3. Some <u>skiers</u> at the top <u>headed</u> for the ski jump. N, V
4. The jumpers <u>glided</u> down a slide. V

5. The best <u>skiers</u> in the group <u>landed</u> on their feet. N, V

6. One skier <u>landed</u> on his head. V

7. A few unlucky jumpers <u>fell</u> into the snow. V

8. Some skiers <u>flipped</u> through the air. V

9. Another skier barely missed some <u>trees</u> in her path. N

10. The safety patrol <u>skied</u> near dangerous <u>parts</u> of the mountain. V, N

11. They would help <u>people</u> in trouble. N

12. Some <u>beginners</u> on the mountain <u>skied</u> to the bottom. N, V

13. The skillful skiers <u>sped</u> around all obstacles. V

14. Most <u>skiers</u> on the slopes had a wonderful day. N

15. They all enjoyed the <u>warmth</u> of the fire. N

EXERCISE C

Prepositional phrases are underlined once; the words they modify are underlined twice.

1. Windmills offer <u>hope</u> <u>for a larger energy supply</u>. Adj.

2. A <u>windmill</u> <u>of great size</u> could serve several homes. Adj.

3. <u>In many places</u>, steady winds <u>blow</u>. Adv.

4. The high <u>cost</u> <u>of wind machinery</u> is a problem. Adj.

5. Remote <u>areas</u> <u>with steady winds</u> produce electricity now. Adj.

6. Another <u>source</u> <u>of power</u> is the sun. Adj.

7. The <u>rays</u> <u>of the sun</u> can heat water. Adj.

8. Water <u>heats</u> <u>at a low cost</u> if this method is used. Adv.

9. Heat collectors <u>operate</u> <u>in sunny climates</u>. Adv.

10. The sun's heat <u>collects</u> <u>in panels</u>. Adv.

EXERCISE D

Answers will vary.

Lesson 65

Identifying Conjunctions

EXERCISE A

Answers will vary. Suggested answers follow.

1. and
2. but
3. either, or
4. Both, and
5. or
6. but
7. and
8. and

9. or
10. Both, and

EXERCISE B

1. I have three brothers, four sisters, <u>and</u> two parents.

2. We get along well, <u>but</u> we do disagree about money.

3. Two of my brothers <u>and</u> three of my sisters have jobs.

4. I don't care much about money, <u>nor</u> am I careless with it.

5. I occasionally borrow money from a brother <u>or</u> sister.

6. I try to pay them back promptly, <u>for</u> I know they need money.

7. A barter system would end all our disagreeing, <u>yet</u> I cannot convince the family of this.

8. No one except me finds my idea interesting <u>or</u> acceptable.

9. My brothers <u>and</u> sisters laughed when I explained it, <u>so</u> I talked to them one at a time.

10. I convinced one parent, one brother, <u>and</u> two sisters, <u>but</u> no one else in the family will budge.

EXERCISE C

1. <u>Both</u> my parents <u>and</u> the rest of my family have given in to me.

2. The bartering will be <u>either</u> a success <u>or</u> a disaster.

3. <u>Neither</u> my brother Fozzie <u>nor</u> my sisters like bartering very much.

4. Fozzie wanted <u>both</u> my favorite pen <u>and</u> my pet duck for his oldest, most worn-out hiking boots.

5. I told him the trade would be fair <u>neither</u> to me <u>nor</u> to my duck, who dislikes Fozzie intensely.

6. "<u>Either</u> leave out the duck <u>or</u> it's no deal," I said.

7. <u>Both</u> he <u>and</u> I made new offers for other trades.

8. I wanted <u>either</u> his backpack <u>or</u> his new T-shirt for my pen.

9. <u>Neither</u> Fozzie <u>nor</u> I could come to any agreement.

10. <u>Both</u> my family <u>and</u> I have decided to forget bartering.

EXERCISE D

Answers will vary.

Lesson 66

Identifying Interjections

EXERCISE.

Answers will vary.

Lesson 67

Punctuating the Ends of Sentences

EXERCISE A

1. Melinda, this is Beth.
2. What are you doing this afternoon?
3. I'm cleaning my room and vacuuming the rug.
4. How long will it take you?
5. It's really a mess this time.
6. Well, hurry up!
7. It may take me all afternoon.
8. I wanted you to go to the movies with me.
9. I'd like to, but I can't finish in time.
10. Let me come over and help you.
11. I couldn't ask you to do that.
12. I'll come right over on my bike.
13. Do you mean it?
14. Of course I do!
15. I'll see you soon.

EXERCISE B

1. **I;** Is that a bear over there in the park?
2. **D;** That's a black bear beyond the evergreens.
3. **E;** Oh, how friendly he looks!
4. **Im;** Don't go near him or you may be sorry.
5. **D;** He may not be so friendly up close.
6. **Im;** Please take a picture of him for our album.
7. **I;** How does the homing pigeon find its way home?
8. **D;** I read an interesting magazine article about pigeons.
9. **Im;** Read this article if you want to learn about them.
10. **I;** Did you know that pigeons can see special light rays?
11. **D;** These light rays are invisible to humans.
12. **D;** Pigeons use their vision to find the sun's position.
13. **E;** How remarkable that pigeons can do this!
14. **Im;** Imagine the world from a pigeon's eye-view.
15. **E;** How different it must look!

Lesson 68

Commas in Sentences

EXERCISE A

1. Will you remember, Wanda, to call the twins, Pat and Michelle?
2. I've bought green, gold, white, and brown crepe paper.

3. Luis, Dan will decorate two of the rooms, and you can help him.
4. Henry, of course, will help too, Luis.
5. If you finish early, you can start choosing the music.

EXERCISE B

(1) "Jerry, I want to ask you something. (2) The Encounter, a new rock group, is performing this afternoon. (3) Unfortunately, I can't use my ticket. (4) I need to replace a filling, and it just can't wait. (5) If you are interested, I'll sell you my ticket." (6) "I wish I could buy it, Samantha. (7) My problem, as usual, is that I am broke. (8) Of course, I could borrow the money from Ivan, my brother's friend. (9) He's not here now, but he should be back soon. (10) Since I can't promise to get the money, you might want to ask someone else."

(11) "If you don't mind, Jerry, I will. (12) Barry, Mike, and June are all crazy about The Encounter. (13) They tried to buy tickets, but the concert was all sold out."

EXERCISE C

1. If you are horror-film fans, ladies and gentlemen, we have some news for you.
2. Do you remember Count Dracula, the stranger from Transylvania?
3. The count is the father of a terrifying daughter, Draculana.
4. These terrible creatures are appearing together in *Daughter Of Dracula*, a new movie.
5. Every scene, needless to say, is packed with action, suspense, chills, and thrills
6. You won't know whether to laugh, cry, gasp, or shiver.
7. We won't give the story away, but you'll definitely be scared.
8. If you go, take a friend.
9. People in Texas, Ohio, and Maine really enjoyed the movie.
10. Another film, *Daughter of Dracula: Part Two*, is being made.
11. As usual, people will wait in long lines to see it.

Lesson 69

Other Uses of Commas

EXERCISE A

1. 2
2. 1
3. 3

EXERCISE B

65 River Road
Potomac, MD 20853
March 20, 1988

Dear Martha,

I just got back from a family reunion in Woodstock, Virginia. We celebrated my grandparent's anniversary on Saturday, March 12. They were married on March 12, 1930. My aunt and uncle flew in from Bangor, Maine, for the weekend. My cousin drove in from San Francisco, California. Then he drove to see his sister in El Paso, Texas. He must have driven over 10,000 miles in his car during his trip!

Woodstock is a friendly town but Potomac, Maryland, has one big advantage. It's my home!

Your pal,
Carrie

EXERCISE C

1. $500,000 Winner
2. Anderson, Rodney
3. 132 Valley Terrace
4. Santa Fe, CA 90670
5. Birthday: October 7, 1966
6. $250,000 Winner
7. Muhs, Neil
8. 6 Jasper Way
9. Boston, MA 01432
10. Birthday: April 26, 1925
11. $100,000 Winner
12. Smith, Janice
13. 863-B Roper Road
14. Gaithersburg, MD 20760
15. Birthday: July 17, 1947
16. $50,000 Winner
17. Zim, Roland
18. 101 Foundry Road
19. Pecos, TX 79772
20. Birthday: March 30, 1958

EXERCISE D

November 25, 1996

Dear Parents,

Come and join the fun on Saturday, December 3. We're holding a bazaar at Leroy Junior High School, 201 Washington Street, San Diego. Books, clothing, and baked goods will be on sale. Help us raise the $4,000 we need for new library books. Our target date for purchasing the books is January 2, 1998. If you can't come in person, please contact Ms. Melissa Raymond. Her address is 136 Mooney Road, San Diego, California 92117.

Gratefully yours,
The 7th Grade Class

Lesson 70

Other Punctuation Marks
EXERCISE A

1. The spelling bee starts at **8:30 A.M.**
2. I signed up (that was my first mistake) last month. or —/—
3. Here are the names of the judges: Vito Cardello, Lisa Wong, and Margaret Fenton.
4. Cara Chen always wins; I'm glad she's not going to enter this year.
5. Can you (I mean anyone) study for a spelling bee? or —/—
6. I'd pay special attention to the medical words (pages 31–42).
7. There are fifty-two words on a page.
8. Your know-it-all attitude sometimes annoys me.
9. Are there two *m*'s, *t*'s, and *e*'s in the word *committee?*
10. My dentist, **Dr.** Mildred **N.** Mann, won a spelling bee.

EXERCISE B
Answers will vary.

Lesson 71

Quotation Marks
EXERCISE A

1. "Let's go to the beach," Ky said.
2. "Would you like a picnic lunch?" Pedro asked. "I'm starved!"
3. "Why don't we invite Harriet?" Ky suggested.
4. Pedro said that he didn't think she was feeling well. **Correct**
5. "She was out of school Thursday and Friday," he commented.
6. Ky said, "Why don't you call her?"
7. "OK, I will," said Pedro.
8. When Harriet answered the phone, she said, "What a shame!"
9. "I'd like to come," she explained, "but I have a terrible cold."
10. She said she had been sitting around feeling sorry for herself. **Correct**

EXERCISE B

1. Many students were reading May Swenson's poem "The Centaur."
2. Others were writing down the lyrics to "America, the Beautiful."
3. "Attention, class!" Mrs. Gordon said. "Listen carefully."

4. "I'm going to put a list of stories and articles for recommended reading on the board," she said.

5. The list included the following titles: "Thank You," by Alex Haley; "A Haircut," by I. S. Nakata; and "Drouth," by Ben Logan.

6. "Should we write answers to the discussion questions?" Lu asked.

Lesson 72

Capitalizing First Words

EXERCISE A

1. <u>dear</u> <u>aunt</u> <u>nell</u>,
2. <u>thank</u> you for the birthday present.
3. <u>when</u> she saw it, my mom said, "<u>what</u> a beautiful bracelet!"
4. "<u>aren't</u> you lucky," Dad kidded me, "to have a rich relative?"
5. <u>are</u> you coming for a visit soon?
6. <u>gratefully</u> yours,

EXERCISE B

1. **I**; Dear Bonnie,
2. **I**; It is snowing hard here.
3. **I**; School is closed today.
4. **C**
5. **C**
6. **C**
7. **I**; Here is a surprise.
8. **C**
9. **I**; Have a happy birthday!
10. **C**

EXERCISE C

1. We waited for the inspector. The atmosphere was tense. Soon the inspector arrived.
2. He said, "The case is over. We have found the thief."
3. "It's not me," Harry said.
4. "Relax, Harry," the inspector said, "because you're innocent."
5. The inspector had a note. Everyone listened eagerly.
6. "Dear Sir," he read. "Max stole the jewels. He buried them in the yard. Sincerely yours, Pat the Rat."
7. "Impossible!" Kay cried. "My dog is a good dog and is not a thief. The thief wrote that!"

Lesson 73

Capitalizing Proper Nouns and Adjectives

EXERCISE A

1. Before **Lewis** and **Clark**, no one knew much about the **West**.

2. Many thought there was a great desert west of **Missouri**.
3. **Oregon** was still **British**, but **Yankees** yearned to settle it.
4. **St. Joseph** and **Independence** were popular start-off cities.
5. **Hiram Sloane** joined a wagon train in early spring.
6. The plan was to cross the **Cascade Mountains** before winter.
7. The party skirted the **Missouri River** and headed northwest.
8. It followed the valley of the **Platte River** to the **Rockies**.
9. It passed through areas that are now **Nebraska** and **Colorado**.
10. In early **October**, it finally got through **South Pass**.

EXERCISE B

1. **Chris Johnson** and I went with **Jason**.
2. We stayed at the **Drake Hotel** near **Pennsylvania Avenue**.
3. We toured the **White House** on **Wednesday**.
4. A **White House** guard told us to visit the **Jefferson Memorial**.
5. We met **Roger J. Collins** from the **House of Representatives**.
6. We visited both the **British** and **French** embassies.
7. In the evening we took a boat ride on the **Potomac River** and went through the **Georgetown Channel**.
8. There was a group of **Swedish** tourists on our bus trip to **Mount Vernon**, **George Washington's** home.
9. **Chris** got acquainted with them because he know some **Swedish**.
10. We also went to **Gettysburg**, **Pennsylvania**.
11. That's where **Abraham Lincoln** made his famous address during the **Civil War**.
12. In **Jamestown**, **Virginia**, we saw a replica of **Fort James**.
13. **Jamestown** was settled by **Englishmen** led by **John Smith**.
14. Before going home, we visited **Aunt Dora** in **Richmond**.
15. **Aunt Dora** teaches at **Jefferson High School** there.

Lesson 74

Capitalizing Titles

EXERCISE A

1. "A Dinner at Poplar Walk"
2. *Julie of the Wolves*
3. *Oliver Twist*
4. *The Old Curiosity Shop*
5. "The Three Sailors"
6. *A Christmas Carol*
7. "A Day in the Sun"
8. *Great Expectations*
9. *A Tale of Two Cities*
10. "The Lady, or the Tiger?"

EXERCISE B

1. *The Queen of Hearts*
2. King Leopold
3. Sir Isaac Newton
4. Mrs. Mary Todd Lincoln
5. General Robert E. Lee
6. Commodore Oliver H. Perry

EXERCISE C

1. Mayor Bailey met with Governor Frey to discuss the bus strike.
2. Officer Patricia Cabot was awarded a medal for bravery.
3. Dr. Robert Conklin proved that chimpanzees can communicate.
4. *Never a Dull Moment* is hailed as the year's best film.
5. The TV play *Children of Tomorrow* will be shown next week.
6. The poem "My Father Is a Simple Man" is one of my favorites.
7. Millions of people watched the weddings of Prince Charles and Prince Andrew.